YOUR SUCCESS – YOUR CHOICE

Personal Adventures and Your Guide to a Happy Life

BY ROBERT C. TRAUTMAN

YOUR SUCCESS - YOUR CHOICE

Copyright © 2023 Robert Trautman.

Authorunit

17130 Van Buren Blvd., Ste. 238,

Riverside, CA 92504

877-826-5888

www.authorunit.com

Because of the dynamic nature of the Internet, any web addresses or links contained in this book may have changed since publication and may no longer be valid. The views expressed in the work are solely those of the author and do not necessarily reflect the views of the publisher, and the publisher hereby disclaims any responsibility for them.

Any people depicted in stock imagery provided by Getty images are models, and such images are being used for illustrative purposes only.

ISBN 979-8-89030-016-4 (Paperback)

ISBN 979-8-89030-017-1 (Ebook)

Printed in the United States of America

Contents

About The Book

A Refreshed Publication

This book is a refreshed publication of my book, "Life's Essential Primer: Adventures, Choices, and The Success They Can Bring", originally published in 2015.

Corrections have been made where applicable, and some new material has been added.

Wherever there is a reference to money, whether it's talking about wages or the current equivalent dollar value of something at the time of writing, I'm referring to the year 2015 (unless otherwise specifically indicated) – this is when the original version of this book was published.

Additionally, any time I talk about some number of years ago in any context, it's referring, again, to 2015 as the starting date (unless otherwise specifically indicated). As such, please add 6 years to those figures for accuracy as of the date of this new publication (2021). Additionally, I've added new material to the 2021 version, and have included "UPDATED" at the start of each section with all new material.

How to use this book

Read, understand, and *embrace* the tips provided in the **Principles, Practices and Philosophy** section. This is where you will find the keys to your own success! I suppose, too, that the book might make a really great doorstop!

Next, for some amusement, and also to check out actual examples of how I have applied this information throughout my life, along with my twin brother when younger, to achieve my own success, please read the **Real-Life Adventures** sections. Though many of the specific activities that I discuss in those sections are rather dated, the principles remain as solid today as when I'd applied them when I grew up in the 1960s and '70s.

Why did I write the book?

An ever-increasing number of friends and acquaintances have urged me throughout the years to record my frequently amusing, perhaps inspiring, sometimes unbelievable, and always fun and unique life experiences for others to enjoy.

The success and happiness I've enjoyed throughout my life is the result of my having unwittingly made good decisions a majority of the time from a very early age. Reflecting on this now, I can clearly identify the motivations that helped me choose wisely and maintain a direct course to success.

With the clarity of hindsight, I can now offer to you not only my own personal voyage as an example within which you'll find amusement and some golden nuggets, but, also, the outright keys to achieve success and happiness in your own life…if you truly want it!

Who should read this book?

- Parents of young children can use the stories and philosophy as a reference to gently guide their children towards making better, responsible, decisions
- Teens & young adults may read the stories and philosophy, and vigorously apply it
- People who want to improve their current lifestyle
- Other people
- Ferrets – although I've been told that they don't read very well

About Principles, Practices and Philosophy

Much of this section is just plain common sense. What makes it important is that many people just don't think about it much, so they end up often making bad choices. It's a compilation of my personal observations, supported by my own very happy and successful life and established facts where applicable. You don't have to agree with all, or any, of it, but I can say with considerable confidence that your chances for a happy and successful future will be *significantly* improved if you do. It is, after all, YOUR CHOICE.

About the Real-Life Adventures

The stories that you're about to read are completely true. I offer them to you here not only as a collection of real-life examples of the application of the principles given herein and the results thereof, but also to provide a bit of levity. After all, who can't use a good laugh? All of the events, activities, experiments, developments, and situations in these stories actually occurred as described, with the people indicated, at the ages and dates given.

Clearly, a book covering every waking moment of a long and prosperous life simply is not practical. As such, I have included only the most interesting and positive events. You'll find anywhere from only a single story, to as many as nineteen in any chapter. Why only positive events? Like most people, I've had my share of missteps to deal with, but, as you'll soon read in detail, I choose not to dwell on the negative. It's part of my recipe for future success.

These stories were not only taken from my own recollections, but also verified by other sources whenever possible. In fact, quite a bit of the material comes from notes, letters, logs, and other scraps that I'd written, collected, and kept since I was 18, with the specific intent of writing my memoirs one day. I can, therefore, attest to its substantial accuracy.

The dialogue, however, is another issue altogether. As I can barely recall what I had for breakfast today, the chances of my recalling the precise words spoken by not only myself, but also by others, as much as 50 years ago are pretty much nil. As such, I've done my best to recreate dialogue that might – or might not – have been spoken between specific individuals, in a style that is consistent with the way they would have spoken. While the specific dialogue might be fictional, it is written in a manner that preserves the truth, accuracy, and intention of each scenario.

The activities in these stories, taken in total, have formed who I am today. It is my fervent desire that perhaps you might find a few tidbits of wisdom within them that will help to make your own life, or those of your children, much more fulfilling.

About Education Alerts

You will find, throughout the adventures section, several numbered "Education Alerts". These refer to a section, ironically titled Education Alerts, in the back of the book. Each of these provides significantly more detail about a concept referred to within the main body of the adventures section. They were moved to the back of the book in order to keep the flow from getting bogged down by details that would interest only a small percentage of readers.

Author Contact Information and How to Request Self-Improvement Excel Spreadsheets

At the end of this book, you will find an e-mail address where reader feedback can be received, and readers may request a current copy of the various Excel spreadsheets that I've developed in an ongoing effort to continue my own self-improvement. You can benefit from these, as well.

HOW TO ESTABLISH YOUR PERSONAL PATH TO SUCCESS

SECTION 1 – PRINCIPLES, PRACTICES & PHILOSOPHY

SUCCESS IS A CHOICE! WILL IT BE YOURS?

First things first; What *is* success? Yes, yes, it *is* a choice. We know that. I mean, I just told you! Didn't I? Okay, so, what *else* is success?

Success can be many things to many people, but I'm going to define success in a very specific way for this book. Now, I'm not talking about the private jets, mansions, and 97-foot yachts kind of success, although that *is* another level of success that I'd ultimately like to achieve in time. No, I'm talking about a *reasonable* level of success that is really quite realistic and *very* achievable by most people who put in the time and effort.

Imagine, if you will, that you have deep friendships while living in your own nice house in a safe neighborhood, doing what you enjoy for a career while earning enough to keep you and any family you have comfortable, with enough time and money left over to experience some of life's extras, including fulfilling many of your dreams. That is *my* definition of success. Anything more is just a pleasant extra!

The level of success – or failure – at any point in your life is the result of EVERY choice that YOU have ever made since you were old enough to exhibit cognitive responses to your environment. As children, our parents will, admittedly, make many important decisions for us, but it's the way that *we choose* to react to those decisions that will start to shape *our* future. If they've made good decisions for us, but we choose, instead, to rebel and do something else, then we need to understand that it is *our* future that we're adversely affecting. Of course, if your parents haven't made good decisions while you were growing up, then you'll have a bit more work to do once you're old enough to make responsible decisions of your own, but you can still achieve your own success if you're determined. When you do have the freedom to start making your own important decisions, then you must choose well if you wish to accomplish your goals and succeed with a happy life.

When you're young (under 18), there really are only a few rather important, fundamental choices that you'll have to make. No, they don't include what you're going to wear, or how you're going to get to the mall. I'll outline them here.

I, of all people will not attempt to dissuade you from taking risks. After all, risk-taking is the spice of life! That said, **never take a *careless* risk!** How's that different from any other risk? It's one that has a high probability of getting you or others expelled, imprisoned, fired, or killed. When confronted with a risk scenario, ALWAYS consider the future ramifications both to yourself and to others who it might affect in the event things don't go quite as you'd planned, and then make your fully informed, logical choice after this moment of introspection. More often than not, such a decision will be the right one, and it will support your quest for future success and happiness.

Obviously, there are a million other decisions that you'll make when growing up (like whether a certain pair of shoes will match your outfit), but few will have the potential to affect your future more profoundly than the following. Expulsion won't look good to any college that you might have wanted to attend, and it will significantly delay any opportunity for success. An arrest, even if sealed as a juvenile, will probably get you expelled from school, resulting, once again, in a delay of your education and, therefore your success, *and* you'll lose the support of a lot of people who might have helped you out otherwise. Death is the ultimate inconvenience, as it's generally quite terminal! If you hadn't achieved your life goals before you do something really stupid that results in that pesky death thing, then, I'm sorry to say, it's all over at that point! Game over! There are no "do-overs" in real life. Therefore, I strongly suggest that you vigorously avoid death if a long, happy and successful life is your goal!

If you've made good choices when you were young, and you continue to select well as you get older, then much if not all of your future should fall nicely into place, producing happiness and success.

It's really never too late to put into practice the principles outlined here to improve the quality of your life. It's just easier to do by starting as a child.

You will note, in the Real-Life Adventures, that, when my brother and I were quite young, we had set a long-term goal of flying. We also had what some might call gifted foresight that helped us to know that it would probably take a lot of money to learn to fly, thus prompting us to pursue our electronics hobby with extreme passion. We knew that we could make a lot of money in electronics, thereby facilitating our dream of flight. This is the process in a nutshell:

1. We dreamt of a lofty goal
2. We determined what it would take to get there
3. We pursued a passion that would convert into a career
4. We obtained the applicable education
5. We achieved our dream, plus much, much more

You need to set long-term goals of your own and consider reasonable means by which you can accomplish these. In addition, also make realistic short-term goals that will help to keep you focused. For my brother and me, our short-term goals were the plethora of electronic projects we'd conceived and built, as well as earning various licenses and other credentials related to electronics. These all helped keep us focused on earning the degrees that would provide us a career in a field that we significantly enjoyed, and it would allow us to afford flight training on our own.

OPTIMISM

Attitude is everything! If you're a pessimist, then it is *your attitude* that is the main obstacle to your own success! If you want to see success in your life, change your attitude to that of the optimist. You've tried, you say? You *would* be more optimistic if everything didn't always go wrong in your life? I put it to you that it isn't everything going wrong that's keeping you pessimistic; rather, it's your pessimism that's making everything go wrong!

ACCEPT RESPONSIBILITY

Now I'll admit that this is a tough one because often your ego, your pride, your reputation, or your public image, can be hurt by admitting that you were wrong. But ultimately, such an admission will benefit you in ways you might not have imagined. It will earn you respect from people around you when you accept responsibility for your words and actions instead of blaming others for your faults.

You may think that you're already taking responsibility for your words and actions – and perhaps you are – but more likely than not you're blaming someone or something else for your current condition.

Some examples:

1. Your complaint: "I can't get good grades!" Your excuse: "My teachers are unfair to me!"

    a. Consider your choice to stay up very late on school nights playing video games causing you to be too tired to learn properly – your responsibility

    b. Maybe you need additional tutoring, but you haven't asked for it – your responsibility

2. Your complaint: "I can't keep any friends." Your excuse: "They become awful people after a while."

    a. Chances are…it's you, not them who is intolerable. For this situation, I like to quote astrophysicist Neil DeGrasse Tyson to provide some context. *"One of the great challenges in this world is knowing enough about a subject to* think *you're right, but not enough about the subject to* know *you're wrong"*

    b. Applying this to you and your friends, it may mean that you're too stubborn to admit that you *could* be wrong, so you strongly hold onto an *incorrect* conclusion to the disbelief and discontent of your friends who can clearly see the *correct* answer. Eventually, the disagreements – caused, in part, by your ignorance of the subject that you *think* you know, and partly from you protecting your ego and pride by not admitting you're *actually* wrong – may become too much, and they move on.

    c.   Taking responsibility for your words and actions means admitting you're wrong when evidence counter to what you *think* you know becomes apparent

3.   Your complaint: "I can't get a well-paying job." Your excuse: "All of the better employers are... (pick one or more: racist, ageist, sexist, don't like: how I dress, how I act, how I smell, how I look, how I speak)."

    a.   More likely it's because *you* didn't pursue any form of a secondary education to make yourself more marketable, and/ or you're still holding onto petty choices in behavior from high school

    b.   Accept that it was *your choice* to not do any further education, or to behave poorly, and now you're suffering the consequences

    c.   With that realization – i.e., accepting that this decision is your responsibility – you may still be able to make the right choice and get into a continuing education situation that'll improve your skills and marketability

4.   Your complaint: "I can't get a well-paying job." Your excuse: "That cop destroyed my life when he pulled me over and charged me with a DWI!"

    a.   Accept that it was *your choice* to drink, and then to drive after having too many drinks

    b.   While a DWI on your record will not help your job search, or even to keep a job, that cop may have actually *helped* you by keeping you from either killing yourself or others on the road! If not that night, maybe another time!

    c.   Yes, you *will* have to suffer the immediate consequences, the fines, possible jail time, probation, travel restrictions, but then it's up to you to take the appropriate steps toward re-building a clean reputation that you can discuss with a future employer. It's better to have made a better choice in the beginning and accept that your future is your responsibility

5. Your complaint: "I can't get a promotion at work!" Your excuse: "The boss doesn't like me."

    a. More likely than not, you have established a pattern or history of blaming your failures on your coworkers instead of accepting the responsibility yourself

    b. Any time that you make a mistake at work, be the responsible person and admit that it was your fault, that you see what you did wrong, and that you can correct it

    c. Taking responsibility for your failures and learning from them is not only a very noble and humble thing, and most bosses will appreciate this, but it will earn you the respect of those around you, including your boss

Bottom line. Every decision that you have ever made throughout your life will affect your future. You are fully responsible for your current situation – where you are in life right now. Even while you're a minor living with your parents or guardians, you are responsible for the way you respond to them, and that ultimately affects your future. It is up to you (your responsibility) to try and make the best decisions you can, and always take responsibility for your words and actions.

ADDRESS DEPRESSION
AND OTHER MENTAL HEALTH ISSUES

A key to succeeding if you're prone to depression is to first recognize and accept that you have depression. It's also important to understand that it is a mental health issue that needs to be addressed. If you know that you have clinical depression or any form of mental illness, you *can still* succeed and live the life you want. It's very important that you keep this in mind, and constantly remind yourself of this fact. To do this, you must have a strong support network, including professional help (therapist), friends, and family. If you're unsure where to turn, check out the resources at the end of the book.

CONSIDER YOUR LIFE AS A SERIES OF SHORT STORIES

Consider this; think of your life *not* as one epic novel, rather, break it down into a series of easily managed short stories – each one with a guaranteed happy ending. Any time that you start into a new endeavor (a new short story), think ONLY that it WILL succeed favorably (the guaranteed happy ending). Sure, there may be some minor pitfalls (every well-written story has some conflict and problems to solve), but by making well-informed choices, you can head them off before they grow into something unmanageable. Maintaining a positive, optimistic attitude will ensure a successful conclusion of each new task. These, in turn, will build upon each other to help support your overall quest for success and happiness.

Here's a real-life example of how this short story thing can work. I was presented with a very complex microprocessor card at work recently, and it had problems. I'd never seen the circuit before, and yet I was responsible for solving the problems and redesigning the card to make it work reliably over the full military temperature range. Now, I could have approached this problem in either of two different ways. 1) I could have become totally overwhelmed and intimidated by the sheer complexity of it all, and the pressure to solve the problem, and maybe even asked someone else to do it, or 2) I could look at it as a fun challenge that would look good on my resume. I chose option #2.

Well, that was just the first part – choosing to take on the task. Once that was decided, I quickly found that I hadn't the slightest clue as to what the problem might be. I will admit that this clueless feeling could have made it seem totally overwhelming to me. The one thing that kept this from happening was that I KNEW that there'd be a happy ending! I had no idea how. I couldn't see it when I started the task. But I *knew* that I would find the problem and fix it, because I'd already scripted ALL of my short stories that way. In my mind, therefore, there is no other way for any of my short

story experiences to end! What really happened? What else? In a sudden flash of insight, found the problem, fixed it with an applicable redesign, and made the card even more robust than ever! Happy ending.

This could never happen, you say. It's happened to me more times than I can count! While it'll usually occur to me while I'm troubleshooting a complex circuit, it can apply in the course of any problem-solving endeavor. Louis Pasteur summed it up well when he said, *"Chance favors the prepared mind."* More prophetic words have seldom been spoken! For instance, when I'm working on a complex problem, I'll test, measure, read, research, re-measure, re-test, review, and relate everything I've learned about the problem in my head. This is the preparation phase. I've filled my mind with as much pertinent information about the problem as I can. The eureka moment might come over night while I'm sleeping – as it's done hundreds of times – or it might take months for it to come to fruition. Either way, it is because I've prepared my mind the best I can to address the problem, that some chance connection is suddenly made, and voila! The answer becomes plain as day.

Here's a situation that more of you might be able to relate to. After working as an engineer for a specific company for about 25-years, they laid me off during one of their many annual downsizing exercises. This would have devastated many people, but I simply looked at it as a chance to explore new opportunities. Some may say it was naïveté, but I was simply confident that the many prior good choices I'd made had sufficiently prepared me to weather this situation with a favorable conclusion. I never once allowed myself to believe that I would fail. Now, obviously, I didn't just sit back and wait for something to come to me. Every day I was actively pursuing new employment, and even trying my hand as a full-time professional photographer at my own studio. The studio income helped considerably, but still wouldn't cover the bills long-term, so I was relieved, but not surprised, when I received an offer to continue my engineering career at a new company. Failure simply wasn't an option, or even a consideration. It never even entered my mind! Remaining an optimist will keep you from becoming depressed, despondent, or worse, and it is your best means towards a successful and happy future.

IT'S OKAY TO BE SMART!

I grew up at a time when being smart in the United States was NOT fashionable. It wasn't considered a positive attribute by many of my classmates in school. In fact, I was severely picked on and harassed by bullies almost daily until my senior year of high school specifically because they didn't like it that I was smarter than them, that I had an intense interest in all things technical, and that I refused to fight back – despite having more than enough strength to do so. Fortunately, I just didn't care what they thought, and I really didn't want to "fit in" with those who would treat others like this. I managed to get through those early school years confident in the knowledge that my technical interests would propel me far beyond anything the bullies could even imagine. And I was RIGHT!

I want to make it *very* clear here that I DO NOT condone bullying in any form. It cuts deeply into your self-confidence and self-esteem, and if you can't visualize your life beyond the next few years, then it could even end catastrophically. Fortunately, for me, I did know that I had a great future ahead of me, ironically because of the very things that the bullies harassed me over. As such, I stuck it out, survived, and used my pent-up anger and desire for revenge towards them as *motivation* to push myself to become as successful as possible. I wanted them to watch me succeed while they failed by their own bad choices. This would be the ultimate revenge for me!

I do not believe in violence or directly seeking revenge, but I really didn't want these bullies to get away with what they'd done without suffering any consequences, either. Therefore, I decided that the best revenge would be *passive, not physical, and especially not violent.* Because of their limited intellect and having no marketable skills, the bullies would remain close to home, stuck in minimum wage jobs for much or all of their lives, while they'd watch with great envy as I became remarkably successful in the career of my dreams, saw the world, and fulfilled most of my aspirations. While I'm really not one to gloat (okay, maybe just a little!), attending my first high school reunion brought me great internal satisfaction as I witnessed precisely what I'd predicted with these former bullies! What I *hadn't* expected, however, was that some were actually *apologetic* about the way

they'd treated me in school. They openly apologized, and, in fact, actually admired my brother and me for not only our career success, but also for the many incredible activities and adventures that we'd experienced as a direct result of our good choices. It seems that they'd finally matured, but they'd still lived a substantial portion of their lives struggling to survive in abject misery because of their earlier choices of shunning intellectual concepts and relying solely upon the superficial, temporary popularity they'd enjoyed in high school. Don't be afraid to be smart!

BOOST YOUR SUCCESS!

Establish a friendly competition with another person. In my case, I competed with my twin brother, Bill, and he competed with me. Together, it pushed us both to continue to explore new and more complex concepts in electronics at a very rapid rate. As young teens, when one of us would design a certain circuit or device, the other would want to improve upon that. It just went on like that, causing each of us to learn new concepts to make our design better than the previous.

This exponential learning gave us both a significant edge over our peers, as, by the time we were out of college, we'd already done more circuit designs, and worked with more kinds of circuits than many engineers will in the first twenty years of their professional careers. This made us very attractive for the engineering market, which propelled us to a very comfortable level of success rather quickly.

CHOOSE A LUCRATIVE FIELD OF STUDY

I fully realize that not everybody has a desire to be an engineer like my brother and me. But, there are many other options, including vocational or trade schools, and in the sciences that will support a comfortable future. I started at a trade school, and then I went on to college after completing that. Why am I pushing the trades and sciences versus the arts? Both from my own experience and observations over 5 years as a technician, and 42-years (UPDATED) as an engineer, and from published data[1], there is a significant disparity between the income of those who've studied a trade versus a high school education only, and also those with a Bachelor of Science versus those with a Bachelor of Arts degree. I frequently tell young people to *work in the sciences and live in the arts*. That is, they'll bring in a rather comfortable income working in a technical field, and then, in the abundant leisure time they'll have by not having to work three or four different jobs just to survive, they can pursue the artistic passions that gives their lives satisfaction. I've provided a brief list of some popular Bachelor of Science disciplines here: Biochemistry, Bioengineering, Cell Biology, Chemical Engineering, Computer Sciences, Cosmology, Developmental Biology & Genetics, Electrical Engineering, Electronics Engineering, Electronics Technician, Immunology, Mathematics, Mechanical Engineering, Medicine, Microbiology, Molecular & Computational Biology, Neuroscience, Physics, Physiology (Anatomy, Endocrinology, Nutrition, Pharmacology, Toxicology), Social & Behavioral Sciences (Anthropology, Psychology, Sociology), and Software Engineering.

REMAIN FOCUSED

Preparation to read this section

Remaining focused on your goals for success seems like a basic and unimposing concept, but it's going to get pretty rough for some of you as we get deeper into it. It's going to sound like I'm preaching – saying that you can't continue to do some of the activities that you might enjoy. I assure you that this is not the case. The purpose of this section is only to put into perspective what certain activities will cost you both monetarily and in lost time *when done in excess*. Remember, all things in moderation. If you elect to ignore this section, well, that's your *choice*. But since you're reading this book in the first place, it suggests that you're interested in achieving sustained success and happiness. Since, *making the right choices* has been a consistent theme throughout, I'm confident that you'll want to read this part, as well. Now, take a deep breath, and push through it.

Avoid excessive intoxicants

It is not possible for you to remain focused on your goal of aggressively seeking success if you're frequently walking (or lying) around in a mental haze. While I do not recommend the total prohibition of all intoxicants, I do suggest *reasonable and responsible use*, particularly for young people – those of legal age for such, of course. Everybody wants to have fun, especially when you're in college, and I was no exception. The greatest difference between many of my classmates and myself, however, was that I didn't go to parties with the specific intention of getting wasted. I actually wanted to maintain my composure, meet women, and even *remember* the evening! I'd have a drink or two, and then, *without toking*, I'd pass along the communal joint to the next person and mingle. I just had a general aversion to fogging my brain in any way that might derail the focused pursuit of my goals for success.

My plan was to get through school, earning a highly marketable bachelor's degree, and establish my career, thus becoming fully independent from my parents, *as quickly as possible*. Only then could I allow myself to occasionally indulge in activities that would have adversely affected my progress through school. I graduated with an engineering bachelor's degree in just three years, at age 21, by attending school year-round and remaining totally focused on my goal of success!

Avoid multiple changes to your major in college

I want to be understanding here and say that I realize that most people won't know what they want to do with their lives when they enter college, but if you've read through this book as a teen and you've applied what I've talked about and even demonstrated to you in my stories, then there really is no excuse for indecision by the time you finish high school! Every time you change your major, you've wasted precious time and money. Now, if you or your family is exceptionally wealthy, and you really don't care that it'll take you eight to ten years just to get a marketable degree, then that's your choice. But, for the rest of us, we simply cannot afford to still be in school, working minimum wage crap-jobs, until we're almost 30! That's more than a third of a typical life span!

Avoid addictions

Any addiction can be destructive if it can't be moderated or eliminated. This is particularly bad when you don't have a marketable college degree, or some other unique talent that'll legally earn you the large sums of money needed to support not only an addiction, but also those pesky living expenses like food, rent, gas for your car, car payments, and utilities, as well. Those who are stuck working part-time minimum wage jobs simply cannot earn what it takes to support addictive behavior – and survive...much less achieve lofty goals and fulfill their dreams! Let's take a closer look at some examples of how various addictions can affect the low paid worker – which represents about 50% of the unskilled workforce[2] under age 25.

A person with a 2-pack per day cigarette habit in NY State[3] will need to work 32-hours a week (after taxes, at the minimum wage rate at the time of this writing) JUST to support this addiction. That's about $200 per week just burned up in smoke! There'll be nothing left over to allow them to buy groceries, gas for the car, insurance, pay the rent, the phone bill, etc.!

If alcohol is your chosen poison, then you'll be spending about half of your minimum wage paycheck on beer (one 6-pack/day), or the entire week's earnings for harder liquor (4-shots/day) at a bar. Statistically[4], about twice as many heavy smokers are also heavy drinkers, compared to non-smokers. In order to buy 2-packs of cigarettes a day, plus a six-pack of beer per day, plus just one shot of hard liquor a day – an amount considered typical for a heavy smoker/drinker – you would need to work 51-hours a week (after taxes) JUST to burn up and drink your earnings!

One who's addicted to drugs like crack cocaine[5] or crystal meth[6], will have to come up with between $400 and $700 per week just to maintain a high! Generally, since minimum wage simply can't supply this sum, it causes such addicts to turn to crime to produce this kind of cash. I think you can figure out what that'll do to any plans you might have had for your future success and happiness, since you'll either be in jail, or dead. If you're reading this book, I trust that this does not describe you.

While I was surprised to learn that marijuana isn't horrifically expensive to buy, there are still two significant reasons to avoid it. Currently, it is still illegal in most states for recreational use. We've covered what'll happen to your path to success if you're in jail or paying off huge fines. Even where it's legal, if used excessively, it'll sap all of your motivation to forge ahead with any plans towards a better life.

Even video game addiction[7] will take its toll if it is not moderated. While there may not be nearly as great a monetary loss playing video games constantly as with some of these other addictions, it will completely tap out any and all of your time. This is time that you *could* have spent studying, preparing for your successful career, or even developing or maintaining a close relationship with a significant other. I've watched relationships dissolve when one person is addicted to video games. I've seen how they've affected the focus of players in school. They lose interest in *everything* except the game. Many excessive gamers will end up obese because they're nearly always sitting at a computer or console playing games and eating fast/junk food – a typically very sedentary activity. I've also witnessed the deep regret that reformed gamers feel once they've "kicked their game habit", and suddenly realize how much of their life they've literally wasted, instead of pursuing their goals for success and happiness!

Fogging up your brain with intoxicants, changing your major frequently, and becoming dependent upon addictive substances or unproductive activities, are all *choices* that people make. These are *not* what I'll refer to as "good choices", as they will *severely* affect the focus on your path to success and happiness. At the very least, bad choices like these will cause you to spend an excessive amount of time in abject misery (i.e., working crappy minimum wage jobs) while trying to achieve your goals. Addictions can also completely remove your drive and motivation to reach for success. Worse yet, they can result in a *permanent* criminal record that no employer will look favorable upon, or, worse still, that always-lurking fatal death thing!

If any of this sounds really harsh or severe, well, that's good. It should. Perhaps it'll help push those with such addictions, or their loved ones, to do something positive in order to moderate or eliminate the addictions, thereby being the first step towards their eventual future success. If you currently suffer an addiction, and want to get it under control, please check out the Resources section of this book.

Avoid Teen Pregnancy

One of the most significant events that will completely derail your quest for success, other than death, of course, is to get yourself, or someone else, pregnant while you're still in your teens! Most teenagers have neither the skills nor the education needed to earn the kind of wage required to care for and raise a child properly. They're also not emotionally equipped to make proper decisions for the child. Not only have they produced a minimum of an 18-year delay to *start* to achieve some level of their own success and happiness, but they'll also very likely have set up the *child* for failure, as well. Yeah, sex is fun, but it can wait until you can *afford* to take that risk!

PERSONAL HYGIENE

I hesitated to put this topic into the book, because it's so very personal. But upon lengthy consideration, I've determined that it's no less important than many of the other subjects. Bad personal hygiene *will* adversely affect your quest for success and happiness in ways that you might never have considered.

You can call it discrimination if you want, but the bottom line is that the human species is naturally wired to avoid people with bad complexions, those who always stink, those who are severely overweight or obese, and those who are notably emaciated. It's not that they're being particularly insensitive; it's that the survival of the species basically *requires* it. We, as human beings, are subconsciously predisposed to seek a healthy mate who will be more likely to produce healthy children who will have a greater chance to survive, thus helping to perpetuate the species. Factors like untreated open sores (acne), obesity, who will often sweat excessively, thus producing quite unpleasant odors, or skeletal appearance, are easily detectable, outward signs of an unhealthy human. Such a person is considered to be more likely to be prone to severe, debilitating and even fatal diseases, which might even be passed along genetically, therefore an unfavorable candidate for a mate.

Since we're prewired to avoid such people for a mate, we will subconsciously (or sometimes consciously) reject job candidates based solely upon their appearance. No. It isn't fair. Yes. It is wrong. But it's also a *fact*. People who *look healthy and don't stink* will *always* be considered first for jobs, and, especially for romantic relationships! Hence, your hygiene *does* affect your prospects for success and happiness.

How to Eliminate Acne Once and For All

I completely understand that acne is a part of being a teen. I had it pretty bad for a short while, myself, when I was 14...that is, until I improved my personal hygiene! It had become quite pervasive all over my cheeks and chin for a good portion of that year. At first, I didn't do anything about it because to do so would mean that I'd have to acknowledge that it was, in fact, problematic...and this embarrassed me to think that I was flawed. Fortunately, in the biology class I was taking that year in 9th grade, the instructor talked about the causes of acne, and how best to control and, ultimately, eliminate it. I feel that it would be a great disservice if I didn't pass this information along to those who can benefit from it.

It is a fact that teens will have oily skin. It's just part of that post-puberty thing. But this doesn't automatically relegate you to having to live with terminal acne… if you simply take a few basic and simple actions. Adults, too, please take note…you should be doing this, too, as there's absolutely no excuse for an adult to have pervasive, long-lasting, or severe acne.

1. Wash your face at least twice a day – once in the morning, and once just before bed
2. Avoid touching your face with your fingertips
3. Don't pick at existing zits with your fingernails without immediate cleaning with soap and water

Washing your face will help keep the buildup of oil and the dirt/bacteria that gets trapped in your pores significantly at bay and will help existing zits to heal.

Your fingertips, especially the nails, are rife with bacteria. If, for instance, you're sitting in class resting your chin on your hands, you're basically directly injecting bacteria into your wide-open, oil-saturated pores. This is called "mechanical acne" and is *very easy* to avoid – don't touch your face with your fingertips or fingernails unless it's to wash it.

I know. Picking at a zit is substantially compelling! You just want to open it up so that it'll drain and, hopefully, heal quickly. Well, that's the thought, but if you're doing it without first thoroughly washing your hands – particularly scrubbing under your nails '- and then cleaning the entire area around and including the opened zit with soap and water immediately afterward, then the only thing you're achieving is the spread of many new zits! Don't pick without washing the area immediately afterward.

Establish a basic, consistent, routine that you follow without exception *every* morning and night. You may arrange your routine however it suits you, but I'll provide my routine here as an example. I take a shower every morning. I realize that many people don't shower every morning, but you should still wash your face in the sink. Since I don't drink coffee, this also serves as my

YOUR SUCCESS - YOUR CHOICE

wakeup method. It's really the best way to be clean and fresh throughout the day to come – particularly if you interact with other people a lot. By washing everything in the shower, I'm cleaning my face the first of the two recommended times each day. After the shower, I clean my ears with cotton swabs, rinse my mouth with mouthwash for 30-seconds to kill bacteria, then I brush my teeth to remove stubborn bacteria. I then apply deodorant, and then I'll shave my face. When I leave the house in the morning after I'm dressed, I'm always fresh, clean, and looking respectable. At the end of the day, I always wash my face just before bed. This will remove the bacteria that were trapped to the oils on your face throughout the day, and keep them from doing their damage while you sleep. All of this, plus avoiding touching my face with my fingers, keeps me looking, feeling, and *being* healthy.

One more thing; always wash your hands after using the bathroom. Failure to do so will not only spread whatever you might have to others, but it'll contribute to more illnesses for you than if you'd washed properly.

Offensive Odors

If you think the last section was overly personal, I've got news for you; the next section is much worse. But, because it's become so pervasive with too many people these days, I simply cannot ignore it. Now, take another deep breath, but you just might want to hold it this time while you read the next paragraph – it's going to get stinky!

I really, truly, did NOT want to get into this, but it seems to be something that severely overweight and obese people just don't seem to understand. Since more and more people in America are becoming obese, it's become an important topic. By virtue of the excessive flesh they have, they'll have lots of skin folds that others simply don't have. Each of these areas is a source of both sweat and trapped bacteria, which, when combined, creates an extremely offensive odor. The worst area, however, is the natural crease that all people have – the butt crack! Yeah. It's disgusting, but it's even more so when people clearly aren't washing there in the shower, and then they end up sweating profusely onto trapped feces there! This produces a really sharp, rancid stench, similar to the smell from common Dry-Erase markers, only much, much stronger. It's overwhelming all around them, and yet they somehow just don't seem to notice it! THIS, alone, will severely affect a person's ability to succeed, as many employers can't tolerate employees who stink. They may not be able to terminate them for stinking, unless they're working around food, but they can, and *will* make the employee's tasks or hours increasingly unpleasant, basically forcing them to quit. Smelling bad is also very detrimental to your happiness, as it's very difficult for anyone to get close to you. This is something of a prerequisite for romantic relationships.

Just exercise good, consistent hygiene, and it'll open up *many* more doors.

How to Lose Weight Effectively, Efficiently, and Safely

(UPDATED) We've established that excessive weight can be unpleasant, not only to the health of the overweight person, but to those around them in the form of unpleasant odors, unless extensive care is taken to wash all of the folds and creases...more than once or twice a day.

If you are comfortable at your current weight – no matter what it might be – you maintain good hygiene, you're eating nutritious meals, and you remain active for good health, then this is your choice, and I am quite happy for you. I've known some plus-sized women who are exceptionally attractive, very confident, and amazing people. More power to them!

But, for those of you who wish to lose weight – for whatever reason; perhaps for a healthier lifestyle, to attract a mate more easily, or to be able to enjoy physical activities that they might not be able to do with excess weight – please read on...

For as long as I was doing gymnastics, I never had any difficulty keeping off unwanted weight. Unfortunately, gymnastics, is:

1) Not offered to adults everywhere

2) VERY hard on the back – which is ultimately the major factor of why I finally had to stop when I was 41

Because I absolutely loved doing gymnastics, nothing else appealed to me as much. As such, I ended up basically doing very little, if any, exercising after I'd quit gymnastics.

As you might imagine the sudden cessation of intense physical activity, plus the natural reduction of the metabolism as one ages, while continuing to eat like I was still doing gymnastics, ultimately resulted in inevitable weight gain.

This is a recounting of my personal struggle with weight gain *after* my carefree years in gymnastics, and how I finally discovered, in 2021, an exceptionally effective, efficient, and healthy way to get rid of the unwanted weight. With restricted activities allowed during quarantine throughout most of 2020, and into 2021 while the pandemic was raging, it caused a lot of people to gain additional weight – myself included. In fact, I made a graph of my daily weight over the past few years (yeah, I just happened to keep such a record!), and I was astounded at how, unlike the typical up and down trends of prior years, my weight in 2020 just continued upward!

Therefore, after reaching a very uncomfortable peak weight in February 2021, I finally took back control of my weight and entered a 5-month weight-loss journey of my own creation.

> *First things first; I am NOT a nutritionist. I am not an expert in nutrition, physiology, kinesiology, or anything related. The information I'm about to provide here is consolidated from my own experience and research throughout my effective weight loss journey and should not be considered medical advice. Always consult your physician before making any significant changes to your lifestyle.*

That said, I can virtually guarantee that you will lose the amount of weight you desire quickly, easily, and safely, all while eating normal foods, without ever feeling hungry, *if you choose to commit* to losing unwanted weight, and follow the guidance I'll provide here.

The process for highly effective weight-loss can be summed up in this very simple statement: **Portion Size & Exercise**

Speaking of portion sizes, you need to understand that most meals that you'll get at restaurants will be somewhere between two and four times larger than the portion size you should be eating for each meal. Take a good portion of the meal home and have it for another meal, or two if you get a meal from a restaurant

The human body is an amazing collection of control systems. A control system is something that self-corrects when sensing a deviation from a set point. Think of the thermostat in your home. You set it to a specific temperature. If it gets too cold (a deviation from the set point) the heating system turns on until the thermostat senses that the ambient temperature has reached the set point. Then it turns off, thereby keeping the temperature very close to that set point. The thermostat provides "feedback" to the heating system to tell it when to turn on and when to turn off. This is called a feedback control loop.

You'll undoubtedly notice that your thermostat might not turn on the heat until it's somewhere between three and five degrees lower than the set point. This allowable variation from the set point is called hysteresis. It defines a range of temperatures that's considered acceptable before turning on the heating system. Otherwise, the instant it turns off the heating system, it'd turn it right back on again, and so on. This is neither efficient nor necessary, and it causes excessive wear on the heating system components. Similarly, your body has a certain built-in hysteresis range, as well as a set point that varies according to your current weight and physical activity.

Your body's prime-directive is "Survival". Technically, "Procreate" is #1, but you can't procreate if you can't survive, so by default, survival becomes #1 in importance.

When it comes to caloric intake needed to survive, your body self-adjusts its set point based upon fairly long periods of consistent intake. Which is to say, when you eat a certain amount per day over an extended period of time (months), your body adjusts its set point to that amount. This means that when you consistently eat more, your body eventually "gets used to" eating more, and it considers anything below a relatively narrow range – the hysteresis range – to be a threat to its survival.

In actuality, when I say that your body "gets used to eating more", what I mean is that it's made internal adjustments to burn more energy, while storing what it can't use right away as fat. Therefore, when you eat more and don't do sufficient activities to offset that extra intake, you'll, ultimately, weigh more. When you weigh more your muscles need to do more work for you to be able to function, thereby requiring more energy than one who weighs less. This need for more energy is equivalent to raising your "internal set point", and it translates into a need for more caloric intake, causing you to eat more. This is what we engineers call "divergent response". It's a runaway condition that is catastrophic in a control system. But our bodies evolved and adapted – from prehistoric times – to fatten up on the latest pterodactyl kill, since it doesn't know when *or if* another meal might be available, and it just wants to survive long enough to procreate...a lot! Okay...I know, early Homo Sapiens didn't coexist with dinosaurs such as the pterodactyl, but it was simply too amusing a scenario to resist.

Ironically, there's currently a larger threat to the body by storing *too much* fat – as is the case with the average American – than starvation, but the body hasn't adapted a mechanism to automatically fix this yet. This is when we need to intervene with conscious will power to take control of our bodies.

The "threat to survival" response can be triggered if you *suddenly and significantly* reduce your caloric intake (i.e., eat *a lot* less all of a sudden). Certain hormones in your body (specifically; Leptin, T3, and norepinephrine) will start to hold onto energy by not releasing stored fat, reduce your metabolic rate to conserve the expenditure of energy, causing you to feel sluggish, and make you feel hungry, causing you to want to eat. All of these, together, become a strong impediment to weight loss. *The key to effective weight loss is to reduce caloric intake gradually* so that it doesn't trigger what some refer to as "starvation mode".

To do this effectively, it's extremely important to maintain a tight control system feedback loop. That is, you record your weight daily, and closely track your caloric and nutrient intake, to be sure you're not approaching your specific caloric level that triggers starvation mode, while providing the opportunity for quick and effective adjustments to your intake and/ or activity level, as needed on a daily basis. This is what we engineers call "convergent response". It's where we can make corrections in a direction opposite the measured effect, (i.e., exercise more and/or eat less when we observe a higher weight) before they get out of hand, thereby converging on the desired result.

For the lack of a better name, I'll call this the "Control Loop Method for Weight Loss". It's really not a "diet", rather, more of a lifestyle.

I'm going to list social relationship categories that can affect the success of weight loss. It is not intended to exhibit any bias towards or against any group of people, nor is it intended to discourage anyone from losing unwanted weight. It is simply a realistic and practical assessment based upon general human behavior, and the knowledge that important personal changes can only happen effectively when those around you support you while making those changes.

For example, if you're in a romantic relationship, it's very likely that you will bend to the desires of your significant other, which *may* not be fully aligned with the direction you need to go for your own progress.

For instance,

Partner #1: "Let's go get a bite to eat at this restaurant."

Partner #2: "But I'm trying to lose weight."

Partner #1: "Come on… you've hardly been eating anything. You should treat yourself!"

Partner #2: "Hmmmm…okay."

With the exception of the occasional "refeed days" (we'll get to that later), this will derail Partner #2's weight loss progress if it happens too often. You need support from your partner.

This doesn't mean you break up. It just means that you need to discuss with your partner the importance of you following a specific path to achieve a healthier lifestyle and ask for their support…and *then* you break up with them! Just kidding. Don't do that.

The percentage figures I'll provide to indicate probability of success are *not, in any way,* hard, scientifically or mathematically based statistics. They're literally just a "gutfeel figure", given only as a way to indicate a *concise relative approximation of the probability of success* that you might expect under each social category. Do not let a low probability of success keep you from embarking on your journey towards better health through weight loss. It only means you'll have more challenges if you don't have the support of those around you, but it can still be done. Support, support, support! That's the key here.

The temptation to just go get a meal at a restaurant is strong. It's much stronger if you're living with others, because they aren't necessarily restricting their caloric intake to lose weight. You will need to fight the urge to abandon your diet, and this will be far easier if those around you fully support your choice to improve your health through a structured diet and exercise plan.

Social category factors that will affect your weight-loss success:

1. 95% probability of successful weight loss: You are single, divorced, or separated, living alone or with roommate(s) who are very independent

2. 75% probability of successful weight loss: You are a minor living with your parents or guardians – support of parents or guardians increases chance of success

3. 50% probability of successful weight loss: You are part of a couple (i.e., dating, living together romantically, married) – support of significant other increases chance of success

4. 25% probability of successful weight loss: You are a single parent on a tight budget with one or more young children and limited childcare or other support – a strong support system and/or greater income significantly increases chance of success

I'm going to be candid here… the most difficult thing about dieting is psychological. If you're used to going out to restaurants for many of your meals like I had become, then it'll take some time to become successful in consistently resisting the urge to head out for your meals after you've begun a diet. But it CAN be done!

Assumptions:

1. You are able to move about on your own without assistance

2. You can get to a gym on a regular basis, and do effective workouts safely

3. You can do additional physical activities such as swimming, tennis, team sports, long walks, hikes, bike rides, even mowing the lawn (not on a rider!) to augment gym workouts in good weather

4. You do not consume excessive amounts of alcohol

About alcohol consumption and the metabolism.

The body cannot store alcohol. Only its sugar content can be metabolized, and that is broken down into carbohydrates and fats while the liver is working to "detoxify" the poison that alcohol literally represents to the body. It does this by converting the ethanol in alcohol into a less toxic compound. The stomach can't efficiently process nutrients because the alcohol reduces the ability of the pancreas to produce the digestive enzymes needed for proper nutritional absorption. The nutrients derived from alcohol, and from food eaten while consuming alcohol, do not affect "satiety", partially because of the reduced absorption, and because it contains no protein. That is, it won't make you feel full – satiated – thereby disabling the body's natural regulation system that keeps you from consuming too much. All of this, together, increases weight from added fat, reduced nutritional absorption, and a greatly reduced metabolism.

Things you'll need to effectively exercise this weight-loss method:

1. A digital bathroom scale, so you can see the small changes in your progress

2. A blender for single-serving smoothies

3. The ability to weigh yourself in precisely the same condition (i.e., naked) every morning before you've had anything for breakfast

4. A membership at a local gym – many good, national gyms charge about $30/month ($1/day)

5. Uninterrupted time (about 45-min/day) available to do at least three gym workouts per week

6. About $12 per day (average, if you're below 200 pounds) for all of your meals, including "refeed days" at restaurants of your choice every week or so

Beyond the one-time cost of $25-$35 for the digital bathroom scale and $50 to $80 for the blender, your only recurring costs are about $13 per day for ALL of your daily meals, *including* the daily cost of the gym membership… IF your starting weight is below 200 pounds. For every 50 pounds additional weight, it adds about $3.00 per day (in 2021). For example, starting at 250 pounds, it'll cost around $16 per day. 300 pounds will cost around $19 per day, and so on. Basically, you can add about $0.06 per pound above 200 pounds to the base $13/day cost.

As such, the daily cost of meals using this diet is least expensive for older, shorter, lower-weight females, with lower activity and more expensive for younger, taller, higher-weight males with higher activity – based upon their respective Base Metabolic Rate (BMR) figures.

I should make it clear here that you'll be buying/making all of your own meals from your regular weekly grocery shopping. This method does not supply or sell meals. This method is only a description of HOW to achieve effective, efficient weight loss safely. The rest is up to you. It is, after all, your choice whether or not to lose the weight!

Why does it cost more if you weigh more?

This is because you can't just drop to eating 1,200 calories a day if you weigh, say, 400 pounds! It is neither healthy nor productive.

For example, a fictitious 25-year-old male who is 6 feet 6 inches tall and weighs 400 pounds and only gets light activity burns 3,876 calories per day. In order to lose 1.5 pounds per week, he'd need about a 750 calorie per day deficit. That is, he'd need to consume 3,126 calories a day. This amount will, of course, be reduced as he loses weight. In comparison, another 25-year-old male, also 6 feet 6 inches tall, but only weighs 250 pounds, will, with light activity, burn just 2,976 calories per day. Therefore, with about a 750 calorie per day deficit to lose 1.5 pounds per week, he will need to consume 2,227 calories per day.

Eating more calories than a lighter person means eating more food. More food costs more. Also, with the 2,676-calorie deficit represented by this 400-pound guy dropping to an absurd intake of just 1,200 calories all at once it will cause a number of hormonal changes (Leptin, T3 (thyroid hormone), Norepinephrine), causing the body to think it's starving, which slows the metabolism and holds onto fat – precisely what we *don't* want to happen for effective weight loss.

> *WARNING: The weight loss method described here can be effective with people of any weight, BUT, if they're above 350 pounds, they will invariably be consuming far too much sodium from the sheer volume of food they'll need in order to function if they don't either have the close guidance of a trained nutritionist, or they prepare all of their meals with very careful and specific focus on the sodium content!*

Here's the process.

Create a Database

Determine the number of calories and primary nutritional information (specifically: Protein, Sodium, Fiber, Carbs, Cholesterol, Saturated Fat, & Total Fat) in each meal you'll consume.

Remember, when I said you had to be committed to this? This is the part that can make or break your success...creating the database. If you don't have a database that makes it simple to track all of this information, then you're basically "flying blind", and you are in great peril of either over- or under-consuming an effective number of calories to lose weight, and the appropriate amount of nutrients to stay healthy during an extended caloric deficit scenario.

You can look up everything on the Internet as you go along and jot it down in a notebook if you wish, but I found it FAR easier just to commit several hours in the beginning to entering all of this information about each of the meals I generally eat into a spreadsheet on my computer. I then update it as I go along.

I created just such a spreadsheet in Excel for myself that contains all of this information for up to 30 multi-ingredient (or a main dish with sides) homemade, from-scratch, meals, 100 individual meal items (i.e., a banana, a plum, a cup of yogurt, a granola bar, individual-item frozen dinners, a slice of chocolate cake, a donut, and a large chocolate chip cookie), and 100 menu items from my favorite restaurants (to make wise choices for the "refeed days" every week or so). I'll explain refeed days in a bit.

You'll notice that I've included some very tasty, snacky items in this list of individual meal items that don't seem to be consistent with a diet. A diet doesn't mean depriving yourself of tasty things. It simply means controlling the portion size of those tasty things. For instance, if I feel like eating a serving of one of my favorite kinds of cookies, that means somewhere between two and four cookies, *not an entire sleeve* of them, like I used to! Just be sure that's not ALL you're eating. You still need to be sure to maintain a proper balance of all of the right nutrients each day.

This spreadsheet indicates not only the total calories and nutrients I've consumed each day, but it offers suggestions for caloric targets based upon my current weight and anticipated level of activity that day. The total nutrients consumed are color-coded to indicate if I've consumed too little, just enough, or too much of any important nutrient – which helps keep me healthy during the weight loss process.

Based upon trends gathered from my daily weight entries, it even projects – with exceptional accuracy – the precise date that I will reach a specific weight loss goal. As a point of fact, I did hit my first weight loss goal on the precise date that my spreadsheet projected, and, as I'm writing this now, I am on track to meet my final weight loss goal date – within a day or so.

This spreadsheet is fully customizable, so if you would like to get a copy of this *very* helpful spreadsheet for yourself instead of trying to build a version from scratch, please go to the end of this book (See: **Request Self-Improvement Excel Spreadsheets**) to get instructions about how to request a copy for yourself. The database portion will be populated with all of the meals and nutrition information that I've already entered throughout my own personal weight-loss journey, but you can either add to that, or start over and enter all of your own. Again – your choice!

Weight Every Morning – Naked

I know, many people say not to weigh yourself more than once every week or two, but in doing so, you're *significantly* reducing your probability of success for effective weight loss. Why is this?

Here's an illustrative example; Let's say you're standing on a wagon. Why a wagon? You'll find out in a moment. Also, for the sake of this analogy, this wagon is secured firmly in place, so it won't roll. You're asked to walk from one end to the other (okay…it's kind of a long wagon, and I suppose it's red!)

– with your eyes closed for a specific amount of time. If you close them for only a second, and then reopen them again as you're walking, you can see that you're approaching the end, and you can make a correction or stop in time, thereby remaining on the wagon. If you close your eyes for, say, five seconds while you're walking, it's very likely that you'll quite literally fall off the wagon. I think you can see why I chose a wagon in this illustrative example now. This will happen – you'll fail with your weight loss progress – if you take your weight samples too infrequently. Daily weighing gives you the ability to make corrections to your intake or exercise, if needed, well before you're totally out of control, thereby ensuring a far greater probability that you'll reach your weight loss goals.

Okay, so why every morning, and why naked? Generally, after a fast (i.e., while sleeping each night), your body weight will be at its lowest of each day. Each meal you eat will increase your weight, and physical activity will help reduce it, but it's always going to be lower in the morning simply because your body continues to burn energy even while you're sleeping.

This also brings with it a certain psychological benefit when seeing a lower weight than you might measure later in the day. The reason to weigh yourself naked is for consistency. You won't have clothes, shoes, a towel, or stuff in your pockets to skew your actual weight each day. It will be as accurate a weight measurement as is possible at home. Speaking of consistency, it's also most beneficial to try and weigh yourself at about the same time each morning. I realize this might not always be possible, but as long as it's very soon after you wake up, and before you eat or drink anything that day, it'll be the most accurate.

Record Your Weight in a Tracking Spreadsheet

RECORD your morning weight immediately after weighing. I put it right into my phone with the date so I maintain a running record, but you can write it on a scrap of paper, or in a notebook if that's your preference. Later in the day, I pull up that entry in my phone and enter it into my weight-loss tracking spreadsheet, which generates a graph of my progress. This visual aid is exceptionally helpful from a psychological perspective, as it helps to encourage me to continue.

How Many Calories from Daily Meals?

It takes 3,495.8 calories of energy to burn (metabolize) 1 pound (about ½ kilogram) of adipose tissue. Adipose tissue is fat plus water – the typical composition of tissue where fat is stored.

Therefore, if you want to reduce your weight by 1 pound per week, you will need to reduce your intake by 500 fewer calories than the number of calories that you expect to burn that day. This is called your "caloric deficit".

Where did the "500 calories" figure come from? If it takes 3,495.8 calories to burn 1 pound, and you want to lose 1 pound per week, then divide 3,495.8 by 7 (days in a week), and the result is almost exactly a 500-calorie reduction (i.e., deficit) each day. Similarly, to lose ½ pound (about 0.227 kg) per week, divide 3,495.8 in half (about 1,748), and divide that result by 7 days in a week to get about a 250-calorie reduction per day.

How can you know how many calories you expect to burn? For this, we will need a slightly more complicated formula, called the Harris-Benedict Equation for determining a person's BMR. You'll recall that this is your Base Metabolic Rate. It was first developed in 1918, refined in 1984, and then revised yet again in 1990 – to account for our more sedentary lifestyle now than was common in the early 1900s. A person's BMR is the number of calories their body will burn over a 24-hour period while resting. Yes, you'll need to convert to the Metric System, if you're using pounds and inches, to use this formula, but it's straight-forward after that.

$$BMR_{Male} = \left(10 \times Weight_{kg}\right) + \left(6.25 \times Height_{cm}\right) - \left(5 \times Age_{years}\right) + 5$$

$$BMR_{Female} = \left(10 \times Weight_{kg}\right) + \left(6.25 \times Height_{cm}\right) - \left(5 \times Age_{years}\right) - 161$$

Obviously, unless you're in a coma, or you sleep as much as the typical house cat, this BMR figure needs to be modified by the level of activity you do each day, in order to obtain a realistic estimate of calories burned. Because "level of activity" is a very, *very* subjective thing, the multiplication factors for different levels of activity vary a fair amount. I've taken the average value of each activity level factor from the many I've found, and provided them here, along with a guideline for the level of activity they're correlated with. To use these factors, multiply the BMR by the factor corresponding to the level of activity you estimate is applicable to your daily activity.

1 x BMR Used for basal activity level (sleeping)

1.15 x BMR Used for sedentary activity (little to no exercise, sitting at a desk)

1.32 x BMR Used for light activity (light exercise/sports 1 to 3 days per week)

1.48 x BMR Used for moderate activity (moderate exercise/sports 3 to 5 days per week)

1.65 x BMR Used for heavy activity (very vigorous, hard exercise/sports 6 to 7 days per week)

Here's a fictitious example:

A person – male – weighs 150 pounds (about 68 kilos). They're 5 feet, 7 inches tall (about 170cm). They're 27 years old.

Their BMR is: 1,612.5 calories, resting

They work out 3 to 5 days per week, which is considered "light" activity, with a factor of 1.32.

The number of calories they can expect to burn each day is: 1,612.5 x 1.32 = 2,128.5 calories

To lose 1 pound in a week, this person should consume 2,128.5 – 500 = 1,628.5 calories per day.

I should mention that the chart of yours, or mine, or anybody's weight loss progress *will not be* a straight line! It *will* go up, it *will* go down, and up again, and return downwards yet again with *every* daily weighing. *This is normal!* It is the *average trend* that's important. If you show less weight at the end of each week, that's progress. If not, then you need to increase your level of activity until you see the proper trend direction. By this, I don't mean to wait until the end of the week to make a change. Remember that wagon analogy? We want a tight feedback loop, so corrections can be made quickly to obtain the desired result. If you're seeing more upward weights each day than downward numbers, THIS is when you need to change something. Waiting until the end of the week will be VERY frustrating and can diminish your chances of successful weight loss.

While the data I've read is inconclusive about a minimum number of calories required for a body to function properly, the figure 1,200 calories per day seems most prevalent. Consuming fewer than 1,200 calories each day for a few days in a row isn't going to be an issue, but it should definitely be avoided on a long-term, contiguous, basis unless monitored by your doctor or a trained nutritionist.

What Nutrient Composition Do I Need?

In addition to reducing calories consumed below those burned each day, you should aim for high levels of protein, fiber, and carbohydrates. You also want low levels on sodium, cholesterol, saturated fat, and total fat. Protein, carbohydrates and fat are called "macronutrients".

It's important to note that I also take a daily multi-vitamin that is formulated to match my gender and age range in order to ensure that I'm getting at least a reasonable number of vitamins and minerals in addition to whatever I'm eating.

How do I know what's too high or too low in these nutrients?

Here are the ranges for each of these nutrients:

1. Protein: 10% to 35% of caloric intake. To convert to grams, divide by 4.
2. Fiber: 10% of caloric intake. To convert to grams, divide by 7.2.
3. Carbs: 45% to 65% of caloric intake. To convert to milligrams, divide by 4.
4. *Sodium: 500mg to 2,300mg. Do not frequently exceed 2,300mg per day.*
5. *Cholesterol: 200mg to 300mg. Do not frequently exceed 300mg per day.*
6. Sat Fat: 7% to 10% of caloric intake. To convert to grams, divide by 9.
7. Total Fat: 20% to 35% of caloric intake. To convert to grams, divide by 9.

For example, if you consider the common 2,000 calorie diet standard, these numbers will work out as follows, but you need to base your specific nutrient needs on your own daily calories that you expect to consume after the applicable caloric deficit:

1. Protein: 50g to 175g
2. Fiber: 28g
3. Carbs: 225mg to 325mg
4. Sat Fat: 16g to 22g
5. Total Fat: 44g to 78g

To do this, I begin each morning with a breakfast consisting of an exceptionally tasty, refreshing, and satisfying frozen peach protein smoothie, made in a blender. You can use whatever fruit you prefer, but I just like peaches in this. This is where I'll introduce an appropriate number of scoops of chocolate flavored whey protein powder in order to get a boost on my daily protein intake.

Protein is the most important macronutrient when losing weight, because it aids in muscle production. I'll talk about the most effective way to produce muscle later, but the reason building muscle is important is because THIS is what will *continue* to require a large amount of energy (i.e., burn off fat) even when you're *not* working out at the gym.

Carbs are also important because they'll help you feel full and satisfied throughout the day during the caloric deficit required to lose weight, reducing the temptation to eat unhealthy snacks.

Fiber is important to keep your digestive system working properly and regular.

For lunch, I've found a tasty, nutrient-rich, high-fiber flavored oatmeal, plus a banana, to be very satisfying and ideal for weight loss. Now, get that vision of the orphans and their disgusting-seeming gruel in Charles Dickens's novel/movie "Oliver Twist" out of your head. Prepared oatmeal, or porridge, is much thicker than gruel, and the type I've been eating tastes like a bowl of thick, warm, chocolate candy bar awesomeness! There's a wide variety of different flavored oatmeal selections in case chocolate isn't your thing.

For dinners, I'll mix it up with a large variety of different frozen microwave dinner meals, or even hot dogs or a hamburger. You might want to prepare meals from scratch for yourself or your entire family. That's fine, too. Just be mindful of the calories and nutritional balance for the servings you consume.

I should also mention that I'm drinking about 2 liters of water a day, plus I'm getting about another 1.5 liters of water through the water content in milk, fruits, and sauces. This is about 3.5 liters a day, which corresponds well with the recommendations (3.7 liters for men) from the US National Academies of Sciences, Engineering and Medicine. For women, they recommend about 2.7 liters a day.

I found that I could lose 1.6 pounds per week, thereby reaching my healthy target weight in precisely 5-months (35 pounds total).

Any time you maintain a calorie deficit, which is required to lose weight, there is substantial benefit to periodic refeed days. A refeed day is when you eat without intentionally restricting your caloric intake. You should do this every week or so. This has the psychological benefit of giving you a break from dieting, and it tells your hormones that your body is no longer likely to starve, so they can resume a higher metabolic rate, essentially re-vitalizing weight loss progress after any slowdown or plateau you might have encountered.

Now don't confuse a "refeed day" with the "cheat days" of popular weight-loss programs. This isn't a day where you can just go wild and eat anything and everything you want. While you *will* eat more during a refeed day than when you're restricting your caloric intake, you should carefully plan what meals make the most sense, so you don't set your entire diet back by a week or more. Oh, and you *will* gain some weight after a refeed day. Expect it. It's okay. It'll come off quickly after the metabolic boost that the refeed day gave you.

Again, with all of these numbers and ranges to consider, having them in a spreadsheet is MOST beneficial!

How Should I Structure My Workouts?

A certain amount – maybe about 20 to 30-minutes – of an aerobic exercise or activity is great for heart and lung health and burning off calories during the workout.

In order to ensure that you don't encounter a plateau where it seems that no matter how much time you spend at aerobic activities, or how little you eat, you're just not seeing the weight loss progress you saw initially, it is imperative that you also include "resistance training" as part of your workout.

Resistance training is working with weights (weight machines or free weights), and it really is *the key to effective weight loss* and continued healthy weight after dieting. Lifting weights, in conjunction with the increased protein you've been consuming daily, aids in building a good muscle mass which will increase your metabolism even when you're not working out. It'll ensure that you don't hit that plateau, and it'll also serve to keep your weight in check *after* you stop dieting.

I am *not* a personal trainer, but I will share MY own personal experience with how to set effective amounts of weight, and number of reps on the weight machines.

If you don't know where to begin with each of the apparatus at a gym, then I recommend getting with one of the gym's personal trainers the first time you go. They'll help you set up a training regimen for your specific body type and abilities.

For ME, the very first time I use a weight machine, I set it to a weight that feels light and easy, so I don't cause any injury. If I can do more than 25 reps at that weight without having to rest, then it's too light – I'll add weight until I'm just starting to strain to get to the 25th rep. A "rep" is a repetition – or how many times I lift or push against the weight. With brief rests between each 25-rep set, I work my way up to about four sets per weight machine for an effective workout. I gradually increase weight as I build muscle over time and the current weights feel easier, in order to keep the progress going effectively.

Again, this is just from MY experience, but my recommendation is to focus on the larger muscle groups – the legs, biceps, triceps, abs (abdominal), and lower back. This will increase tone in those areas, as well as to produce new calorie-burning powerhouses that'll help you remain at a stable weight after you stop dieting.

Now, I'm not saying that you need to become a muscle-bound bodybuilder who has grotesque amounts of bulbous muscle mass all over. I'm just suggesting that you gain some tone in your muscles. It'll not just help to burn off calories even while you're not working out, as indicated above, but you'll feel amazing with strength and ease of movement that you'll have forgotten you had ever had before!

Summary of the Weight Loss Process

1. *Consult with your doctor and/or a nutritionist before starting into any long-term caloric deficit situation with strenuous physical activity involved if you have any chronic health issues and/or are severely overweight*

2. Create a database of the calories and nutrients in the foods you like to eat (only at the start, plus periodic updates as new foods are added)

3. Set a couple of weight-loss goals. What weight do you want to achieve ultimately, and what weight would be a good intermediate goal to start shooting for?

4. Determine your daily caloric deficit based on the amount of weight you want to lose per week, and what your weight loss goals are (needed only once, unless you change your weight loss rate later)

5. Weigh yourself every morning at the same time, and make note of that weight – plot a graph of your daily weights as you go along

6. Take a daily multivitamin that's appropriate for your age and gender

7. Determine your expected daily caloric burn (your BMR times your activity level factor)

8. Eat three meals, plus up to three snacks throughout the day, each chosen from your database to boost protein, carbs and fiber, and minimize sodium, cholesterol and fats

9. Your total daily calories from meals and snacks should be about

equal to your caloric burn minus your caloric deficit

10. Do 20-30 minutes of aerobic workout at the gym or by walking, hiking, riding a bike, whatever, at least three times a week

11. Do 20-30 minutes of resistance training (weight machines or free weights) with as much weight and as many reps as you can without causing pain or damage – but it *should* be quite tiring! – at least three times a week

Commit yourself to becoming more healthy, more fit, and more toned!

USE CREDIT WISELY

These days, you don't exist as an adult if you haven't established credit. This means that you'll have to use credit responsibly to build *good* credit, and not get buried by it, thus contributing to *bad* credit. Whenever you use a credit card to pay for something, be sure to pay it off as quickly as possible. Be aware that the credit card companies are set up so that if you make just the minimum payments that they suggest it will guarantee *perpetual* payments! That is, because they charge interest on any unpaid balance, when you pay just the minimum, all you're paying is the interest, and never touching the actual principle! Always pay off your credit balance as quickly as possible, by paying as much as you can when the bill comes due.

Counter intuitively, when you start getting behind on paying one credit card, other companies will invariably offer you new cards. It's like they're sharks. At the first sign of blood (falling behind), other sharks are attracted! Of course, people are naturally inclined to use the new cards that have no balance on them yet, to buy more stuff, or to take out cash advances to pay off the maxed-out card(s). This is what the credit card companies count on, but it's also the very thing that you should NOT do...if you wish to succeed. Otherwise, you'll become so buried in debt that you'll be forced to work more jobs, reducing the time you might have had to further your education towards your career goals...or you might end up having to declare bankruptcy, which will remain on your credit report for many years. Don't get buried in credit!

ESTABLISH AND STAY WITHIN A BUDGET

(UPDATED) I know...the "B-word" (budget) is one that most people don't want to hear, talk about, or use, but I can guarantee that those who don't actively establish and stay within a budget will never achieve financial comfort. What about millionaires and billionaires, you ask? I assure you that *even they* have budgets – the primary difference is that it's only their team of accountants who worry about paying the mortgages on their various mansions, yachts, private jets, butlers, and maids... not them!

A budget shouldn't be viewed as a scary thing. It SHOULD be your friend – especially when you're just barely bringing in enough income to survive.

In its simplest form, a budget is nothing more than a balance of your income with respect to your fixed monthly bills (i.e., mortgage/rent, utilities, phone, cable, vehicle loan payment, insurance, credit card) and basic living expenses (i.e., food, daycare if relevant, clothes when needed, gas for a vehicle, occasional entertainment).

You can buy or just download applications specifically designed as a budget, either for your computer or phone. You can keep a budget in a simple Excel spreadsheet of your own design like I do. Or you can scrawl it on a used paper napkin if you like. It doesn't matter. They all do the same thing – only a spreadsheet or application will definitely make it MUCH easier to update and see instant results.

A budget works best when your income is consistent and regular. If it varies from week to week, then you'll need to either average it out, or take the lower amount to ensure that you won't exceed your income on those weeks. You'll enter the amount of your income *after* all taxes and deductions – the amount that you actually receive on your paycheck or what's directly deposited in the bank.

Next, add up all of your fixed monthly bills. Finally, make an estimate of what you spend on living expenses each month. The total of the fixed bills and your estimated living expenses MUST be less than your income for the same period – usually considered over a month-long period. If it isn't, then you'll need to cut some of your expenses. This might mean not spending as much on new clothes each month, not eating out as much, or it might mean canceling the cable, or another bill that you can remove and do without for some while. It might mean getting a better-paying job, or working a second job, getting a roommate to share costs, or getting others in your family to contribute.

Ultimately, if you can maintain a positive difference between your income and the total of your bills and living expenses, then you can put that left over money into savings where it will grow, thereby helping you weather large, unexpected expenses like car repairs.

One very important thing to be aware of, related to saving as much as practical with each paycheck, is that you can't spend all (or most) of what might be left over each week. Not ALL of that money is there just to spend. There will be some bills – particularly your mortgage or rent – that will very likely take contributions from several weeks throughout the month in order to build up the proper amount by the end of the month when it'll be applied to the following month's payment. If you've spent each week's contribution on other things, then you won't have the amount needed at the end of each month!

In time, once the income from your employment grows from raises if you've performed well, and you may have paid off a vehicle or credit card, freeing up even more money, then you can save even more, and pay off more debt if you've accumulated any. This is how successful people achieve their dreams.

CONTAIN/RESTRICT FOUL LANGUAGE

I am, by no means, a prude. In fact, one of my favorite comedians of all time was George Carlin – most well-known for "the seven words you can't say on TV", most of which, ironically, are found on prime-time TV these days with considerable profusion. If you're a standup comedian performing a routine, and you can make profanity be funny, or you're among close friends in the privacy of your home or dorm then fire off a blue streak to your heart's desire. BUT, I *do not* want to be sitting in a restaurant and hear you loudly proclaiming how tasty your feces are (i.e. "Hey! This sh*t tastes amazing!"). You DO know that's what it means, right? No, it has never meant anything else!

Illegal in most states

Did you know that it is a misdemeanor offense in most states to utter profanity in front of a minor? Sure, it may not be enforced everywhere, or consistently, but do you really want to take that chance? That means that the restaurant scenario above *could* land you in jail for up to two years if there happened to be a family with young children nearby. Again, jail time will substantially affect your chances for success and happiness. Think before you use profanity. Is it really an acceptable place for it?

Also, when a person uses profanity excessively, such as nearly every time they open their mouth, others will think of them as being uneducated. When I was very young, I was taught that intelligent people can think of socially acceptable words where less educated people might use profanity instead because they don't know any better. Do you want to be judged by others as being stupid? This certainly won't help in your quest for success!

There's still another judgment going on when you use excessive foul language. People will perceive you as violent, or a criminal, and avoid you with great caution. Is this the attitude you want people to get when they meet you in public? Violent criminals are seldom given decent opportunities that might lead to a successful future. Remember, the way you act – not just your language, but your gestures in particular – can be perceived as being quite threatening, which will severely affect your quest for success.

Now I want to be very clear here that I am NOT suggesting or promoting racial profiling when I talk about judging others for your own safety. It doesn't matter if you're white, black, brown, red, orange, yellow, or green with purple polka dots, if your body language, in combination with your verbal language, appears threatening to another, then they have every right to consider you a threat and treat you accordingly. This may be as benign as others simply choosing to avoid you, or it might cause you to lose a job, or not get a job. If you're *very* aggressive, making disturbing, rapid gestures that most would consider threatening, and speaking like a true Vulgarian, then your actions could even get you killed in the wrong crowd. Except for organized crime, success relies upon a non-threatening demeanor.

GOOD PRESENTATION

"i well b there l8r today or tm imma c som ppl 1st ill let u kno if its to late an wanna wait till tm can my frend get pics 4 hr bf i dnt think sh has a ride 2 ther"

Translated for those of us over 18; "I will be there later today or tomorrow. I'm going to see some people first. I'll let you know if it's too late, and I want to wait until tomorrow. Can my friend get pictures done for her boyfriend? I don't think she has a ride to there."

This linguistic travesty is representative of *far* too many text messages and posts on social media that I see frequently from young people today. I generated it directly from multiple samples of actual posts and text messages that I've read recently. While the roots to this severe kind of abbreviation might have come from the 140-character limitation of Twitter or the cumbersome nature of texting with old cell phones that had only numeric keypads, its perpetuation outside of these situations, as well as the outright misuse of words can only be the product of mental and literary laziness.

Like it or not, you're being judged by everything that you write and by the words that you speak. We can't help it. It's basic human nature. Until we spend enough time to get to know someone, that's really all we have to go on. Therefore, a disproportionate amount of whether you succeed or fail in life comes entirely from *the way you present yourself*, regardless of your education. That is, one can be highly educated, and choose to act like an idiot, or have a basic education and appear very intelligent and confident just by the way they communicate with others. Guess which of these people will go further? It's the one who communicates well.

You might argue that you only communicate like this among your friends. I contend that, not only will you lose the ability to communicate properly if you continue like this – even "just with your friends" – but that a LOT more people are reading your messages than you might intend. This is particularly the case anytime you post on Facebook, MySpace, Tumblr, Twitter, LinkedIn, or any of the 205 other currently active social network sites. Social media, by definition, widely publishes your raw words just moments after you type them. Young people, old people, potential employers, current employers, employees perhaps, relationship candidates, your parents, your children if applicable, and even members of your church if you attend, might see what you've written. Why is this such a bad thing? There are a number of reasons.

If you're looking for a job, it's extremely likely these days that one or more of the employers to which you've applied will perform at least a cursory background check by searching social media – because it's easy. This is, in fact, a very common means used by employers today to determine if an applicant seems like a good fit for the company. If they find consistent themes of drunkenness, drug use, or irresponsible behavior in the pictures you post, or frequent cryptic messages demonstrating very poor communication skills, laziness, and excessively foul language, it doesn't look good for your prospects of being hired by the better employers. Similarly, some employers will routinely look to social media to check out the behavior of their *current* employees. If they find activity that isn't consistent with the morals, philosophy, or the mission statement of the company or their customers, then they'll have cause to terminate such employees. Clearly, this isn't a good way to succeed in life!

When other people your age or younger read these posts, they're likely to emulate what they've seen, perhaps to try and fit in, or because they're just too young to know any better. Either way, it perpetuates *very* poor writing skills, producing new generations of poor communicators.

Prior to social media, the only widely published material that was available for people to read was in the form of newspapers, magazines, and books. Each of these was rigorously reviewed and edited so that, by the time it reached the public, it was fully vetted for accuracy, spelling, grammar, and sentence structure. Such reading provided solid examples of good writing style that served well to augment a student's own writing skills.

Today, while it's likely that more people are reading and writing than ever before, the *quality* of much of the writing that's being read is absolutely deplorable! In addition to the totally unstructured wild ravings seen on social networks and text messages, more and more books are being self-published, often lacking the full editorial review that was a staple of traditional publishing. All of this, in combination, serves to dumb-down our society as a whole.

Good presentation isn't limited only to textual communication. It's certainly very important in spoken communication, as well.

"Nuculer", "Realitor", "Jewlery". You've heard these words spoken frequently. They're nearly ubiquitous, even spoken by apparently well-educated people in very high and visible positions in our society – but they're wrong!

These are only a few of the many words that people frequently mispronounce in everyday speaking. Many will equate this to lower intelligence. This is because it takes only a brief glance at the properly spelled words (i.e., nuclear, realtor, jewelry) in nearly any properly vetted writing like traditionally published books, high quality magazines, THIS book, and similar, to see the proper pronunciation, which, presumably, any intelligent person would do. The mispronounced words are clearly the result of only *hearing* the word and mimicking the sound, instead of *reading* the word and, thereby, knowing the proper way to say it. These people clearly aren't illiterate, but they *are* "low-literate".

I've listed several words, acronyms, and phrases here that are very commonly mispronounced or misspoken.

Improperly Spoken Words:

1. Nuclear: Say Nu-Clee-Er, *not* Nu-Cu-Ler. There's nothing between the "C" and the "L".

2. Realtor: Say Real-Tor, *not* Real-Itor or Real-Ator. There's nothing between the "L" and the "T".

3. Jewelry: Say Jew-El-Ree, *not* Jewl-Ree. There IS an "E" between the "W" and the "L".

4. Athlete: Say Ath-Leet, *not* Ath-El-Eet. There is nothing between the "H" and the "L".

5. Foliage: Say Fo-Li-Age, *not* Foil-Age. It's about plants and such, not an age of aluminum foil.

6. Silicon Valley: Say Sili-Con Valley, *not* Sili-Cone Valley. It's a semiconducting crystal, not rubber.

7. Library: Say Lie-Brar-Ee, *not* Lie-Berry. It's a place where books might be found.

8. Moot: Say Moot, *not* Mute. It's unnecessary to discuss, not one who cannot speak.

9. Supposedly: Say Sup-Pos-Ed-Lee, *not* Sup-Pos-Ab-Lee. There's no "B" in this word.

10. Granted: Say Gran-Ted, *not* Gran-It. This is something you're willing to offer, not a rock.

Redundant Acronym Syndrome (aka: Pleonasm):

1. ATM: Don't say "ATM Machine", as this would be "Automated Teller Machine Machine".

2. PIN: Don't say "PIN Number", as this would be "Personal Identification Number Number".

3. LCD: Don't say, "LCD Display", as this would be "Liquid Crystal Display Display". I say "LC Display".

4. PDF: Don't say, "PDF Format", as this would be "Portable Document Format Format".

5. CD: Don't say, "CD Disk", as this would be "Compact Disk Disk".

6. DVD: Don't say, "DVD Disk", as this would be "Digital Video Disk Disk".

7. USB: Don't say, "USB Bus", as this would be "Universal Serial Bus Bus".

8. AC: Don't say, "AC Current", as this would be "Alternating Current Current".

9. DC: Don't say, "DC Current", as this would be "Direct Current Current".

10. EMP: Don't say, "EMP Pulse", as this would be "Electro-Magnetic Pulse Pulse".

Incorrect Phrases:

1. Say, "I *couldn't* care less", not "I *could* care less". The intent of the phrase "I couldn't care less" is to indicate that you're at the very bottom of your ability to care about something. You simply cannot care any less. Saying "I *could* care less", however, indicates that

you've still got quite a bit more caring to go before you no longer care.

2. Say, "For all *intents* and purposes", not "For all *intensive* purposes". It's all about intent, not very strong purposes.

3. Say, "I did a full *180*-degree change", not "I did a full *360*-degree change". Know your angles! If you turn through a full 360-degrees, then you've effectively ended up in the precise position in which you began – hence, no change. To make the most significant change possible, it's necessary to turn only halfway, or 180-degrees. You'll now be facing in the opposite direction from which you began.

4. Say, "Six *of one, or a* half-dozen of the other", not "Six *and one* half-dozen of the other". The correct one refers to just six items and indicates the non-necessity of choosing "six" over "half-dozen", as they're both the same. It is an allegory to any similar sampling. The improper version refers to 78 (6.5 dozen) "other" items, with no reference at all to any sort of a "one" reference item.

5. Say, "I *have gone* to the store," or "I *went* to the store", but not "I *have went* to the store." "Went" is the past tense of "to go", while "Gone" is the past participle of "to go". "Gone", used as a verb (an action word), must always be preceded by an auxiliary (helping) verb such as "have", in order to convert the two words to a past tense meaning. "Went" has no need for an auxiliary verb, as it is already past tense.

6. Say, "Ultraviolet *radiation*" or "Infrared *radiation*", not "Ultraviolet *light*" or "Infrared *light*". "Light" by definition, requires that a human observer experiences a psychophysical response to it via the combination of retina and brain. Since UV and IR cannot be sensed directly by the unaided human eye, they, therefore, cannot be labeled "light".

7. Say, "I don't have any," not "I don't got none." The intent is to indicate non-possession, yet to say, "I don't got none", which includes a double negative, turns the statement into, "I do have some." This will completely change the intent of your statement.

By saying these words, acronyms and phrases properly, you will be presenting yourself in the very best possible way, thereby contributing to your future success and happiness.

This is your choice; you may either follow the spiraling path of literacy decay in our society, or you can stand out as one of the few who maintains proper literary and spoken standards. By standing out in this positive manner, you increase your chances for success while also helping to encourage more young people to write and speak properly. By continuing to communicate poorly, people only increase their chances for failure and help to perpetuate poor communication.

THE TWENTY-YEAR CYCLE

When I'd begun my engineering career in the fall of 1979, I had a number of offers from eager employers months before I'd even graduated with my bachelor degree. Talking with some established engineers later on, I'd hear them lament about the terrible engineering layoffs in 1970. I, therefore, felt quite fortunate for the turnaround in the engineering job market by the time I'd entered it.

Around 1990, I'd heard about the difficulties that new engineering graduates had experienced getting a job. It was also correlated with many engineering layoffs. Then, around the 2000 timeframe, engineering companies were grabbing up engineers again like candy. As 2010 approached, many companies were downsizing to recoup profits. This meant massive layoffs again... including my own! I was fortunate to have reestablished my engineering career with another company soon afterwards, but it's very hard to ignore this historical data and the trends it reveals – and then apply it to the future.

I call it *the twenty-year cycle*. That is, every twenty-years, since at least 1920 (i.e., 1940, 1960, 1980, 2000, 2020, 2040, etc.), the economy is good, and companies will vigorously try to fill engineering and other positions. But, every *other* twenty-years since at least 1930 (i.e., 1950, 1970, 1990, 2010, 2030, 2050, etc.), the economy has tanked, and engineering and other positions will be hard to get or to hold onto.

(UPDATED) The year 2020 had started out right on track with this cycle, showing excellent rates of employment and a strong economy…and then the Corona Virus ID:2019 (COVID-19) global pandemic – considered the worst since the 1918 Spanish flu pandemic – hit. COVID-19 began in China in December 2019 (hence the identifier, 2019). It spread to other countries finally hitting the United States in January/February 2020. We have started getting it under control by May 2021 after the rapid development and strategic, tiered deployment of a vaccine. This meant that the oldest – typically the most vulnerable – and hospital workers got their vaccinations first. Every couple of weeks, they'd allow a decade younger group to get their vaccines, until May when they opened it up to all adults. It hadn't been approved for children yet, at that point.

But, from mid-March 2020 until about June/July 2020, ALL restaurants immediately closed their dining rooms, converting to take-out or delivery, only, to help reduce the spread of the virus, causing massive unemployment for those four months when waitstaff wasn't needed. They were able to re-open their dining rooms with significantly reduced capacity, mask-wearing, substantial disinfecting processes at tables, and special seating barriers in place in the summer, re-hiring a portion of those who'd been let go in March and April.

Any other companies not considered "essential" were shuttered (some permanently!), and those that survived remained closed all year, and into 2021, causing even more unemployment. Fortunately, many companies were able to establish remote – work-from-home – situations for their employees who didn't have to be physically in-plant to perform their jobs (such as my engineering job), helping to mitigate the potential of even greater unemployment.

The unemployment rate peaked in April 2020 at 14.7%, representing 20.5-million people suddenly without employment – ostensibly the worst unemployment since the Great Depression in 1929. The year 2020 was definitely not an average year, but throughout 2019, January – mid-March 2020, and, later, past mid-2021 is surely looking favorable to conform to the twenty-year cycle. In fact, April 2021 through June 2021 is reported to have the highest number of job vacancies in need of filling since the year 2000!

The take-away here, at least if you're going into engineering, is to graduate college near an even decade if you want to start your career right away, thus increasing your probability for greater success.

THE MORTAL MOMENT

From my own experience and those I've heard of others, I believe that everybody experiences at least one notable situation throughout their lives that causes them to suddenly realize that they are, in fact, mortal. I call this the "Mortal Moment". You'll read, in detail in Chapter 10, about my first Mortal Moment when I was fourteen and walking untethered on top of a 3-story house, helping to install an enormous antenna. That one was significant only until I'd tied a rope between the chimney and myself, so it didn't end up causing me to substantially alter the way I approached life. But, there was a far more life altering Mortal Moment (#2) when I was about twenty-five, and Bill and I were hiking through the Santa Cruz Mountains. We took a trail that brought us to an elevation of perhaps seventy-five to hundred feet above the forest floor. It's there that we chose to do a free-climb on a particular rock face that rose vertically from the inside edge of the narrow trail. The outer edge of the trail dropped off precipitously. I was about fifteen feet above the trail when I had my Mortal Moment. I suddenly envisioned falling from my current position. I knew that I'd only suffer some minor scrapes and bruises by the time I met the trail below, so that wasn't the issue. It was what I considered *next* that caused me to immediately, and *very* carefully climb back down. I pictured not just falling onto the trail, but then either bouncing or rolling off the narrow ledge of the trail, and then falling to the forest floor much further below! That totally ended my free climbing days! With the possibility of death *that* close, it was no longer fun to me. Now this is what Mortal Moments are supposed to do! They *should* cause you to reevaluate the activity if it has a fair probability of terminating your further pursuits of fun activities. Now, mortal moments are *not* intended to traumatize you to the point of avoiding ALL activities with some degree of risk – only those which could be considered a "careless risk". Remember, "reasonable risks" are the spice of life!

WHAT *IS* THE MEANING OF LIFE?

Philosophers have pondered this very question for literally millennia, and, as far as I'm aware, nobody's yet come up with a viable answer. Well, that's all about to change. Before we can answer this question, however, we must first determine what, specifically, is meant by "the meaning of life".

Some will argue that it's asking why life, in all of its manifestations, exists at all. If that's the intent of the question, then the answer is simple: There is *no* reason, plan, intent or other purpose for life to exist. It exists only because it can! It's the result of trillions upon trillions of random elemental combinations over 13.8 billion years in 3.3 trillion separate galactic environments. Eventually, a basic, self-regenerative building block comprised of only a few simple elements coalesced, and life sprang forth. In fact, one day we will discover that life is not only an exceptionally *simple* process, but it is almost impossible for it NOT to occur on its own with enough random interactions. As an old physics instructor used to say about many concepts of physics, "It's intuitively obvious to the most casual observer." As such, I don't know why we haven't discovered it yet. Maybe we're just looking too deeply. We just can't see the forest for the trees.

Others may interpret the meaning of life to mean, "Why are *we* here"? That is, why each individual human being exists. Well, the bottom line is that there is no actual *reason* that you or I exist except that our parents were feeling a bit randy one day, so they did what comes natural to any species with a desire to perpetuate, and then nine months later, well, there we were. But, do not confuse *reason* with *purpose*. While there may not be a profound *reason* that we each exist, there IS an important *purpose* for every individual to live his or her life. Personally, I believe that it is *this* question – what is our *purpose* in life – that most people want to have answered. That *purpose* is, quite simply, to have the opportunity to create both a living legacy, and a *positive* durable legacy, while perpetuating the species.

A *living* legacy is our children. They are our most personal legacy, as they carry our genetic code and some of our influence into the future, which can benefit forthcoming society, if we, as responsible, well-educated, loving parents, have raised them well.

A *durable* legacy is where our name and some significant action we've taken are both carried into the future by some media that lasts well beyond our lives, and even those of our children. It's permanent, lasting, durable. Think of carved cave drawings. They've lasted millennia.

A *positive durable* legacy is the result of those who are creative, on-track, sure of themselves, givers, intelligent, and well-motivated to do something to help our society *while* helping themselves. These people will live exceptionally satisfying and rewarding lives filled with love and joy among the many who care about them. Even after they've passed on, they'll be regarded by future generations as great people with both amazing insight and gifted foresight.

An example of a positive durable legacy would be Leonardo Da Vinci's extremely insightful writings exploring mathematics, anatomy, architecture and engineering, as well as his beautiful and inspiring artwork. Now, I'm not saying we all have to do the things that Da Vinci did, or even cure cancer, solve world hunger, or eliminate chronic stupidity, but it wouldn't hurt if everyone at least *tried* to do something of significance sometime during their lifetime.

Speaking of chronic stupidity, this, too, is a choice. People can be ignorant in certain areas due to a lack of education or experience, and that's fine. They can learn and no longer be ignorant. But *willful* ignorance – making the conscious choice *not* to learn when it's available – is what fosters chronic stupidity. Choose, instead, to learn new things anytime that you can.

For a positive durable legacy, you might take a leadership role helping the homeless in your community, resulting in someone writing an article about you. You're helping future society, and your name and what you've done has been recorded in print, causing it to last into the future – it's durable. You could write a book that entertains, enlightens, instructs, or, in some way benefits readers now and into the future. Books are definitely durable media. You could write poetry, or paint beautiful artwork. These are very durable, as well. Perhaps sports are more to your liking. Become the very best in your specific sport of interest. Ultimately, you will become an inspiration for others. Actors and actresses will be remembered well into the future through their movies, plays and other entertainment. Similarly, musical performers will be remembered for their musical contributions. If you're more inclined towards the sciences or engineering disciplines, like I am, then a durable legacy could take on many forms. For instance, you might discover some new planet, organism, process, or technique. You might invent a device that benefits mankind well into the future. You could simply become the very best at whatever it is that you do so that you'll be successful enough that you can help educate future generations either by directly teaching them in the classroom, or indirectly with generous foundations, scholarships, articles, or books.

The list of activities and accomplishments that will create a positive durable legacy is limited *only* by your imagination.

That said, creating a positive durable legacy is *not* easy. It takes work – hard work – to do this, but the rewards for future society, as well as for those of us who've accomplished these goals, are amazing! They also beat out the alternatives.

One of two alternatives to a positive durable legacy is to produce NO durable legacy at all. Sadly, most people will fall into this category. They'll go through life in a sort of fog. They're unmotivated with no real direction and no great aspirations. They make no notable contributions to society, and possibly won't even experience any deep relationships with others. They seem to be *waiting* for something to happen, or for someone to lead them somewhere. They don't seem to understand that it is *they* who need to take the initiative in order to *make* things happen in their lives. Frequently, they'll end up just existing without ever having lived a meaningful life. They're born. They exist for some while. And then, they're gone, and essentially forgotten, with nothing to show for the time they were around. This greatly saddens me, as there's absolutely no reason that anybody should live a meaningless existence, and then die essentially unnoticed, when life has SO MUCH to offer, if you just take a look around and *actively* take notice!

There will also be those who have the thoroughly counterintuitive belief that "real life" only begins once they die. They believe that they're just biding their time here on Earth while waiting for the opportunity to "eternal life" with their deity-of-choice after they die. They sacrifice throughout their entire lives, expecting the ultimate payoff once their deprived Earthly existences finally come to an end. In doing so, they've likely created no durable legacy, and very possibly not even a living legacy. I don't like being the bearer of bad news, so I won't give away the ending here, but I might just suggest that these people get out there and do *something* fun and a little bit daring (and legal!) with their lives before it's too late!

Even worse than leaving no durable legacy at all, is to create a *negative* one!

A negative durable legacy is the result of those who are uneducated, stupid, selfish, hateful, takers who engage in violent criminal behavior, and will be hated by all of decent society. They are vile losers who will never know genuine love or compassion, or have true, unconditional friends. The negative durable legacy they create will serve only as a warning to future generations of what *not* to be. You *do not* want to be in this category!

These are the people who try to gain wealth by forcibly taking it from others. They take unfulfilled lives routinely, without a care or any thought of the decades of loving, nurturing and education that their victims as well as the victims' family and friends have invested in them, or what these innocent people might have contributed to society had they lived. They refuse to take responsibility for their own actions, and always blame others for their bad situation – not willing to accept that it's their own decisions that have put them in their present bad situation. They instill fear and revulsion throughout society. They are the people who murder during the commission of an otherwise minor crime because they're selfish, stupid, greedy, and angry. They're also the psychopaths who take innocent lives just for their own sick and twisted enjoyment.

There is still another category of murderers that I feel needs separate treatment here since there's been such a huge resurgence of it in the past couple of decades. This is a particularly vile and disgusting group because they actually believe that the supreme deity that they and their children worship has sanctioned their senseless killing of thousands of innocent people! I call this category *faith-motivated murder*!

Those of us who've attended church at any time throughout our lives can attest to the fact that religion *purports* to be a means by which good people are brought together in a collective environment of trust, compassion, and love. Regrettably, by the existence of the Catholic Church's Spanish

Inquisition, the puritanical Calvinists with their witch-hunts, and, much more recently, Islamic extremists who kill anybody who doesn't denounce their non-Islamic faith, to say nothing of numerous outlandish cults, we've seen that this simply is *not* so. The common factor in all of these situations is the self-centered and *very* dangerous belief that anyone who doesn't believe as these deranged zealots do is evil and must be eradicated.

What they're explicitly saying is that if others don't believe in what they believe in, then they have some sort of express permission directly from their deity-du-jour to kill those non-believers. This is SO wrong on SO many levels! Anyone who kills in the name of God, Jesus, Allah, Vishnu, Jehovah, tall trees, small furry animals, or any other spiritual manifestation that they believe in, is still a murderer. Not a martyr, not a hero – but a disgusting, hated murderer! What's more, they are substantially contributing to the vilification of the religions and deities that they claim to worship. As such, I wouldn't be the slightest bit surprised if the continued actions of these deranged faith-motivated murders create such a stigma in the name of their faith that good people of these religions will turn away from them because of the implied "guilt-by-association" aspect. As such, these murderers are killing not only people, but the very religion that they're apparently killing to protect!

My recommendation is that everybody should be allowed to practice – or not practice – his or her desired religion and/or belief structure all that they want to as long as it doesn't affect anybody else. Stop proselytizing! Stop taking it upon yourself to convert or eradicate non-believers! If someone doesn't choose to believe as you, so be it! Let them! If you believe that others who don't believe as you do will burn in Hell when they die, let them! *It's none of your business what another person believes in, or chooses not to believe in.* Live and let live!

Unfortunately, as long as greed, lust for power, strong selfishness, psychopathic afflictions, and twisted extremist interpretations of religious doctrine exist, there will be those who choose to create a negative durable legacy. Many others will also continue to live bland lives with no direction, and will be forgotten with no durable legacy at all. A few will have the inspiration, foresight, and drive to give their lives substantial meaning, thereby creating a positive durable legacy. Applying what you'll read in this book, thereby achieving a successful, happy life, will improve the odds that you'll enjoy the latter-most category.

Finally, we get back to the root question; what is the meaning of life?

After much consideration, I have determined, quite simply, that *the meaning of life* is to *live a life of meaning!*

Of course, others just passing through our galaxy will distill it all down to the simple product of six and seven; that's okay, too!

ABOUT DEATH

This is a particularly serious topic, which is why, in order to get you to read it without getting all depressed, and so that I can write it effectively without ripping my eyes out, I'll be treating it in the same manner that I do all serious subjects, with humor!

Similar to the meaning of life, people have pondered death for just about as long as there have been people around to ponder such things.

So, what does happen when we die?

I feel compelled to warn you that you probably won't like the answer, which is why most religions have constructed such elaborate fictions to cover up the reality. While the prospect of having "eternal life" romping around up in the heavens and being reunited with all of your departed loved ones might have considerable appeal and possibly even cause people to *want* to die rather than to fear it, I'd much rather fear it than be lied to and waste my only opportunity for a full and meaningful existence right here! Imagine for a moment that you're a priest or nun who's taken a vow of celibacy and poverty, as you've been taught that your ultimate reward will be eternal life *after* you die. You've sacrificed throughout your entire life, resisting temptation and living a life of worldly deprivation as your religious teachings have taught you in order to be rewarded with this great scenario after you die. How would you feel if we somehow proved to you that you'd been *lied* to your whole life – by the very organization to which you've given everything?

Well…sit down, and hold on, because that proof is about to be revealed.

I will not try and persuade anyone to believe anything they don't want to. I do not proselytize. I really don't care if you choose to believe what I believe. That's the job of religious leaders and zealots. What I will do, however, is to provide accurate, factual information, and allow you to make your own decision.

Now, before you go off classifying me as some sort of lunatic, I would like you to consider the logical, clinical, and physiological actions that lead to death. While cessation of the heart will generally *lead* to death, a stopped heart does not mean that one *is* dead. Only once the brain is starved of oxygen will the physiological aspects associated with death begin to present. Since oxygen comes from the blood that's pumped through the lungs by the heart, death will often result once the heart stops…but, not necessarily! If there's some other means of providing either blood flow or oxygen to the brain tissues (like CPR, or a heart/lung machine), then cessation of the heart will not cause immediate death.

Fainting is physiologically identical to death, with one exception – it's momentary, and you recover.

It is the sudden, brief loss of blood pressure, hence oxygen starvation, to the brain that causes one to black out in a fainting scenario. Usually, however, it's gravity that causes you to recover! That is, generally when you faint, you fall to the ground. This brings your head to an attitude that requires far less blood pressure to provide enough oxygen to bring the brain back to a conscious condition, thus allowing you to come to. But, if your head isn't lowered fairly soon after a fainting incident, or if your heart were also to stop, then death, and all of the inconveniences that it brings, may well ensue.

Therefore, anyone who has fainted has experienced what it feels like to die… only you've lived to tell others about it. When I was a kid, I had several such episodes – enough that I was eventually able to make significant sense of what I was experiencing, including accurate timelines of when certain sensations – and lack thereof – occurred. I basically took each opportunity to make a nearly clinical analysis of the process from an inside perspective.

As I'd begin to lose consciousness, I'd experience tunnel vision. No, this isn't television inside of a tunnel. This is the effect of blood draining from the periphery of the retinas and also from the occipital lobe of the brain where vision is processed. As such, my field of view would become black around the edges, appearing like I'm looking down a tunnel. Eventually, I'd feel complete apathy, like nothing seemed to matter. Everything is okay, and I was just going to willingly accept the end...and then... nothing. *Absolutely nothing!* No sensation of any kind, no pain, not even of the passage of time. No thoughts of anything or even of nothingness. No dreams or visions of anything or of nothingness. Just nothing. Nonexistence. Full stop! That's all she wrote!

Obviously, I have no conscious recollection of this "nothingness", since I no longer existed, mentally, at that point. But I was able to assemble the logical conclusion *afterward* when I'd realized that several minutes of my life had suddenly gone unaccounted-for... as if just an instant had passed for my brain.

If this condition were allowed to persist such as by not getting my head to a lower position, then non-revivable termination – aka death – *could* soon occur.

Some minutes later, which, to me felt like no time had passed at all, I'd begin to come to. This process also has its own interesting characteristics. Once blood pressure starts to be restored to the brain, it will also infuse the retinas from the center first. Between this and dilated pupils, a brilliant white tunnel (over-exposure of the retina to the ambient light) will first be sensed, growing in diameter as blood reaches the periphery of the retina, until the full field of view is filled. Concurrently, the pupil will contract, and normal vision will begin to be restored. You'll recall that I'd usually hit my head on the way down once I went unconscious. Therefore, this bright tunnel will appear in combination with total confusion and intense pain, as well!

Reports of tunnels leading into a bright light have consistently been documented from all who have had "near-death experiences", as well. Many of those who have been influenced by their strong religious beliefs will equate this bright tunnel with a glimpse of heaven or angels when, in reality, it has a very logical, physiological explanation.

Now, those who embrace religion in one form or another might not want to hear this, but there is just one logical conclusion that can be drawn from the data, and it fundamentally conflicts with most religious dogma. From my own personal experiences, correlated with said reports of near-death survivors, established scientific facts about the physiology of the brain specifically, and the body as a whole, *I* can only conclude, logically, that there is *nothing* after we die. No dreaming. No consciousness. No purgatory. No haunting. No afterlife. No heaven. No hell. No 70 - 72 virgins. NOTHING! Therefore, if you've been putting off living a full Earthly existence with the expectation that you'll have an eternity to live on in the afterlife, finally enjoying yourself, I think you might just want to reconsider that. That's just what the established facts indicate.

THE BIG LIE

Mankind has feared death for about as long as there's been human life. Therefore, it shouldn't be at all surprising that wise people, perhaps with good intentions, chose to make up stories to tell their children in order to reduce the fear of death. These stories eventually morphed into legends, and then into scriptures, and have become the basis of most religions today. Basically, they say that if you're good your entire life, you'll be rewarded when you die – usually with an "eternal afterlife" in a pleasant place, free of stress, strife, concern, worry, and fear. Conversely, if you're bad, you'll be punished – usually with an "eternal afterlife" in the most extremely unpleasant of places imaginable. It's more than just a little bit obvious that these are nothing more than behavior control tactics designed to prey upon people's deepest beliefs, desires, and fears, designed to cause good behavior. Now, don't get me wrong; I am *all* in favor of a well-behaved society, but I think it should be by their own, informed choices, not based upon a very big lie that coerces us throughout our lives to behave under the threat of supreme punishment, and promises things that simply *will not happen* when we die! THINK FOR YOURSELF! Do not accept anything exclusively on blind faith...especially when "miracles" are needed in order to make the stories make sense!

THE SOUL

For those who'll argue that it's not the body, rather the soul that will live on, let me describe what the soul *actually* is. Think of your computer for a moment. It's built with hardware that runs software to perform certain functions. The WAY that the software-directed-hardware interacts with you, the user, is like a personality. This is essentially the description of a soul.

Similarly, the human body has a skeleton, muscles, brain, a vascular and nervous system, other organs, and all physical aspects that are like the hardware, while the process of information collection, correlation, and action based upon that information, can be thought of as the software. It is the WAY that a person acts – i.e., their *behavior* – based upon the correlated information that forms their personality...their soul. It is completely intangible, and yet a very real part of what makes us...us!

Knowing this now, does it make sense for a *method* to live on? I will, however, accept two interpretations related to one's soul living on after death. People who were close to the deceased will remember how they acted, their personality, their behavior, for many years after they've passed. Many more will carry the memory of the deceased if they've created a durable legacy. With those two exceptions, the soul simply cannot live on as a form of independent *consciousness*.

PATH TO SUCCESS, SUMMARIZED

1. Understand that success IS a conscious choice
   a. Success doesn't just happen
   b. You must make the choice whether or not to put in the work and effort to make it happen
   c. The earlier in your life you decide you want to succeed, the more likely it will happen
2. Maintain an optimistic perspective
   a. This will keep you motivated
   b. Pessimism will jeopardize your chances of success
3. Accept responsibility for your words and actions
   a. You will gain respect from those around you
   b. By accepting that you are the only one responsible for your future success or failure, you will be able to make better

decisions toward a successful future

4. Get help for depression or other mental issues

    a. Un-addressed depression can completely crater any attempts at finding success

    b. All mental issues need to be addressed and/or treated

5. Break your life down to a series of short stories

    a. Trying to get through one epic novel can be daunting, but it's easy to read a short story

    b. Break your life down into small chunks and treat each one like a short story that has a guaranteed happy ending

    c. These short stories will generally correlate with each new activity you begin

6. It's okay to be smart

    a. Don't hide your intellect just to "fit in" with some group of people who don't value it

    b. Use your intellect to your advantage to create your own path to success

7. Boost your success

    a. Hold informal, friendly competitions with others who have similar knowledge or talents

    b. Instead of getting angry if your peer outperforms you, do something more impressive

8. Choose a lucrative field of study

    a. Start into a hobby that interests you when you're very young

    b. Determine if the talents required for that hobby can be translated into a career

    c. If so, begin to set up your future education to support an efficient path towards such a career

    d. Consider if a trade school or college will be more applicable for your education

e. FYI, historically a career in the sciences, or business will outperform 95% of those in the arts, but the trades can also bring in very consistent, decent income

f. Work in the sciences or business, and live in the arts

g. Remain focused with your educational path towards your chosen career

h. Avoid changes to your major

i. Avoid addictions and teen pregnancy

9. Establish and maintain good personal hygiene

a. Eliminate acne for better presentation to a mate and/or employer

b. Eliminate offensive odors

10. Lose unwanted weight effectively and efficiently

a. Excessive weight will make you feel sluggish and unmotivated

b. Excessive weight can restrict you from many fun activities

c. Excessive weight can reduce your chances for romantic and employment opportunities

11. Use credit wisely

a. Getting buried in debt will not help your pursuit of happiness

b. Wise use of credit can open many doors through a good credit score

12. Establish and stay within a budget

a. Staying within your budget will help you build wealth towards your goal of success and happiness

b. Failure to use a budget is very likely to keep you from achieving your goals

13. Communicate like a gentleman or lady

a. Know when and where foul language can be appropriate – and especially where it is not

    b.   Be concise but unambiguous using intellect and manners in your communications

14. Understand the 20-year cycle for professional employment

    a.   The economy appears to be best for hiring professionals approximately every 20 years (i.e., 1980, 2000, 2020)

    b.   The economy appears to be worst for hiring professionals during the opposite 20 years (i.e., 1970, 1990, 2010, 2030)

REAL-LIFE ADVENTURES
SECTION 2 – THE ELEMENTARY SCHOOL YEARS

Introduction

A long time ago, in a basement not so far away, two kids explored strange new concepts, and boldly built stuff that few kids had built before...and even fewer since! Anyway, I am Bob, and my identical twin brother is Bill. These stories – adventures, if you will – are humorous accounts of things that we *actually* did while growing up as twins with a great interest in electronics and flying.

Our family wasn't wealthy; not by a long shot. But we weren't poor, either. Our parents were obsessively frugal – a result of their having grown up experiencing the effects of the Great Depression. Most of our clothes were hand-me-downs, and we simply weren't given anything new except a few specific toys and clothes on birthdays and Christmas. Even then, there was a substantial, and quite thorough, vetting process to ensure that money wasn't wasted on something we didn't *really*, truly want, or need. Therefore, we had to be very creative with what we did have – invariably finding imaginative "re-use" in just about every toy we had. This led naturally to the numerous adventures you're about to read.

We also have two other brothers: Craig & Jim. They were many years apart from us – Craig was much older, and Jim much younger – and they had vastly different interests from those of Bill and me. As such, despite their being a part of our family, they'd might as well have been living on the moon for all the interaction we had with them. With no disrespect or animosity intended, they simply didn't seem to exist to Bill and me within our comfortable little bubble of imagination and adventures while we were kids.

This book covers *my* life, but since nearly every experience and adventure was shared with my identical twin brother, Bill, until we went our separate ways after college at age 21, to *not* include him, or to say "I" or "me" when describing most of the events during that early timeframe, would simply be inaccurate and misleading. As such, within this book, I have included him in the stories up until our college graduation, and any mention of "we" and "us" will *always* refer to Bill and myself. "My brother" will always refer to Bill. All other brother references such as older brother, younger brother, other brothers, or one of those other two guys who seemed to share our parents' home, will refer to Craig and/or Jim.

Our parents, Doris and Don, were both born just before the Great Depression. They were further shaped by the hardships imposed by both World War II and the Korean War. As such, they were ultra-frugal when it came to money, and strict disciplinarians, but also good parents. Dad was an Army sergeant with training in radio repair during WWII. After the war, he became a traveling industrial chemical salesman, spending days at a time on the road. He sold cleaning agents and systems to large dairies throughout New York State, Pennsylvania, and Ohio. Mom worked as an accountant at a factory that manufactured signaling systems during WWII. She also volunteered as a pilot, doing domestic search and rescue with the Civil Air Patrol both before and during the war.

Once our parents began our family, Mom, like most women in the 1950s & 1960s, became a stay-at-home-mom. Of course, that term didn't even exist at that time; it was assumed that a mother would stay at home to raise her children. In fact, with less than 20% of mothers of young children (under 6) a part of the outside workforce, the term "working mother" was actually the novel term of the day.

We had a decent roof over our heads, good food in our stomachs, a caring family environment, and intellectual stimulation both from our mother, and in the form of books that encouraged independent and analytical thinking.

The majority of these stories will take place in and around the home where we grew up, located in a not very urban suburb well outside of Buffalo, NY. This town was, in every way, precisely like any big city is not. Our tales begin shortly after we'd turned five – the earliest age that I have more than just one or two very sketchy memories. They continue in detail through our college years in Columbus, Ohio, with several additional stories after college to provide closure and demonstrate the ultimate achievement of our goals through the good choices we made throughout our lives.

CHAPTER 1 – 1963; AGE FIVE

Imagination, Attempting Flight, Parks, Tinker Toys, & Pennies

Kids "Flying"

It was the summer of 1963, before President Kennedy was assassinated, before Beatlemania hit the states, and even before Baby "dirty danced" with Johnny at Kellerman's. Gasoline was just $0.29 per gallon, and the popular TV shows – in fuzzy black & white on one of the three US and three Canadian channels we could receive – were: "The Andy Griffith Show", "The Flintstones", "Mister Ed", "The Avengers" and "The Dick Van Dyke Show".

IMAGINATION

We played outdoors in the *real* world a lot! We interacted with *real* people, and we had *real* friends. Even though we used our imaginations extensively during many of these real-world activities, there was nothing simulated or virtual about this activity. Because we were so very active all of the time, there wasn't the slightest threat of becoming overweight, much less obese like many of the video game addicted youth of today. Similarly, there was no button to press that would eliminate all prior transgressions to allow us to start over fresh. There were consequences, sometimes severe, for our actions. Of course, we sometimes took chances, but we were very careful about them, and we learned to behave properly, or we *knew* that we would suffer. There were six words that we absolutely dreaded hearing; "Wait until your father gets home!" When we heard our mother say that we knew we were in for it. It was really the waiting, the anticipation, our imagining of the spanking that we were destined for, that was always far worse than the punishment itself. This was especially effective since our father traveled out of town much of each week for his job. For us, this often-extended anticipation of punishment was a very effective deterrent against bad behavior.

ATTEMPTING FLIGHT with IMAGINATION

Our family had just moved to this house on the Clarence/Williamsville, NY border a couple of months prior, and the unpacking left a number of large cardboard boxes for the trash. Others just saw a stack of dismantled boxes, but Bill and I saw wings! Having dreamt numerous times of hovering just above our driveway or the house itself, we were virtually obsessed with the idea of flying. We took a couple of pieces of cardboard from the trash and headed out to play.

"Let's go out back and try to fly!" I said to Bill.

We'd shaped the cardboard so it'd fit under each of our arms, and then we headed to our furthest back yard where the wind would be strongest, and there'd be far more space in which to run. See the Kids "Flying" illustration at the top of this chapter.

"RUN! Faster!" Bill shouted to me as I headed full speed into the wind and jumped.

"Did you see that?" I exclaimed. "I flew!"

In reality, all I'd done was jump a few feet while feeling the pressure of the wind pushing on the cardboard under my arms. Bill and I made several similar runs, and we were quite convinced, in our five-year-old brains, that we were flying, if only for an instant. Either way, it was exhilarating enough to continue to fuel our desire to attain more sustained flight.

Speaking of jumping, Bill and I tried every conceivable method that was available to us to get slightly more airtime in our numerous attempts at flight. We'd jump out of trees and swing from ropes into the air. These were all most exhilarating, but still not sustained flight like we craved. We wanted desperately to run, jump, and remain just above the ground, like we always did in our recurring dreams of flight. We were determined to find some way to *really* fly! This was a major goal that we'd both set in our lives.

IMAGINING FLIGHT at the PARK

Our next "flying" endeavor would introduce us to the concept of helicopters at a nearby park that same summer. Now, when I say helicopters, what I really mean at this time is a small kid's ride with helicopter-like seats that would take us in circles around the center of the ride platform.

Returning to 1963, we'd engaged our imaginations, and set off on the strategic mission.

"Bill, do you see the squadron yet?" I spoke into the walkie-talkie.

"Not from my location." Bill replied.

"There's a rise up ahead." I said, "Let's meet up there."

"Roger that."

We soon converged at the top of the hill, revealing to us the entire airbase just beyond. It was filled with helicopters. We knew what we had to do.

"I see a small breach in the fence straight ahead." I told Bill, "We can make our entry there, but watch out for sentries."

We headed for the fence and quickly climbed through the opening, and then took cover until we could be sure we wouldn't be seen as we made our way to the line of waiting helicopters.

"I'll take this one." Bill said, indicating the first one in the line. "You find one further back so the guards will have to split up once we start the machines."

In our preparation for this mission, we'd memorized the pre-flight checklist for this particular type of helicopter. We skipped the outside fuselage, engine and rotor checks in order to avoid detection, so it went along much more quickly.

"Circuit breakers in. Fuel shutoff valve on. Carb heat off. Master battery switch on. Ignition!" I said to myself as I went along.

The powerful piston engine roared to life, and I set the idle speed to 55% RPM while flipping the clutch switch closed and plugging in the headset I'd need to communicate with Bill in the other chopper.

Between the din of the engine and the silence inside the noise-canceling headset, there was no way for me to hear if Bill had succeeded in starting his helicopter. A glance forward, however, provided my answer, as I saw his rotors start spinning.

"Come on!" I voiced out loud to the aircraft as I was waiting for the clutch light to go out.

While just a matter of seconds, it seemed like an eternity before the clutch was fully engaged, the light went out, and I could finally roll on more throttle to warm up the engine at 80% RPM. I looked around me to see if any guards had been alerted. In fact, it looked like an entire platoon was headed towards the flight line – splitting off half towards where Bill was urgently waiting for the same processes to complete, and half towards me!

The engine gauges slowly crept up towards the green regions, but I was simply out of time. I rolled on full safe RPM and pulled up on the collective lever while pulling slightly back on the cyclic lever, hopping off of the ground just as the enemy approached. Looking up ahead, I saw that Bill had done the same.

We both performed maximum-performance take-offs, straight up, and then, after achieving some forward speed, banked hard, putting a hangar between the troops and us. Gaining altitude beyond the range of their weapons we came back around and began strafing the airfield, with particular focus on the ammo dump. But we couldn't get close enough before we realized that we had company and had to break off. Several other helicopters had taken to the air and were heading towards us with guns blazing!

Since our walkie-talkies were rendered useless in the noisy environment, I switched the helicopter avionics to the private frequency that Bill and I had established ahead of time. "Helicopter Six-Three Juliet, this is Six Niner

Delta. Let's split up and come up around behind them."

"Six Nine Delta, roger that." Bill replied.

The maneuver took the other pilots completely by surprise, making it easy for us to bring them down with our guns. Coincidentally, one of the helicopters crashed directly into the middle of the ammo dump, causing an explosion so massive we both felt the concussion wave from nearly a mile above it!

Our mission accomplished, we headed back to our own base several kilometers away.

When the tiny ride at Glen Park slowly came to a stop, and the attendant opened the gate, our mother helped us climb out of our respective helicopter cockpits, and our imagined world faded away. This park was known for its picturesque falls, but it also had a small area of amusement rides for young children. It was, therefore, a great place for us to engage our imaginations like in the above scenario. I'm sure they had other rides as well, but I only remember the one with the helicopters because it was *not* a fully passive experience like most rides. With the pull of a lever in the cockpit, the helicopter would rise upward several feet. Lowering the lever produced the opposite effect, of course. They also had a gun-like apparatus mounted on the cowling, facing forward on a swivel base. To complete the illusion, it would make shooting noises when we pushed a button!

FANTASY ISLAND AMUSEMENT PARK and TINKER TOYS

Later in the summer, our family traveled to Fantasy Island. After our seaplane set down, the proprietor and his short associate cheerfully welcomed us, and then we were escorted to our rooms. Soon afterward, strange things began to happen... Sorry, wrong Fantasy Island!

Okay, we drove the 20-minute trip to Grand Island, NY where the Fantasy Island *amusement park* was located. This was a rather large amusement park with roller coasters, Ferris wheels, fun houses, and many of the thrill-rides typical of most of the larger parks... but no waterfalls like Glen Park. Of course, if we wanted falls, then another 15-minute drive would take us to arguably the most famous falls in the world; Niagara Falls. At this park, we were still too young to ride much more than the Ferris wheel and the kiddie rides, but both of these recent park visits would still make a significant impression upon us, both near-term, and much later on.

We'd been playing with Tinker Toys for a couple of years by then – the original wooden ones with the tasty, easy-to-swallow pieces. Until then, we'd kept the assemblies rather basic, but, after attending these parks, we were inspired by the fascinating mechanical marvels represented in the rides at these parks to build far more complex mechanisms. We then set about duplicating all of the intricacies and functionality of various attractions from the amusement parks we'd recently attended. We were dually fascinated by that really long chain being pulled over a big gear at the top of the roller coaster, and the clicking sound it made as a train of cars were pulled up to the top. We NEEDED to make something like that at home!

"Whoa!" Dad exclaimed when he walked into his den one day after he'd been out on the road a few days. Carefully watching where he stepped, he asked, "What IS all of this?"

We'd been quite busy since the visit to the amusement park on Fantasy Island. Bill and I had spent much of each day, while Dad was working, building Ferris Wheels, Merry-Go-Rounds, and a crude roller coaster. When he came home, our completed wooden carnival sprawled across much of the floor. Despite the difficulty it imposed upon him to walk through his own den office area, I think he was far too impressed by what a pair of 5-year-old kids had accomplished to complain – well, for a few days, anyway. After this, we were asked to keep our projects confined to a small area on one side of the floor, where it wouldn't obstruct entry and exit to and from the den. Such is the life of young, creative kids!

THE MISSING PENNY

Despite our parents' frugality, they did give us a weekly allowance. Their desire to teach each of us fiscal responsibility was stronger than their thrift. You can't learn to manage money if you have no money to manage. Now, when I say they gave us each an allowance, I'm not talking about something that could buy a new sports car each week... No. We each got just a nickel per week at this age. Before you say, "well everything was a lot less expensive back then, so a nickel had a lot more buying power back then", consider this;

how much can you buy for thirty-eight cents today? This is what a nickel in 1963 translates to in 2014 currency. You won't be buying any sports cars with that! A nickel just isn't very much money, no matter how you look at it, but we saved our nickels, and spent some portion carefully.

Our mother was not only painfully frugal, but also a Certified Public Accountant. Therefore, as you might expect when dealing with monetary sums as vast as those that we were earning from our weekly allowance, we had to be very careful with our bookkeeping. This meant that we had to undergo a detailed financial reconciliation with our mother *every* month. I imagine that the dreaded IRS audit is nothing in comparison to that which our mother conducted with us. It was not unusual for us to spend hours trying to locate the cause of a one-cent discrepancy in our accounting! Of course, I suppose it *was* fairly significant since a penny represented, at that time, 20% of each of our individual weekly incomes – or the equivalent of an entire workday's pay to an adult!

Ultimately, the one of us who'd misplaced that penny would be grilled for the rest of the evening until one of two things happened. Either a miraculous epiphany would happen, and its disposition would suddenly be recalled, or 7pm would arrive. Epiphanies of that sort weren't common, but bedtime always came along, and it trumped all other activities in our family. You would think that we could have saved ourselves long periods of torment just by fabricating where that penny had gone, but we'd learned long prior that lying would serve only to cause FAR worse torment later. You see, our parents were psychic – or so we were convinced. Also, our mother had a memory better than the proverbial pachyderm! Based upon the few times that one of us had lied to our mother about other things, I'll present a fictitious scenario here representing what *would* have happened IF one of us had ever lied to her during this important financial reconciliation:

Bill and I were sitting next to our mother on the living room couch. There were lined sheets of paper with scribbled figures on them, and a couple of dollar bills and some change setting in two separate piles on the coffee table.

"Zee ledger shows von dollar undt seventy-five cents, undt yet you count just von dollar undt seventy-*four* cents!" my mother said to me in an odd pseudo-Germanic accent. "Veer ist zee missink penny?"

Now, I feel that I should mention that our mother had no accent at all. She doesn't even have any German ancestry on her side of the family. Yet, this is how I remember the grilling we'd sometimes endured at these monthly audits. I suppose it's because I subconsciously equate it to being interrogated by the Gestapo during WWII – or at least the "Hogan's Heroes" version!

I'd reply helplessly, "I don't know where it went."

Bill and I were notoriously bad at ensuring that we'd received the correct change from any purchase at a store when we were very young. We tended to trust the person making the change since it was difficult for us at that time, and therefore, invariably, we'd be short-changed and not realize it sometimes until these infamous audits!

She'd have me count, and re-count, and then count again, each time coming up to the same amount – short by a penny! She'd make suggestions.

"Perhaps zee candy was seeex cents, not five?" she'd taunt tantalizingly, possibly just hoping I'd grab the bait instead of admitting the truth that I just didn't receive the right change back. But, to admit this, could have even greater ramifications, and I wasn't keen to find out what.

This would, therefore, go on for hours. With no conclusion in sight as the clock was nearing seven o'clock, I knew I'd be in for another evening of complete misery the next night if I didn't come up with something viable before I went to bed!

"Okay! Now I remember! You were right. The candy WAS six cents." Phew!

She made the adjustment in my ledger and closed the books. Crisis averted... or so I'd thought.

Twenty-seven years, and two albino ferret-sightings, later...

I'm married, with two point three kids, a dog, and we're living in a beautiful, brand new home in the Midwest. My wife and I have friends over, and I begin to recount the missing penny situation to the couple that lived next door.

They were both amused and aghast at the big deal I'd told them that she'd made over one stinking penny. One of them said, "That's just ridiculous!"

"Yeah," I said, "I finally just agreed that the candy was more expensive that time. I just didn't want to admit that I'd messed up with the change again!"

At that very moment the phone rang. It was my mother! I'm convinced, after Bill and I left our parents' home after college, that Mom had invented and installed some sort of super-powerful thought-receiving machine and she'd been pointing the antenna at each of us ever since, just waiting to catch us in a lie!

And it happened!

She started off with, "I was just thinking about that candy you used to get when you were a kid. Remember, the stuff that cost six cents?"

"Um...yeah." I replied tentatively, unsure where she might be going with it. "What about it?"

"Did you know that it never cost six cents?" She said.

And there it was! I'd been found out, but I figured there was nothing she could do now that I was no longer a kid living under my parents' roof.

Boy was I wrong! She grounded me!

Can you imagine what it's like to be grounded by your mother when you're an adult with a family living thousands of miles from your parents? What do you tell your boss?

That was, of course, a fictional story, but the monthly audits when we were young were very, very real!

And this is why I just DON'T LIE!

CHAPTER 2 – 1964; AGE SIX

Amazing Picture Books!

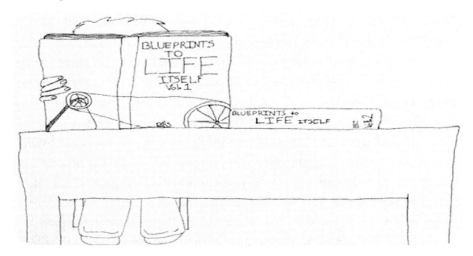

Blueprints to Life Itself

In 1964 the average house cost $13,050, the typical annual income was about $6,000, a new car cost about $3,500, Chrysler produced their 300K, a 360hp, high-performance convertible, and gas cost $0.30 per gallon. The Vietnam War began for the US, and the Boston Strangler was captured. The BASIC programming language was introduced, Ford manufactured the first Mustang, China exploded its first nuclear bomb, and our little brother, Jim, was born.

THE AMAZING MECHANICAL PICTURE BOOKS!

This was the year that Bill and I were given the blueprints to life itself... or so it had seemed.

"Are you ready?" Bill asked me as we each prepared to open up one of the two enormous hardcover books Mom & Dad had just given us. See the Blueprints to Life Itself illustration at the top of this chapter.

Just looking at the cover art on these amazing books, we were already in awe, and intended to treat the interior with a suitable amount of reverence.

"Okay…on the count of three!" I replied. Cracking each book open in sync with the other, we dove into a world of incredibly detailed drawings of all things mechanical that made our minds reel!

These huge volumes were profusely and gloriously illustrated with highly detailed, photo-realistic, multiple-view and cut-away color drawings of all manner of mechanical contraptions. These amazing drawings ranged from very early bicycles and motorcycles to cars and trucks with many different purposes, to elaborate farm implements and construction equipment, to simple boats through luxury ocean liners, and maybe even a ferret or two…but probably not. We pored endlessly over these books, studying every drawing until we'd absorbed the minutest details. In the process, we developed a deep intuitive sense of how an incredible range of mechanical devices worked. To us, this was like discovering life's deepest secrets! These books were a couple of very few items in our lives that were responsible for our building a strong understanding of, and appreciation for, all things mechanical. This would soon translate to electronic apparatus, which would begin the path towards our inevitable engineering careers.

With the significant clarity that these books had provided us about how so many apparatus functioned, interacted, were assembled, and moved, they certainly felt like the plans to life itself, but, alas, they were not. Of course, if we were evil geniuses, then I suppose we'd have put these plans to use in a quest for world domination! Now, I'm not saying that we *had* any such ambitions, but, *if* we did…well…I suppose then we'd have had to find an evil lair, and they're just not that easy to find. I mean most of the good evil lairs have already been taken by the nemeses of various superheroes!

CHAPTER 3 – 1965; AGE SEVEN

The Mud Pile, Erector Sets, & Reinventing Toys

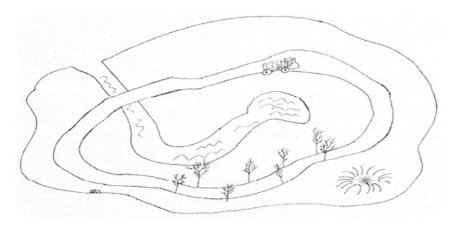

The Mud Pile

In 1965 the average house cost $13,600, the typical annual income was about $6,450, a new car cost about $2,650, Chrysler produced their 300L, a 360hp high-performance convertible – the last in their 300 letter series in this decade – and gas cost $0.31 per gallon. The Watts race riots broke out in southern California, there was the Northeast Blackout, where seven states in the northeast US and parts of Canada were plunged into darkness due to a massive power outage that lasted up to 13.5 hours, and the 1965 Voting Act guaranteed African Americans the right to vote. Popular films in the theaters were: "Mary Poppins", "The Sound of Music", "Goldfinger", "My Fair Lady", and "What's Up Pussycat?"

THE MUD PILE

About this time Bill and I had discovered an ideal plot of land on the edge of the woods that came to the back of our parents' property. We felt that we could develop this area into a regular gated community...for our toy vehicles, of course. Really, it was just a mostly flattish area devoid of foliage, causing our parents to unwittingly give it a name when they said it was nothing but a mud pile! Ironically, it was mere feet away from the brand-new sandbox that our father had just installed, but I guess we were the types who'd rather play *outside of the box.*

We gathered up some of our trucks and construction toys, a tablespoon for excavating, and, of course, our imaginations, and then we headed out to "The Mud Pile". Our mother had taught Bill and me about adobe bricks commonly used in the southwest as construction material for houses. From this, we knew to put grass, straw, or other fibrous materials into the mud mixture when constructing portions of our Mud Pile metropolis that needed some amount of structural integrity, such as overpasses. We'd mix this all together, form the basic shape, and then let it dry into a hardened substrate under the sun. This created effective bridges...until it rained, of course.

While I was working on perfecting more robust spanning structures, Bill was busy digging his pit with the tablespoon. We had shovels at our disposal, and occasionally we'd use our father's small folding Army shovel, but most of our construction projects in the Mud Pile just weren't big enough for a full-sized shovel. In retrospect, a garden trowel would have probably been the most effective digging implement for our purposes, but the only one around was that which our mother used in her gardens...all of the time in the spring through fall seasons, frequently while wearing a very weathered leather flight jacket. Because of this, we viewed this trowel as a virtually sacred implement. As such, if we'd actually used it once and left it out to rust, broken it, or lost it, the universe would surely have collapsed upon us the very moment she found out; hence, the spoon!

Now if you're wondering why he was digging this pit, you wouldn't exactly be alone. In fact, I think the only reason ever mentioned was to see how deep he could go. I suppose this made sense... to a seven-year-old. The idea was to dig until he'd reached one of these three things; a continuous rock surface, water, or China – whichever came first. From our then-limited knowledge of the world, we rather expected to smell the aroma of fresh chop suey at any moment! After weeks of this grueling tableware excavation project, and still no hint of Asian cuisine, he finally announced that he'd gone as far as he could, meaning as far as he could reach. The pit had taken on an odd angle, almost like the shape of his arm when bent. I peered into it.

"Looks pretty deep," I said.

"I think it's nearly to China!" He replied gleefully.

"Probably" I agreed.

Bill then posed the question we were both thinking; "What do you think we should do with it now?"

"Fill it in?" I posited.

"Yeah, okay."

So, that was that! The entirety of this pit was a hole about one foot in diameter at the surface, which reduced down to around three inches diameter at the deepest point. It was no more than about eighteen inches below the surface; not exactly a record-breaking excavation, but really not too bad for a seven-year-old.

Over the span of the next three or four years, we'd created a small metropolis out there, complete with tree-lined roads, tunnels and overpasses. The trees were real maple trees, courtesy of the overabundance of rotary wing maple seeds that spun down and covered quite a bit of area among our front lawns. We just planted these seeds at regular intervals throughout our make-believe towns, and in a remarkably short period, we had tiny 3-inch high maple trees sprouting about, providing a modicum of shade along our roadways. Of course, every time it'd rain, many of the roads and other defining features would be washed away, so our village was constantly in a state of heavy construction...not entirely unlike what the highways are like these days, only on a much smaller scale! See the Mud Pile illustration at that top of this chapter.

CHRISTMAS and ORDERLY GIFT UNWRAPPING

Shortly after waking up on this particular Christmas day, Bill and I assembled at the top of the stairs, as instructed the night before, waiting for our parents and other brothers to wake up so we could all head downstairs and feast our eyes upon the pile of gifts that we'd envisioned would be distributed all around the tree.

After what seemed like an eternity, everybody was up, so we galloped down the stairs, heading towards the unmistakable glow of the tree lights. It wasn't long before our eyes seemed to light up with a similar intensity, once we spied the many wrapped presents beneath the tree.

"Stop!" Mom called out just before any of us boys had actually touched any of the tantalizing boxes wrapped in multi-colored paper, ribbon and bows. She fetched some scraps of paper and a pen from her desk in the den.

"Okay, now…" she continued once she was comfortable in a seat near the tree. "I want each of you to take turns unwrapping each gift, while I write down what it is, and whom it's from."

Pointing to a small package closest to the perimeter, she said, "Craig, take a look and see who that one is for."

If it was his, then he'd be allowed to unwrap it. If it was for one of the rest of us, it'd be passed on to the appropriate person to open it up, all in a very orderly process. While we just wanted to dive under the tree and rip open all of the packages, this methodical procedure actually extended the duration from only a minute or two of total chaos, to sometimes upward of an hour. Doing so this way, it seemed to give us a much greater appreciation for the gifts we got.

ERECTOR SETS

One of the gifts that appeared beneath the tree this year was an Erector Set for each of us; Bill and me. For the edification of the uninitiated, Erector Sets – at that time – contained hundreds of lovely knife-edged metal beams of various lengths and curves, each with holes punched along their entire length. Because these holes "puckered" the metal, it created the effect of a cheese grater! Beyond the fermented curd-shredding aspect, the holes would also allow the pieces to be screwed together with standard 6-32 machine bolts and nuts in order to assemble all manner of menacing machinery. While successfully avoiding the severance of numerous major limbs by the sharp beams, we developed considerable manual dexterity by handling the tiny connecting hardware. Our Erector Sets opened up an entirely new construction medium for us! The various devices, vehicles and structures that we constructed provided significant lessons in structural integrity, shear forces, and logical construction procedures… if only we'd noticed. We were seven! We built stuff because it was fun! Still, it was virtually impossible to create and play with these various and sundry apparatus without these structural lessons taking root on a subconscious level, which allowed us full access to them once we were old enough to fully appreciate them.

We built large-wheeled vehicles with rubber-band suspension systems on independent axels that would be the envy of many a monster truck enthusiast today. Cranes were a personal favorite of mine. They'd even fold down for transport like the ones you see now. We also constructed all sorts of farm implements based upon the diagrams in our coveted books, and from actual farm equipment we'd see locally and on our maternal grandparents' farm. The Power Take Off (PTO) on farm tractors was of particular interest to us. This suggested a deviously simplistic means by which we could use the rotating mechanical power from our other toys to provide torque to our elaborate new constructions. We certainly hadn't abandoned the amusement park fascination when we graduated from Tinker Toys to Erector Set. The constructions just became more realistic. A roller-coaster built with metal, and powered by an eviscerated toy car, for instance, was much smoother and far more functional than one with wooden pegs and sockets!

REPURPOSED TOYS

Upon the infrequent occasions when we'd get a new toy, such as the small battery-operated car mentioned above, we'd stare at it for a long moment, grinning from ear-to-ear. Other kids might be thinking about making it drive all about the house or racing against those their friends might have. That's other kids...normal kids; kids who hadn't been infected with an insatiable curiosity and had the vivid drawings of all things mechanical indelibly etched into their minds from amazing books! That grin was the result of seeing the car for what it really was; an intricate collection of individual parts *temporarily* arranged in the configuration of a car. To appear somewhat normal, we'd briefly put on a show of playing with it in its current form, but we knew it was only a matter of time before these parts would find many other uses once removed from the confines of their vehicular function.

CHAPTER 4 – 1966; AGE EIGHT

The Number 8, Bells, & Electromagnets

In 1966 the average house cost $14,200, the typical annual income was about $6,900, a new car cost about $2,650, and gas cost $0.32 per gallon. Vietnam protests abound, Miranda Rights/Warning was introduced, and miniskirts with a hemline at the upper thigh are introduced. Color television becomes popular, Star Trek (the original television series) airs its first episode, and the disposable diaper was created.

EIGHT!

I remember disliking that age, not because of anything that happened, but just because the figure "8" is very round, and looks...well... "fat", to an 8-year-old. Okay, to *this* 8-year-old, anyway! Despite my concerns of the full-figured figure, neither Bill nor I had an ounce of fat on us. It just wasn't possible for it to settle in when we were constantly running, playing made-up games outdoors, climbing trees and ropes, riding bicycles, and playing in the woods during much of each day's daylight hours in the spring through fall, and building snow forts and other vigorous outdoor activities during the winter. That's also when former drill sergeants taught gym class in school. Yes, really! We were constantly drilled in military marching procedures and exercises as if we were in basic training, with a bit of dodge ball thrown in for good measure. I remember we were very good at dodge ball. We weren't what you'd call particularly keen on "sports" in general – we really had no interest in baseball, football, or any other team activities – but we certainly were quick, and that's really what counts in dodge ball. We were also exceptionally strong – the result of climbing trees all of the time. In gym class, while many would cringe when it was time to climb the ropes, we'd scurry up to the very top like monkeys, sometimes without even using our feet. Outside of gym class, instead of fighting with the ever-present bullies, we'd established some measure of respect, if only temporarily, by always winning against them at arm wrestling.

THE BELLS, THE BELLS!

Our house had two electric bells on the outside. One bell, mounted fairly high up, just under the eves, was hooked up to the phone line. Any time our parents or any of us kids would be out in our large yards – which was frequent during the two or three weeks each year when there wasn't snow on the ground (Hey! It's Buffalo!) – this bell would announce an incoming phone call. Since there were no answering machines or cordless or wireless phones at that time, most people would let it ring enough times (10 to 20) to allow someone to run back inside to answer. The other bell was installed on a side wall of the house next to the back door, right beside the milk chute door (See Education Alert #1) that entered the kitchen.

Craig – our older brother (remember him?) – had actually hooked up this second bell, and ran the wires through the edge of the milk chute to the inside where our mother could flip a switch to make the bell ring. Again, Bill and I would usually be playing outside, so when meals were ready, Mom would turn on this bell to alert us to come in. I can't recall the circumstances about what caused its removal, but I do remember the intense glee I felt, and the intense irritation my parents felt, when Bill and I had the opportunity to hook up this amazingly loud, clanging, electromagnetic device to a 6 Volt lantern battery in our play area in our father's den, and observe how it functioned electrically, mechanically, and… yeah…annoyingly!

This experiment, though brief (until our father suggested that we remove the gong portion that produced the loud clanging sound), fueled our interests in building our own electromagnets. We built them in all sorts of forms from a simple nail with coils of wire wound around it, to much more elaborate ones with a hollow core. This latter configuration would "suck" ferrous metal like screws and nails inside it, and suspend them in the center! Years later we'd learn that this central region was where the invisible lines of magnetic flux changed direction from north to south, and from south to north poles. Therefore, it was neutral there, with the north and south poles pulling evenly upon any metal that found its way into it.

We also observed levitation of non-ferrous metals like aluminum when an alternating current was applied to an electromagnet. While we'd later learn that this demonstrated the effects of eddy currents and Joule heating in a moving electromagnetic field, what mattered most to us at the time was that we could make metal "float" in the air, and it was fun!

MUSICAL MISINTERPRETATION

In mid-May, as our mother's birthday was approaching, I wanted to make her a special card. She was an expert pianist, and sung in the church choir, so it seemed logical to include something to do with music. I, therefore, made the mistake of asking her what musical notes meant. If I was going to draw them, I wanted to be sure they were accurate. Of course, since I didn't want to give away the surprise of this special card, I didn't mention *why* I wanted to know. She, naturally, interpreted this as a deep interest in music, so she immediately began giving both Bill and me piano lessons!

Now, I want to point out something to parents. If you want your son or daughter to hate everything to do with some activity, subject, or interest, try to teach it to them, and make them practice it frequently! It's virtually guaranteed that they'll push back, rebel, and ultimately want to do just about anything *except* that one thing that you want them to do! That's what happened when Mom tried to teach us the piano. Ironically, we DID have some interest in playing a musical instrument, but not the piano at that time – simply because our mother was an expert with it and had absolutely no patience for non-experts. So, we both ended up playing the clarinet.

CHAPTER 5 – 1967; AGE NINE

The Ontario Science Centre

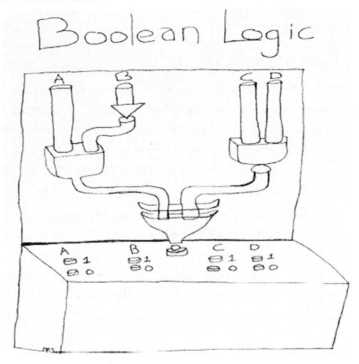

Boolean Logic

In 1967 the average house cost $14,250, the typical annual income was about $7,300, a new car cost about $2,750, and gas cost $0.33 per gallon. The Israel six-day (Yom Kippur) war occurred, improved car safety after National Transportation and Safety Board (NTSB) was created, and race riots happened in Cleveland, Newark & Detroit. The popular TV shows were: "Star Trek", "The Prisoner", "The Saint", "Doctor Who", "Hogan's Heroes", "I Dream of Jeannie", "The Beverly Hillbillies", "The Lucy Show", and "The Monkees".

Nothing happened this year.

Now, I'm sure that *something* must have happened this year. I mean, it's not like me to misplace an entire year, but at the moment, that's about all I can recall of being nine. Well, that, and I'd never seen a ferret at that point!

Okay…actually one thing DID happen that year, but it wasn't in any way related to any of Bill's or my adventures – rather, lack of adventures – that year. But since it would provide great fun to us in future years, I'd might as well mention its beginning here.

THE ONTARIO SCIENCE CENTRE

The Ontario Science Centre in Toronto opened its doors to the public. I don't recall when we first went there, but I'm sure, knowing my parents, that it wasn't long after they opened. But, I DO know that we went MANY times thereafter. Therefore, I'll say that we went there the first time *this* year. Hey, why not? It's better than leaving an entirely empty chapter…AND, it's my story!

The Ontario Science Centre was the most fantastic and amazing place Bill and I had ever seen as kids. They had a number of specialized rooms. Each room was about the size of a football field – or so they'd seemed to us young kids – and contained fully interactive exhibits about biology, communications, electricity, earth sciences, space, and others. The two rooms that Bill and I enjoyed most were the "Communications" and "Energy". Big surprise!

HUGE PARABOLIC REFLECTORS

In the Communications room, each of us would climb up to a platform at the focal point of a huge parabolic reflector on either end of this enormous, extremely noisy room.

"Can you hear me now?" I whispered into the reflector, with my back to the far side of the room.

"Loud and clear!" Bill replied from his position at the other end of the room, as if we were standing just a foot or two from each other.

MECHANICAL LOGIC GATES

In another demonstration device in that room, we'd also send a number of Ping-Pong balls down through mechanical logic gates in such an order as to achieve the proper output condition using Boolean logic. Ancient, very crude, black & white TV cameras (brand new technology at the time) were everywhere among the exhibits at the Centre. This was fascinating to us considering our strong interest in electronics, television circuitry, and video in general. See the Boolean Logic illustration at the top of this chapter.

PERSISTENCE

The Energy room had hundreds of exhibits involving electricity and magnetism. We could generate electricity by pedaling a bike connected to a large alternator, which would power a bright floodlight that would allow our image to be seen on a television monitor in front of us. We could go inside a darkened room that had its walls coated with a high persistence phosphor. Each time a strobe light flashed, our shadows would be projected onto the walls, and, because of the persistence, the image would be frozen there for several seconds after we'd moved on. They had experiments with magnets and lenses, and many other fascinating concepts.

LASERS

The Energy room also had some of the most spectacular (to us) demonstrations. One of these was a huge carbon dioxide laser, originally built for Expo 1967 in Montreal by General Electric of France. It was probably about 20 feet in length and rated at 100 Watts.

The lights in the large auditorium-like room dimmed as the sound of pumps could be heard near the long, 8-inch diameter glass tube. They'd first introduce helium, then nitrogen, and lastly carbon-dioxide gasses into the tube. Brilliant colors danced through the clear tube as each gas made its way down its length. Once the CO_2 had reached the proper pressure, the photon energy inside the tube would begin to lase.

Let's put the power of this laser into perspective. A 1-milliwatt (mW) laser pointer will blind you if you point it into your eyes. That's just 1/1000th of a Watt! A laser beam of around 50-75mW will sting bare skin. A beam less than 100mW will cut some dark plastic materials such as electrical tape. At 100W, this CO_2 laser is *a thousand times* more powerful than that!

It should be no surprise, therefore, when the technician would wave a 2x4 stud of lumber through the beam, that it would burst instantly into flames! This was one powerful laser! What made it even more exciting is that the beam from a CO_2 laser is in the ultraviolet portion of the electromagnetic spectrum, thereby making it invisible to the Human Visual System. Since we couldn't actually see the beam, it was almost like magic when the board would seemingly spontaneously start to burn!

They also had a much lower-power helium-neon laser (probably about 5mW) with a bright red beam that they'd modulate with music and play through a speaker after the modulated beam was detected on the other side of the room. Sending music over a beam of light was, for us at that time, just about like magic!

ELECTROMAGNETISM and BIG SPARKS

As amazing as the laser demo was, the electricity demonstration was easily our favorite. It began with an electromagnet powerfully hurtling an 18-inch diameter aluminum ring high up into the air, where it would remain, hovering, until the AC power was removed from the gigantic coil of wire. Before the allure of this new form of sorcery began to fade, they moved onto the high voltage demo by switching on an enormous Tesla coil that makes sparks three feet long! After that, they'd introduce an audience favorite; the Van de Graff high voltage generator. They start off by drawing some very loud and rather nasty looking foot-long sparks from the bulbous top collector of the static generator to a long, grounded rod. Naturally, after such a menacing display, they invite children to step up onto a high acrylic platform and place their hands upon the huge metal sphere where the sparks had come from earlier! I suppose they ask children to do this because they're not prejudiced by the knowledge of what half a million Volts might do to them! Anyway, once it's powered up with the child's hand fixed firmly upon the metal surface, their hair stands up on end. They're quite literally ecstatic! This is the classic electrostatic pose.

Needless to say, Bill and I thoroughly enjoyed each visit to the Ontario Science Centre...even if nothing at all happened that year!

CHAPTER 6 – 1968; AGE TEN

Johnny Astro, The Ping-Pong Table, Picture Tubes, & The BB Gun

Removing a Cathode Ray Tube

In 1968 the average house cost $14,950, the typical annual income was about $7,850, a new car cost about $2,800, and gas cost $0.34 per gallon. Martin Luther King Jr. was assassinated, North Vietnam launched the Tet Offensive, and Anti-Vietnam war protests persisted. The first successful heart transplant was performed, vehicular airbags were invented, and the Emergency 911 telephone service was started in the US. The popular films in theaters were: "The Graduate", "Guess Who's Coming to Dinner", "Valley of the Dolls", "The Odd Couple", "Planet of the Apes", and "Rosemary's Baby".

JOHNNY ASTRO

This is the year that I got a Johnny Astro for Christmas! In the late 1960s, it seemed that toy companies were determined to perpetuate the age-old gender roles for kids. For instance, for boys they made Johnny West, western action figures, Johnny Seven, military-style toy guns, grenade launchers, etc., Johnny Lightning, small matchbox-like cars, Johnny Apollo, astronaut action figures, and, of course, my Johnny Astro, an outer space-like action toy. The only popular toy other than dolls that I can recall for girls was the Suzy Homemaker set. Back then, the very thought of a boy playing with a toy typically intended for girls, was simply inconceivable. Some girls seemed to make the transition into boy's toys with much greater success and far less fanfare, but they were few and far-between. When you found them, though, you'd be wise to keep them around!

The Johnny Astro was set up to look like a movable radio telescope antenna connected to a control console. The "antenna" contained a fan. By varying the speed of this fan and changing the position of the antenna via an ingenious mechanical linkage system from a novel joystick, we could move gondola-equipped balloons from the home base on a Moon-like landscape, to one on a Mars-like landscape...as if there was an atmosphere on either, or in-between, sufficient to support such a concept. Apparently, as children, we were just to *ignore* this gross fallacy! The balloons moved because the Johnny Astro device exploited the concept of laminar airflow, which would "capture" a balloon within the flow, and not allow it to move outside of it until it reached a position where the flow was too weak. This was great fun... until the rheostat used to vary the fan's speed burned out. Of course, to us this just meant that the remaining functional parts – namely the motor with attached fan blade – would be "re-purposed", finding its way into one of our other projects.

THE PING-PONG TABLE

We finally outgrew our play space on the den floor and found a much more suitable space in the basement. I think our parents were happy to be able to re-claim the previously occupied real estate of their den. Craig had already claimed one area of the basement with his elaborate Strombecker 1:32 scale slot car racetrack over by Dad's workbench and Mom's washer, dryer, and mangle rotary ironing appliance. He'd also made use of a larger space beneath the Ping-Pong table on the other side of a wall closer to the basement stairs. He put together a complete train track set there with functioning train crossing gates at "roads", and a locomotive engine that actually blew smoke – most likely quite toxic – out of its smokestack as it chugged along. This left only the top of the Ping-Pong table to support our more advanced experiments. I mean, it's not like a Ping-Pong table could possibly be used for anything else! Right? But it needed more light.

Our father had given us permission to install a long fluorescent tube on the wall near the Ping-Pong table. He didn't give us details of what he'd envisioned, so we considered it to be like any of our regular projects... a demonstrator of sorts. As such, we mounted not only the long tube on the front of the wall, but the ballast transformer and the starter, as well – obviously! We were really rather proud of it. Our father... not so much. When he first looked at it, I think he was a bit surprised, maybe even upset that we'd put all of the "behind the scenes" circuitry up front, yet he never asked us to change it, and that's the way it remained forever after. After this, though, he was very much more specific with instructions any time he'd ask us to make any improvements around the house.

TVs, TUBES, and BIRTH CONTROL GLASSES

Our parents were long-time members of the local United Methodist church. Our entire family attended each and every Sunday... religiously. For Bill and I there were two reasons for this. First of all, we were told to, and back then you did what your parents said – well, *we* did, anyway. The other reason was because it simply hadn't occurred to us *not* to go. As we got older and could think for ourselves, however, we found that religion had no appeal for us; so attending church with our parents became more of a social venue for us, instead. This was because there was a youth group there where we could do social activities with others near our age in a non-academic environment.

On one particular Saturday the church held a community garage sale downstairs in the "fellowship hall" area. Our father was an avid garage sale seeker. He loved to get great deals on used items, even if it meant driving all of the way across town to find people selling their worn wares. There was, therefore, no question about what we'd be doing on that particular Saturday afternoon. Imagine our glee when Bill and I saw, tucked near the back of the room filled mostly with junk in our opinion, this beautiful console TV with an amazing ten-inch round screen! Getting closer, our excitement suddenly deflated. Was it because it was Black & White? Was it because it was just a ten-inch screen? Was it because the enormous wooden cabinet might barely fit in our father's car? Was it because the tag said, "Doesn't work"? No...it was the price tag! At $8, it had might as well have been a million! Eight dollars represented *sixteen weeks* of our *combined* allowances! It's also equivalent to about $55 in today's currency.

This is where our father's negotiation prowess came into play, as he talked the price down to just $4 with the seller. That was still a significant investment for us, but at least we had that much in the bank, and felt that it was worth the expenditure for the opportunity to tear it apart and learn all of the magical secrets of the circuitry inside a television receiver. This was our first experimentation TV!

The first obstacle we encountered once the acquisition process was completed...okay, so this would actually be the *second* obstacle, as getting it home was no easy feat... was to get this behemoth console television set down the stairs to our new basement lair where we could begin playing with it. Back then TVs were furniture first, functional second. This meant that the cabinet in which the tiny display and chassis was mounted, was larger than some cars today! With guidance from our father, Bill and I successfully carried our new procurement down the basement steps and placed it beside the Ping-Pong table. After a brief test of the TV, as is, we decided to pull the chassis out and set it onto the table for better access. In this particular model, unlike most others made later, the picture tube was mounted to the chassis instead of to the cabinet. This meant that we could remove the entire chassis and picture tube, as a complete, self-contained unit, by taking off the front knobs, disconnecting the speaker, and unscrewing a few large bolts underneath.

Now, we had absolutely no intention of "watching" this TV. We already knew, from the seller, that the TV didn't work, but, even if it had worked fine, with all of our activities and interests, we truly had very little time remaining to spend it, in a nearly vegetative state, in front of the hypnotic, bluish glow of a TV. We were focused on what was inside! A television receiver contains almost every kind of electronic and electrical circuit that exists. With oscillators, amplifiers, power supplies, blah, blah, blah, (I know that most of you are really not interested in these details here, but for those who are, please check out Education Alert #2 for the complete list!) a TV represents a complete, advanced course in electronics. Considered another way, a television's *circuits, not* its programming, represent the source of all knowledge... in electronics.

Okay, let's just be honest; while it *is* true that a television's circuits are an exceptional educational resource, we were far too young to appreciate it at the time. In reality, what we saw in our minds were "sparks"! Big sparks! Frankenstein's laboratory kinds of sparks...only without the monster... probably! But we couldn't make any sparks at all until we learned how to create them safely and effectively in a manner that wouldn't damage the circuits too much. Burnt out circuits would severely limit our ability to make *more* sparks, and we certainly didn't want *that* to happen! This, therefore, drove us to learn as much as we could about the circuitry.

This particular TV had its entire electrical schematic diagram pasted onto the interior wall of its room-sized wooden cabinet, but it was presented in a symbolic language that was about as cryptic to us at the time as hieroglyphics of an ancient civilization might be to those who haven't studied archeology. We'd seen enough basic schematic diagrams in library books already to know that we were looking at something rife with meaning, and that it would soon reveal the function of the circuits in front of us, but until we could decipher the diagrams, its secrets would remain hidden from us. We'd need to hit the more advanced volumes at the public library to have any hope of interpreting the enigmatic message contained therein!

Age has very little bearing on education if there is sufficient interest. Bill and I had an intense interest in learning whatever we had to at that time in order to make our envisioned sparks a reality with this TV, but nobody had bothered to tell us that the information we were teaching ourselves was normally taught at the collegiate level. With no concept of these senseless barriers, we just learned it. Very soon, we were able to determine the precise problems with this TV. We confirmed that the Cathode Ray Tube (CRT, commonly known as a picture tube) was bad, and would have to be replaced if we had any intentions of using it like most people would. But we've never been most people, so we just wanted the tube out so we could use the rest of the circuits on the chassis for our experiments without the imminent danger of CRT implosion (See Education Alert #3) in its exposed condition, unprotected by the cabinet.

Since this old TV was among the first manufactured – sometime in the 1940s – it had neither the integral safety glass on the front, nor a tension band around its wide perimeter. Additionally, we'd just removed it from its third and final protective measure, its cabinet, turning this tube into a veritable ticking time bomb! Picture tubes don't *ex*plode when broken. They *im*plode. This is because of the extremely high vacuum within. Of course, that's all rather academic, since if you're anywhere near such blast, I'm fairly sure you won't quite notice, or care, that the large, heavy, jagged chunks of glass flying in your direction had, in fact, been propelled inward instead of outward for the first few milliseconds of their lethal journey. You'll hardly even have time to say, "Not again."

We'd heard stories where glass from an imploded, free-range (i.e. placed in a field and shattered by a rock), picture tube was found about 100 feet away. Because we had no intention of becoming such a casualty, we had to remove the tube, destroy it safely, and then put it into the trash before we could start playing freely with the circuits on this chassis.

I feel compelled, at this time to point out that this is only one of the many perils associated with picture tubes. A disconnected picture tube has a nasty tendency to store high voltage in it – basically *forever*. Even after its second-anode connection has been discharged, which we knew to do, it'll still accumulate enough of a charge in the span of only a few minutes, just from the air, to provide enough of a bite to startle an inattentive technician; possibly resulting in a dropped tube, and then there's that annoying fatal implosion thing again!

With all of these hazards neatly wrapped up into one large, evacuated bottle, our father insisted that we take certain safety precautions before proceeding with its removal. The sum total of these precautions amounted to us wearing our seldom-worn glasses. So, let's take a step back here and assess the situation. I was about to cradle a huge, heavy, glass bomb charged with more than ten thousand volts in my arms after Bill helped me to remove it from the chassis. I would hold this fragile fragmentation device that's exceptionally susceptible to implosion, and known to hurl large, jagged chunks of glass hundreds of feet in an instant, tightly against my chest, but I was "safe" because I'd be wearing my glasses! I hope I'm not the only one who now sees the absurdity in this.

That's my thought now, but to a couple of young kids who had no concept of their own mortality, it seemed perfectly logical at the time. We absolutely did *not* want to go blind, but the possibility of death had never even entered our minds! Now, from a *vanity* perspective, suffering through an implosion – so long as we kept our eyesight – seemed far preferable to wearing those horrible black plastic frame glasses. Our only consolation was that nobody would ever see us in them there in our basement at that moment!

We would later learn that the military issued that very style of glasses to servicemen because they were extremely cheap....which explains why our parents got them for us. Our mother said, "Your father wears this style, your older brother wears the same, and you'll wear them!" We really had no choice about *getting* them at that time...but we did have a choice about *wearing* them! I also later found out that the military personnel had a very specific name for this style of glasses, and it wasn't exactly flattering. It came from the experiences of many a lonely soldier. They called this type of frame "birth control", since anyone who wore them at that time was guaranteed never to get a date, or experience any of that other romantic stuff that follows! But I digress.

So...we were in the basement about to remove the picture tube from a TV. In addition to his making us wear our "nerd" glasses, our father decided to "assist" us during this procedure. Now, when I say he assisted, what I mean is that he supervised. Since he knew no more about picture tubes than Bill or I did – in fact notably much less – his supervision mostly consisted of just being an adult presence in the event that something bad happened.

A picture tube is shaped very much like a funnel... a very large one made of glass and sealed on both ends. This doesn't make it a very useful funnel, but then funnels don't make very good picture tubes, either. The screen where you view the picture is at the wide end, while the other end is long and narrow, referred to as the "neck". It's inside the neck that things get really interesting. It contains a structure known as an "electron gun" – literally a particle accelerator. Electrons are the subatomic particles produced in the electron gun. When modulated (made stronger or weaker), accelerated (faster), and deflected (moved) in a controlled manner, they paint a picture that appears as a series of light and dark spots on the phosphor-coated front screen, and voila! A TV picture appears!

In order to move the high velocity electron beam about to construct the picture, a set of electromagnetic coils are form-fitted around the neck area of the tube. The assembly in which these coils are installed is called the deflection yoke. I had to tell you that so you'd understand the dilemma we faced next.

This yoke assembly was attached to a tall metal structure protruding from the chassis. This meant that we'd have to thread the long neck of this heavy, fragile, bitey, glass implosion bomb through the very tight inside diameter of the immovable yoke assembly until the tube was clear of it! Both Bill and I had a grip on the delicate tube-with-teeth from different positions so that at least one of us could monitor and minimize the lateral movement of the neck at the yoke while the other took most of its weight and pulled it forward. See the illustration titled Removing a Cathode Ray Tube at the top of this chapter.

The concern was that the smallest movement away from perfectly straight through the yoke would apply severe stresses to the fragile glass neck of the tube. Too much, and it'd snap! It was a very tense couple of minutes as we worked it through the very tight yoke aperture. But after much sweat it was finally clear, and we could relax a bit. I suppose it never occurred to us to just unscrew the yoke assembly from the chassis first! Ten-year old kids don't always think of *all* of the options, and besides, that would have been *far* too easy!

We still had to take it outside and destroy it in a controlled manner, as we knew the trash collectors wouldn't pick up an intact picture tube. This is because it posed a significant risk of injury or death to them if they were to toss it into the truck causing it to break.

We had a BB gun. Like many of our toys, it was a hand-me-down from when Craig had once used it. Unlike little Ralphie in "A Christmas Story", we hadn't shot out anybody's eyes, including our own, yet. We'd used it in the past just to shoot targets, but its primary purpose was about to change. We knew that the picture tube would no longer be a danger to us, or the trash collection people, once we'd allowed air back inside of it – hopefully in a controlled manner. We'd learn the "proper" method to let the air back in years later, but right then we knew of no other way to do this safely than with a BB gun and a good distance between us and the tube. And so, we placed the tube at the edge of our back yard, took aim from afar, and shot. With equal measures of relief and disappointment, there was no catastrophic implosion…just a slow, loud sucking sound through the tiny BB hole in the front of the tube. We chose the front because it was the thickest part, which, we reasoned, would be less likely to fracture or shatter with the BB strike. Several minutes later, once the air pressure had equalized, we took it to a trashcan and began breaking it up with a shovel. While the use of a shovel suggests a chaotic, mindless hacking, we were nearly surgical with the strikes, as we wanted to preserve the electron gun for further study, and we wanted to inspect the phosphor-coated screen. This was how we learned. What we found lying inside truly surprised us. There was a nearly perfect solid glass cone, about an inch tall, with a small dimple at the apex. This piece, we surmised, was liberated from the point of the BB's impact. Each shot through the thick front screen portion of such a tube produced yet another of these "CRT Jewels", as we decided to call them. We collected several.

For years, this is how we'd dealt with dead picture tubes to make them safe for the trash pickup, but despite – or maybe because of – the danger of an implosion, we desperately wanted to witness one first-hand. Finally, when we were 17, we set up the conditions that we felt would provide us with this result without posing too much danger to us. We'd just removed a huge, 24-inch picture tube from an old TV. The tube was about three feet long and weighed about 60 pounds. It'd be the perfect candidate for our implosion experiment…we thought.

We took it out back to a gravel portion of our driveway where we'd placed a heavy, metal, 85-gallon trash container. It took both of us to heft this excessively awkward, fragile glass tube into the air towards the awaiting barrel where, in theory, it would smash with a spectacular implosion on the bottom, while being mostly contained. Seemed safe enough to us! Still, we both ran for cover the moment we let it fly. We heard it strike the barrel, and then...nothing! No smash. No crash. No whoosh, pop, bang, or any other sound we'd expected from an implosion. When we looked back at the scene of the intended implosion, what we saw truly startled us. This enormous tube was still quite intact. In fact, it was setting at an odd angle as if to defy us. It had wedged itself hard against the sides of the metal container! Now we knew, at this point, that we were dealing with the equivalent of an unexploded ordinance after the intended detonation; Very dangerous. It was undoubtedly weakened, and the slightest additional stress could make it shatter. So we got out the shovel, and pried it out!

Round two. With increased caution, we got a grip on it once more, aimed, and threw the weakened tube at the trash container again. This time it glanced off of the solid metal rim, rolled once, and dropped 3 or 4 feet to the gravel drive! It struck the ground neck first – the most fragile part – throwing up a generous divot of grass from beneath the 1" x 2" rectangular stones, and then it came down hard on its side and just rocked there lazily in the driveway, still undamaged, as if mocking us! Our third, and final toss yielded the same result as the first, only this time it was so tightly wedged it wouldn't give. This left us just one option; Get out the old BB gun!

REAL-LIFE ADVENTURES
SECTION 3 – THE JUNIOR HIGH SCHOOL YEARS

CHAPTER 7 – 1969; AGE ELEVEN

Christmas, The Auto Lab Kit, Sunday School, & The Secret Foliage Lair

Visible Transmission

In 1969 the average house cost $15,550, the typical annual income was about $8,550, a new car cost about $3,270, and gas cost $0.35 per gallon. This was the year of the first manned moon landing, and Woodstock. The ARPANET (predecessor to the Internet) was created, the UNIX programming language was developed, the microprocessor is invented, and the Pontiac Firebird Trans Am muscle car is introduced. The popular films in theaters were:

"The Love Bug", "Funny Girl", "Butch Cassidy and the Sundance Kid", "Midnight Cowboy", "Chitty Chitty Bang Bang", and "Easy Rider".

CHRISTMAS TIME and THE AUTOMOBILE LAB KIT

We loved the Christmas holiday season. I suppose I *should* say that it's because people celebrate the virgin birth, and the spirit of giving is in the air, but that'd be a lie. We were 11, and it was *all* about the toys! Sears, JC Penney, and some local stores would send out their large, colorful catalogs with expanded toy sections sometime around October. Because we knew that we could choose only two or three of the many hundreds of toys displayed upon those magical pages that gave off the familiar smell of ozone from the static electricity they'd generate as each new glossy spread was revealed, we savored each page, affixing all of the brilliant pictures solidly into our minds. This not only helped us to memorize precisely where to find the toys we'd be allowed to request for Christmas as it got closer, but such intense, frequent study of so many toys would help us figure out how to build our own toys similar to some of those shown!

Our parents grew up during the Great Depression, so naturally they were very practical-minded and frugal. When it came to Christmas, this is when their frugality shone the brightest. They had each of us kids make detailed lists so they wouldn't end up buying something that we really didn't want. Now just making a list for Christmas is hardly original. It was the *amount* of information they had us provide on these lists that made them somewhat unique. As an engineer who's worked on quite a few military contracts, I now recognize that our childhood Christmas lists were nothing short of government material requisition forms (See Education Alert #4)! On our lists, we'd provide the exact part or stock number, and brief description of the toy we wanted, the vendor where it could be purchased, the page number in the applicable catalogue, plus the quantity, the unit cost, the extended cost, and total cost. We'd include alternate selections in the event that our primary selections weren't available, or they'd put our requisition over budget. In this way, our parents were quite assured that we'd done our due diligence in determining our options for the requested toy and were truly interested in it. This virtually eliminated any chance of their spending money on a toy that we didn't actually want.

Despite this in-depth vetting process, that is precisely what Bill and I feared would happen with this one toy we'd requested for Christmas that year. We were having second thoughts after submitting our order forms to Mom & Dad, and that was bad. The description of this particular toy in the catalogue read as follows:

"Remco Auto Lab Kit: Accurate replica of auto chassis has operating 3-speed transmission and differential, brakes and steering mechanism. See-through differential shows ring and pinion gears. 22C9547X. 3 lbs. $4.99"

This description had us virtually drooling in anticipation of assembling and playing with such a detailed, functional automotive toy. Two things bothered us, though. Unlike the big, colorful Sears catalogs and such, the Allied Electronics catalog in which this toy was spotted was still largely B&W newsprint. It was due to this too-small, fuzzy, detail-free photo, and the way-too-cheap price, that we began to develop doubts that it'd turn out to be anything like we'd imagined from the amazing description. We started to convince ourselves that any functional model that we'd envisioned would have to cost a *lot* more than that.

Once we'd made this decision, we approached our parents and asked them to remove that car toy from each of our lists. As it was past the ordering cutoff date – yes, there was a cutoff date, too – they were non-committal. They didn't say yes. They didn't say no. They just listened and thanked us for our consideration about saving $5 from each of our lists. We'd done what we could, so, with clear consciences, we went about our business and continued to count down the days until Christmas, when we'd open our toys.

When Christmas morning came, we eagerly opened each wrapped gift in turn, while reporting to our parents what it was, and who had given it to us. Gift unwrapping, as you'll recall from earlier, was no free-for-all in our house! Each of us had to account for each gift so we could properly thank those who'd given them. As I was unwrapping a fairly large, flattish box I saw the words "AUTOMOBILE LAB" emblazoned across the top. Surprised to see the toy I'd cancelled, I hesitated only a moment before pulling the paper off of the reminder of the box. This is when my concern turned instantly into absolute joy! Seeing the large, detailed, full-color picture on the front of the box suddenly brought back my recollection of the entire written description.

It was actually correct…and most amazing!

It took only a brief search under the tree for the second one to be located for Bill. These kits had a white plastic chassis 14 inches long and 5 inches wide that supported a fully functional 3-speed stick-shift transmission (with reverse!) made up of nine bright orange plastic gears inside of a clear plastic housing (See the photo titled Visible Transmission at the top of this chapter. It's in 3ʳᵈ gear here.), rack and pinion steering system, and accurate, functional drum brakes (again, orange pieces inside clear plastic housings) on each of the back wheels, connected to the actual brake pedal! It also had a functioning differential torque distribution system with authentic ring and pinion gears, as described, and a universal-jointed drive shaft. The accuracy and precision of this amazing "visible car" was incredible! Every gear, every lever, every little piece of this car had to be assembled, greased up as applicable, and glued or screwed together before it could be used, and it was exceptionally fun. Despite our asking for this item to be removed from our Christmas lists, I can now say, with great confidence, that this $5 Remco Automobile Lab kit was one of very few items that made a *significant* impression upon us, and taught us an immense amount about vehicular systems, the interaction of gears, and mechanical apparatus as a whole! This also helped prime our engineering careers.

ELECTRIC MATCH GAME

This year we'd added a third reason to attend Sunday School; building an electrical apparatus!

A new couple, Art and Judy Pranger, had moved from Alaska to the thriving metropolis that was our sleepy little town. All things are, of course, relative. As soon as they found our church, they volunteered to teach the grade 6 – 9 class, which actually consisted only of Bill, myself, and a girl our age, Charlene. So, in reality, it was just a 7ᵗʰ grade class.

Art was either an electrical engineer, or an engineering student, so when it came to activities, they took on a slightly different look than typical. Ordinarily, activities in a Sunday school class had typically consisted of gluing vaguely shaped Biblical characters cut from construction paper, along with a liberal amount of cotton balls, onto more construction paper, with a few popsicle sticks thrown in for good measure. Not this class!

In this class we designed and built an electrical "match game" board, with Biblical phrases, names and/or events on it. For Bill and I, this was great fun, as it fully engaged our electronics interest. I'm not sure what Charlene thought of it, but she helped out like she was interested. This project was built completely from scratch. In fact, we even wound the transformer that stepped down the AC wall power to a low 6.3 Volts, ourselves. This allowed the device to be plugged into the wall for power and be operated safely.

We learned quite a bit by building this project...well, except the Biblical verses, of course. We found that it takes a LOT of fine wire, concentration, and time to wind the two coils (primary & secondary) needed in a basic transformer, and then assemble all of the "E"- and "I"-shaped thin metal laminations in alternate positions to form the ferrous core. The stepped-down output voltage was clearly defined to be the ratio of the primary turns to those of the secondary. We also learned that smoke would result when taking shortcuts like cutting down the number of primary coil turns in order to save winding time! Fortunately, Art had the foresight to bring along another transformer – one that was factory-built – so, after clearing the smoke and removing the charred remains of our self-wound transformer, we installed the new transformer. This yielded the desired results, and it didn't even burn up this time! Whoohoo...or oh well, depending upon your perspective!

THE SECRET LAIR

Bill and I still spent a lot of time playing outdoors. In the summer we rode our bikes just about anywhere we needed to go, climbed trees like monkeys, ran back and forth across our large lawns playing made-up games, and we explored the woods behind our property. In the winter, we dug tunnels in snowbanks, rode sleds down hills, and trudged back up those same hills, and ice-skated on the patio and local frozen-over ponds. We were always physically active, but we were equally active with our imaginations!

We built a secret foliage lair back in the woods. Using our parents' long-bladed hedge trimming shears and blunt-nosed pruning shears (for the thicker stuff), we literally carved out a virtual town through the thick bushes, trees, and undergrowth. We had elaborate, interconnected, maze-like paths, "factories" where we'd carve up crab apples as if they were a mass-produced product, and even a "sunroom" – basically an area where the overhead canopy thinned out, allowing an unobstructed view to the sky directly above while still protected from view of anyone outside of our complex. Of course, no secret lair is complete without a well-disguised secret entrance! We accomplished this by attaching a vine to a low-hanging tree branch and pulling it down until its leaves touched the ground. It was held in place by a fairly large rock. When we'd want to open the entrance from the outside, we'd tug on the vine, dislodging the rock, and the branch would fling upward, opening wide for entry! We had to stoop to enter, but once inside, we'd pull the branch back down and lock it in place with another rock inside, effectively hiding the entryway, and we could resume our normal posture.

Because we were fairly short, and the foliage dense, most of our pathways were actually tunnels through the thick, intertwined branches and leaves. Since we "manufactured" these carved crab apples, we had to establish something to exchange for these items. Our currency was leaves. Due to the fact that we were inside a city formed by leaves, this currency really didn't have an enormous value, but at least it was easy to amass a fair quantity of this worthless tender! In our imaginary town, money did, in fact, grow on trees!

CHAPTER 8 – 1970; AGE TWELVE

The Stink of Selenium, Sound to Light, EMP, Sorting Resistors, Bicycle Electrical Systems, and Croissant Roll Rings

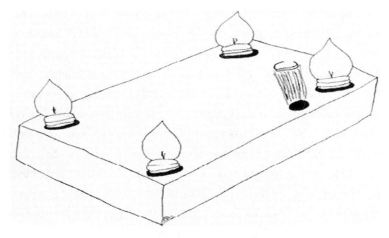

Sound to Light

In 1970 the average house cost $23,450, the typical annual income was about $9,400, a new car cost about $3,800, and gas cost $0.36 per gallon. The Apollo 13 mission to the moon was abandoned after an oxygen tank exploded, the US invaded Cambodia, and the Beatles disbanded. The popular films in theaters were: "M*A*S*H", "Patton", "Woodstock", "Hello Dolly", "Catch-22", and "On Her Majesty's Secret Service".

THE KNIGHT KIT and BURNT SELENIUM

Our older brother, Craig, had been given a rather expensive electronics experimentation lab the prior year. It was made by Allied Electronics and sold as part of their "Knight Kit" line. It was advertised to support "100 experiments", and cost $29.95 at the time. This translates to nearly $200 in today's dollars! Our parents rarely spent that kind of cash on anything, so when Craig lost interest in the kit after a rather short while, it was a given that it would be passed down to Bill and me this year. Nothing was wasted in our family!

Because we didn't know any better at the time, we just called the experimentation lab the "Knight Kit". I suppose it's kind of like calling all facial tissues today, "Kleenex", and copy machines "Xerox", despite the fact that the actual manufacturer might be different.

This Knight Kit provided us with a plethora of fascinating electronic experimentation possibilities and introduced us to an all-too-familiar smell, produced in a very new way. We discovered that selenium stinks when it's burned. In fact, it smells very much like the very worst fart you could ever imagine! Why were we burning selenium? Considering the horrendous stench it produced, I can say with great confidence that it was *not* intentional! But we were 12, and probably weren't all too concerned about a loose wire or two finding a place in a circuit that it shouldn't. In this case, a grounded wire happened to wipe across the exposed metal plates of the layered selenium rectifier mounted on the back of the kit. Selenium, like silicon, is a semiconductor material, and was deposited between these metal plates to form the diode-rectifier function. The sparks caused trace amounts of the selenium at the edges of these plates to vaporize, thereby liberating the incredibly pungent stink! But, since we could now create liberal amounts of this stench at will, it became rather fun to do so when somebody would walk by…particularly Craig.

SOUND, LIGHT, and THE EXPLODING KIT

We were in junior high school at the time. That's right, *junior high*, not *middle school* like everybody calls the grades after elementary and just before high school today. Anyway, everybody took a music class back then, and I was certainly no exception. This class was held in a very large room shaped something like an amphitheater. The instructor would frequently play recordings of various musical performances through the stereo system. Setting on a high platform attached to the front wall facing us, was a strange device with a microphone in front, and a stack of colored lights protruding from the top. I'd watch in rapt fascination, as higher-positioned colors would illuminate when the music reached a crescendo! The teacher would often encourage the class to sing along, with the specific intention of causing the device to illuminate the very highest colored light, indicating the loudest sound. We never did reach that top light. I think they'd calibrated the device in such a way that it'd have taken a sound pressure wave from nothing short of a jet engine to get it to light, but that really didn't matter to me. I was fascinated by this device, and I needed to build one for myself!

The concept was simple; Turn sound into light! The process? Not so simple... well, for most 12-year-olds, anyway.

With my limited resources to obtain exotic electronic components, I had to use what I had laying around. I figured that I could achieve a similar result with some relays, resistors, and light bulbs. Oh, and of course, an amplified sound source sufficient to drive it all... which brings us to another story, first.

Bill had isolated the audio amplifier circuitry from one of the television chassis we'd gutted, and connected it to the speaker terminals from the stereo system upstairs in the living room. This stereo was a huge piece of furniture that took up nearly the entire width of the wall next to the stairwell leading both upstairs, and, below that, down to the basement. As such, this provided convenient access to our basement lair, by running wires through a small hole in the floor, down to the lower stairwell. With this amplifier arrangement, we were able to listen to music at any volume we desired in the basement with the stereo set at a barely audible volume upstairs, thus not bothering anybody.

One day we'd turned on Bill's amplifier in the basement before we'd turned on the stereo upstairs. That day we discovered something truly fascinating! The speakers upstairs acted like really good *microphones*. We just had to turn up the volume control of our amplifier and we could hear *everything* that went on in the rooms above us with great clarity. We also decided to try exchanging the connections on our amplifier between the input and output. This allowed us to be heard through the stereo speakers by talking into one of our speakers, using it like a microphone, in the basement.

We were quite confident that this reversal concept would work, but we'd never actually tested it...until this one day when our mother had the Avon lady over. Imagine their surprise when, as Mom was listening to the sales pitch – every word of which we could clearly hear in the basement – we switched the amplifier around and said "Hi!" to them through the stereo speakers! At first they were both very confused. The stereo wasn't turned on, and yet voices were coming from it. Of course, had we been prone to practical jokes – which we were not – we might have continued with the charade and left them to wonder. But, after hearing their confused queries, we announced that it was just us, and described how we were doing it.

So, that was the amplifier story. I had to tell that one in order to set up this next one. This same amp would be used to drive our new sound-to-light converter devices. The first such project was of my own design, and it was, admittedly, quite crude. I fed the amplified music signal into a series of relays, separated by low-value resistors. As the music would get louder, more relays would be engaged, thus illuminating more light bulbs in the chain. This is how we made our first sound-activated light show. It worked quite well, but we wanted something a bit more elegant – less "clunky". This led to the second version.

The next sound-to-light converter that we built – our very first kit – was much more refined. Normally, we designed all of our own circuits completely from scratch, but this kit allowed us to explore a more elegant solution than the first version, so we decided to give it a try. It was a completely electronic system, using a kind of solid-state switch called a Silicon Controlled-Rectifier, commonly abbreviated SCR. Another significant difference with this kit was that it operated directly from wall power – something that we'd consistently avoided with all of our prior projects due to the inherent danger it posed; high voltage plus high current. We'd always worked with very low voltage, with high current, or very high voltage with low current, but never before with high voltage *and* high current. With this potential hazard, our father, once again, felt a need to supervise. Our first concern was that the SCR had no markings on it whatsoever. This left us no choice but to install it into the circuit precisely as the kit diagram showed. Instead of allowing us to use our own knowledge, experience, and judgment to ensure that it was connected properly, we were essentially blindfolded, and, forced us to put complete faith in the instructions. Faith and I, simply don't get along, so what happened next wasn't exactly a surprise.

As we were nearing the completion of this project and about to turn it on, I'd like to describe the process of applying first power to a brand new, untested circuit – any circuit. This is something that we did instinctively when we were 12, and we continue to do it even today! Despite substantial confidence in the circuits we've designed, and those that we've built, there's always a very small amount of doubt that translates to a certain degree of trepidation just before the first power is applied. It *could* burn up or any of many components *could* explode! Whether wearing safety glasses or not, we'd invariably assume the following posture; arm outstretched, just barely reaching the power switch (or power plug), head turned mostly away with eyes straining to see over a shoulder raised to protect the face! We'd switch it on, or plug it in, and be ready to immediately remove power! Despite the tension and buildup to the first application of power, it's *almost* always uneventful...a bit of a letdown, really. It works as it was designed to, and nothing explodes...well, usually! But, a boring, routine power-up wasn't in the cards this time!

Once the smoke had cleared some, and our ears weren't ringing as much from the gunshot-like blast, we peered down at what was left of the project, with the power now removed. There, in the top of the thick, ribbed plastic enclosure, was a neat hole about a quarter of an inch in diameter. Pulling it apart, we could see that it was the SCR that had quite literally blown its top! We now had confirmation that the diagram was, in fact, wrong. See the illustration titled Sound to Light at the top of this chapter.

After peeling the metal lid of the device from the ceiling, we went to our recent stock of SCRs and located one that we felt would work in this circuit. Because this part had a number on it, we could look it up in a catalogue databook to confirm the orientation. This gave us great confidence about its connection this time. It was a quick repair to remove the bad part and solder in the new. With this assurance, tension with the next application of power was significantly reduced, and we were soon sending music through the device and watching the colorful lights flicker in relation to the sound! We also had our long-standing avoidance of kit assembly directions reinforced that day.

This is my philosophy towards step-by-step instructions. I must be sure to have a complete understanding of the end result the kit is trying to achieve and use the instructions only as an occasional reference. If I don't fully understand the intent of any particular step, then it is a virtual guarantee that the device will *not* function as desired. It doesn't matter if it's a complex electronic circuit, or a bookshelf. It's imperative to understand the *intent* of each and every step. This is because such directions cannot anticipate every contingency, so they'll often assume that certain things are done *in between* steps – things *they* don't even have to think about, but without that, it won't turn out right. I've found that step-by-step instructions almost always cause people to stop thinking, as they *completely* trust the directions to guide them.

THE EFFECTS OF EMP (ELECTROMAGNETIC PULSE)

Our basement, like many, had no ferrets, but it did have a sump pump. It sits virtually idle throughout much of the year but earns its value in the springtime when ground water seeps up through the limestone caverns beneath the house and into the basement sump. One night this particular spring, unbeknownst to us, the motor burned out during a particularly heavy use. We awoke that morning to discover about three feet of water in the basement! Our father installed a new pump, and even set up a second one as a ready backup, and the water was soon pumped out, but Bill and I wanted to do something more. We wanted an early-warning system that would alert the family of any water above the sump. By this time, we'd become very familiar with the latching characteristics of the SCR solid-state switch, and we'd also figured out how to cause audio feedback, without using a microphone, by specific wiring inside of a small transistor radio. It was, therefore, a fairly natural progression to combine the two; to cause the tiny red plastic-cased radio to howl in the living room with a warning tone once a pair of sense-leads in the basement momentarily closed a circuit to the SCR, such as when water came between them. Voila! We'd built a crude, but functional "flood alarm" which could be heard fairly easily throughout the house.

Of course, like most early warning systems, it never activated by that which it was designed to sense, but that's only because we never had another flooding situation. That's not to say that it was never triggered, though! We'd soon learn the annoying effect of a high-energy Electro-Magnetic Pulse, or EMP, such as from the detonation of an atomic bomb somewhere in the neighborhood, or, somewhat more frequently, a very nearby lightning strike. Now, while we *were* deep into the Cold War era where a nuclear attack was expected at any moment, thus precipitating the "duck & cover" routine where we were led to believe that we'd be completely safe huddled underneath our flimsy desks at school, such an attack never materialized. This does cause me to ponder now what these amazing desks must have been constructed of that they'd apparently stand up against a hydrogen bomb blast at ground zero! Or maybe we were just lied to. I wonder. But I digress. So, apparently, it was the nearby lightning strikes that kept on triggering our flood alarm!

Now we didn't actually know about EMP at that time, but we certainly did observe its effects, and had easily correlated it to a high-energy event such as lightning striking within about 50 feet of the house. At times, if the lightning was particularly fierce, we had to pull the battery off of the flood alarm until the storm had passed sufficiently to keep us from having to reset it every few seconds!

Presently, some of the military systems I've designed and tested have integral EMP detection circuits – using an SCR. I don't think they're looking for lightning strikes, though!

RESISTANCE IS FRUITFUL

Until fairly recently, a specific type of circuit component called a "resistor" came only in a tiny, brown, cylindrical case with two axial leads and three or four colored bands around its circumference. Resistors control the flow of current in a circuit, much like the diameter of a pipe controls the flow of water. The colored bands indicate its resistance value in Ohms, represented by the capital Greek symbol for Omega. The resistance unit is named after the German physicist, Georg Simon Ohm. We were about to become overrun by resistors!

Herb Zinter was one of the older members of the church that our family attended. A retired engineer himself, he'd taken an interest in our early enthusiasm with electronics. He was cleaning out his house of several decades of accumulation of electronic equipment and parts, including thousands of random, unsorted resistors. We gladly accepted an apparatus or two that he'd offered us, and the bags and bags filled with resistors, but we just didn't have the room to take everything. With the resistors, he also gave us a fairly new-looking, empty, "resistor caddy", made of sturdy cardboard. It was basically a tiny chest of drawers – each drawer was about 2-inches wide, and an inch tall. Two or three separators further segmented each tiny drawer. Each small compartment would hold about a hundred resistors. There were probably 20 drawers in a 5 x 4 arrangement, and 60 or 80 compartments among them. Each compartment was assigned a different standard value of resistor. Those values were noted on the front of each drawer.

Bill and I already knew the resistor color code – that which correlated a numerical resistance value to the set of color bands on the resistor – but with so many resistors to categorize, we needed help. For this, we enlisted the aid of our six-year-old little brother, Jim. We first had to teach him the color code and how to read it on each resistor.

This little sorting exercise firmly burnt the resistor color code into my mind, and I'm sure Bill's and Jim's too. To this day, I can't think of a color without automatically correlating a number with it! (See Education Alert #5)

PERSONALIZED BICYCLE

I cannot recall the precise provenance of the red 26" bicycle that Bill got. It might have been passed down from our older brother, Craig, or from our father. I just can't remember. But I do know that the one I got was a brand new blue Schwinn racer 3-speed. It cost $50...that's like $300 in today's dollars! Of course, having a cool new bike was nice, but it needed something more; something to personalize it to me. I proceeded to install a headlight (with generator, of course), a tail light that went brighter when I applied my brakes – acting as a brake light – and blinking turn signals. Did they make such things for bikes back then? Of course not! All they made were bike generator systems with a headlight and a basic taillight. I was able to locate a taillight that also had turn signals built in, but they didn't blink, and the taillight didn't indicate braking. I first had to make a few custom modifications of my own for these to happen!

I'd also been playing with a selenium solar cell for a while, so it made sense to mount this to the side of a small, sensitive, panel-mount voltmeter, and strap it onto the handlebars of my bike. Okay, it made sense to the 12-year-old me! I thought that it was immensely satisfying to watch the needle of the meter fluctuate as I rode through a variety of lighting conditions, particularly under trees with sunlight filtering through them. Oh, and, true to form on any respectable aircraft, I'd even installed a "master switch" on my handlebars to switch on/off the entire electrical system!

CROISSANT ROLL RINGS

Since Bill and I climbed everything in sight, anyway, Mom suggested that we hang a pair of gymnastics rings from a tree branch in one of our side yards. Turns out she'd done gymnastics a fair amount when she was a kid. Even though girls don't formally do the rings, she did play on them a lot. With this experience, she'd be able to describe to us how to do certain moves on our newly installed rings.

Like most of our clothes and toys, these rings were second-hand, and far from optimal. But, we were determined to make them work for us. We'd scavenged them from an old, rusted swing set. Being made of aluminum, they were about the only part of the swing set that was not crumbling into dust. As they were intended for small children, they were only about five inches in diameter, with a thickness of just 3/8-inch. Standard gymnastics rings are just over seven inches inside diameter, with a thickness of one and a quarter inches, usually made of wood.

Since the very thin metal would dig into our hands, we decided to add some thick padding to the bottom where we'd grip them. We wrapped duct tape around that portion until it was built up to something between one and two inches of thickness. The tape was thickest at the very bottom of each ring, and thinned out on the edges. Not only did they take on the appearance of grayish croissants, but they also had a nasty tendency to roll when we hung onto them. Ultimately, this simply made us grip them tighter, thus building up our forearm muscles that much more.

One maneuver that Bill and I perfected on these rings was called the "double-leg cutoff". No, we weren't about to amputate our legs. It was just a dismount, but since it would propel us high into the air, we really liked it. We would begin in an inverted straddle holding onto the rings. We'd then swing our legs down and back, and then up front again to gain momentum.

A pull with our arms at just the right moment would effectively amplify the momentum in the swing. Just as our legs swung through the position where our hands were, we'd release our grip, and fly upward in a back straddle flip, eventually landing on our feet on the ground.

POURING MOLTEN ALUMINUM

The gas jets in the crucible gave off a dull roar behind us while my shop partner and I busily packed damp sand into our mold frames. One frame was packed solid and flat. This would be the bottom portion. The other frame had an aluminum eagle form in it. If the sand had the proper moisture, and was packed hard enough, it would pick up every detail of the eagle form once we removed it to assemble the two sand filled mold frames together. We'd also introduced a tube-shaped section in the molded sand to facilitate the pour.

With about 30 students in our metal shop class, this same process would be repeated with each 2-student team over the next three weeks, just for our class. There were at least three or four classes. It was the only day that we'd be given permission to miss our two prior classes. The preparation for the pour to create a cast aluminum eagle took time and patience. This meant that we had to start the process early in the morning, well before the time of our shop class. Although the instructor was present the whole time, he was teaching the other classes. This left my shop partner and me essentially on our own in the back part of the shop. We'd watched the instructor's demonstration and taken notes weeks prior, so now it was a simple matter of doing it ourselves.

Wearing long leather aprons, asbestos gloves, and face shields, we periodically skimmed off the slag from the top of the molten aluminum in the crucible. We were soon ready for the first pour. My shop partner was going to go first, but his sand mold hadn't been packed hard enough. As a result, it fell out of the mold frames when he tried to lift it into position. He had to start over. My sand mold was robust and ready to go, so we positioned it where the pour hole was facing upward, and then we picked up a pair of long metal tongs. Once both tongs had a firm grip on the crucible, we very carefully maneuvered it over my sand mold. Once in position, we did the pour. It took less than half of the available contents. Most of the remainder would be used in his mold once he'd re-packed it.

Waiting a couple of minutes for the aluminum inside the mold to cool, I punched through the sand, allowing it to fall out, leaving only the roughcast eagle. It had seam lines, and a short appendage from the pour tube, but those things would be ground down once it was cooler.

My partner's second attempt with the sand mold was good, so we put it into position, and repeated the pouring process, nearly emptying the crucible.

Once our pours were completed, we fetched our instructor to have him shut down the crucible, and then we headed off to our next class. Just another day at school.

CHAPTER 9 – 1971; AGE THIRTEEN

Ham Radio, Morse Code, Phosphorescent Persistence,
The Discount Coin, & Binary

Morse Code Practice

In 1971 the average house cost $25,250, the typical annual income was about $10,600, a new car cost about $3,600, and gas cost $0.40 per gallon. The NASDAQ stock index was begun, the voting age in US was reduced from 21 to 18, and the Sylmar 6.6 earthquake hit the San Fernando Valley in California. The popular television shows were: "Mary Tyler More", "McCloud", "The Odd Couple", and "The Partridge Family".

HAM RADIO

We loved Hamfests! No, these aren't gatherings of pork-loving folks. They're large events held by amateur, or "ham", radio operators, with the intent of buying and selling electronic parts and equipment among fellow hams. It's basically an enormous garage sale, exclusively for electronics. Combine Bill's and my interest in all things electronic with our father's zeal for bargains, and it should come as no surprise that he'd eagerly agreed to take us to several such gatherings over the next few years. My brother and I had been building up our savings by repairing the TVs of people from all around the neighborhood, so when the local annual hamfests came around, we had some cash available to buy new used equipment for our growing electronics lab. Much of this equipment helped us troubleshoot broken radios, TVs and such, but mostly it helped us experiment and learn much more about electronics. While it was just plain fun for us to play with all of these parts and equipment, the learning was unavoidable!

LEARNING MORSE CODE

We were introduced to the concept of ham radio through these hamfests. We soon learned, too, that one of our neighbors, Mr. Endres, was a ham radio operator, which came in handy later on when we went away to college. Instead of paying for an expensive, long-distance, collect phone call each week ($1 - $2 per *minute*!), Bill and I would sit at the school's ham radio station (supervised by a licensed operator), and Mom would either head across the street, or she'd call Mr. Endress and he'd do a phone patch to the radio. Communication that costs us nothing beats an expensive phone call every time! The idea of talking to people around the world from a radio in our own home was also very compelling. We read up on it to see what was involved. In order to transmit speech (as opposed to only using Morse code), it was required that a candidate pass a technical examination with 30 questions covering many aspects of radio transmitters and receivers, FCC rules and regulations, and accurately receive Morse code sequences transmitted at a rate of 13 words per minute. The written test was a breeze for us, but the code portion was a killer! Thirteen words per minute may sound pretty easy, but it isn't! Think about it. Each alphabetic character is comprised of between one and five elements; dots (short tones), and dashes (long tones). Each word has five characters. This means that you're hearing an average of nearly four tones *per second*, interpreting it as the associated character, and writing it down. That was very difficult for this 13-year-old.

Before we could have any hope at all of passing the code test, we first had to *learn* the code. For this, Bill and I enrolled into a code class at a local community center. Mr. Andes (not Mr. Endres) was our code instructor for that class. He was an active ham radio operator, and an electrical engineer working at the big electronics firm in our town. He encouraged us to build a Code Practice Oscillator (CPO) to enable us to continue practicing the code at home. Our CPO was basically a small block of wood, upon which we'd mounted a simple circuit (an oscillator and amplifier) to produce audio tones, a 3-inch speaker, and a standard code key. We would sit opposite each other at a table while one tapped out coded characters, and the other received. After a reasonable set, we'd switch roles. This was very effective at increasing our code capability.

One evening while Bill and I were doing our nightly code practice at the dining room table, our mother sat down and asked if she could try her hand at it. See the illustration titled Morse Code Practice at the top of this chapter. We gave each other a wary glance, thinking that nothing intelligible would come from the code key. Our mother was a very intelligent woman, but she had no technical background, and we'd never known her to show any interest in Morse code. Therefore, to say that we were *quite* surprised at the flawless code she tapped out at a rate well beyond our grasp, would be a *gross* understatement! When asked where that came from, she replied, "Everybody had to know Morse code during the war" (this was in reference to WWII). This was our first clue to something much bigger, and far more interesting, but she wasn't about to "tip her hand" at that time, nor had we caught on.

Once we'd practiced sufficiently, we went downtown and took the Novice class amateur radio license technical written exam, and the associated code reception test, at 5 words per minute (WPM). We both passed both exams easily and were soon issued our first ham radio licenses: WN2EFE and WN2EFF. With that class of license, we could communicate with anyone around the world on most of the short-wave radio bands using Morse code – only. The only problem at that time was that we didn't have a short-wave transmitter! That would have to wait.

PERSISTANT IMAGES

Mr. Andes, our Morse code instructor, worked for Mennen-Greatbatch, Ltd. in Clarence, NY. They manufactured medical monitoring equipment – specifically, EKG (heart monitoring) machines that had 5-inch CRT displays. During our code training classes, he soon became aware of our intense interest in electronics experimentation. He ultimately salvaged a pair of defective 5-inch cathode ray tubes destined for disposal. He gave them to us as a parting gift when we'd completed the class.

By this time, we were quite familiar with cathode ray tubes, the picture tubes in TVs, but we'd never had any quite like these. The phosphor screen had a notable "persistence". This meant that the screen glowed bright green for a while after being excited either by an internal electron beam, or simply from ambient light striking it. Regular TV picture tubes had a persistence of about $1/30^{th}$ of a second; just long enough for the electron beam to scan a full picture. These 5-inch CRTs had a persistence of about eight-seconds!

One of Bill's projects at the time was making a xenon flash tube fire like a strobe light. With this, we got the bright idea to flash the intense strobe onto the flat, long-persistence screen of our new CRTs with the room lights out. This produced a brilliant yellowish-green glow that faded slowly. Next, we decided to put a hand, and then other opaque objects, against the screen and strobe the light. This would freeze the shadow of the item into the phosphor screen for a few seconds! This was great fun to us, as we imagined it to be something like a crude x-ray device.

RADIO SHACK and THE BRONZE DISCOUNT COIN

Back in the 1960s and early 1970s, Radio Shack actually sold lots of neat stuff for the electronics hobbyist. Year after year since then, they've continued to reduce their hobbyist component stock, first in favor of stereo systems, and later, computers and accessories, until they no longer had anything left to stimulate the minds of creative young people. Fortunately, other companies have come to the rescue for creative hobbyists, but back then Radio Shack was the place to get the parts we needed to build our projects.

Bill and I would ride our bikes up to one of the two local Radio Shacks and spend hours there perusing the walls filled with thousands of electronic components. These included: resistors, capacitors, diodes, transistors, transformers, inductors, silicon controlled rectifiers, photocells, relays, transducers, tiny light bulbs and sockets for indicators (See Education Alert #6), simple integrated circuits, and many other items, each with a large assortment of different component values. I suppose this might seem like a severe case of window-shopping, and, in a way, I guess it was. Despite our

TV repair income, we still had very limited money to spend at that age, so we had to make very careful choices when buying parts for our various projects. In order to do this, we spent that time basically memorizing the walls filled with parts, their values, and, in particular, their prices. This gave us the advantage of designing our fun electronic devices with parts that we knew were readily available, and at a cost that we could afford. To this day, I practice a similar process at my engineering job – only I'm not physically perusing the walls at Radio Shack. Most other engineers design their circuits exclusively from datasheets, and then produce a Bill Of Materials (BOM), which they send off to Procurement to buy the parts without ever looking up the parts at vendors to even see if they're even available to be purchased. With my method, I've already researched the available stock at various vendors well before I put together a BOM. This way, I'm certain that the parts will have short lead times and low prices – which generally isn't the case with the other method.

In July of 1971, Radio Shack celebrated the opening of their 1,000th store across the nation. To commemorate the event, they held a drawing for ten lucky winners at each store to receive a specially minted bronze coin that gave the holder 10% off of any purchase for a full year. I was one of the coin recipients! For quite some time, I'd lusted over a specific step-down transformer that I'd seen high up on the wall, but its $9.99 price was just beyond what I could reasonably justify. With the discount coin, I was able to knock off a dollar from that price, making me feel like I was getting a really good deal! Because of its position upon the pegboard wall, one of the employees had to go in the back and fetch a stepladder to pull down the black dust-covered transformer I'd been eying for so long. With this transformer, and some diodes to turn the AC output into DC, I no longer needed batteries for many of my experiments!

THE DECIMAL-TO-BINARY CONVERTER PROJECT

We had recently discovered the binary number system (See Education Alert #7) and were fascinated by the elegant simplicity by which it represented decimal numbers with just zeroes and ones. Simple semiconductors, such as diodes, had also become very familiar to us, so it was no great stretch to incorporate a matrix of diodes to create a decimal to binary encoder. For those who are interested, and to annoy the rest, a diode conducts electricity in only one direction. It's like a one-way (check) valve in plumbing. With just 28 diodes, connected in a proper matrix configuration, ten switches fashioned from cut scraps of tin secured with screws, and four light bulbs, all mounted on a crude, wooden "lean-to" (two small pieces of scrap plywood paneling), we built this simple computing device. It could be powered by either a 6 Volt lantern battery, or, due to a neat power supply rectification system we'd built into it, 6.3 Volts AC such as from my brand new step-down power transformer. In binary, the right-most digit represents a decimal value of "1". The next one over, has a value of "2". The next is "4", and then "8". Each subsequent digit takes on a value that is double that of the one to the right. Now, assuming that an illuminated lamp represents a binary "1", and an extinguished lamp equals a "0", this is how it operated.

Press the 1 switch: Read 0001

Press the 2 switch: Read 0010

Press the 3 switch: Read 0011

Press the 9 switch: Read 1001

REAL-LIFE ADVENTURES
SECTION 4 – THE HIGH SCHOOL YEARS

CHAPTER 10 – 1972; AGE FOURTEEN

Conducting Glass, Yellow Smoke, Indicator Tubes, Jacob's Ladder, Steering Electrons, Conditioned Reflexes, Ant Traps, Corona Discharge, CB Radio, & Bullies

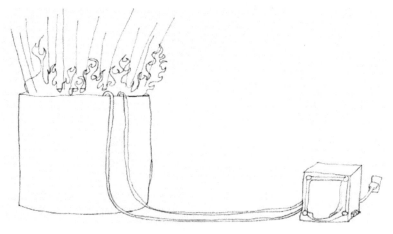

Building the Better Ant Trap

In 1972 the average house cost $27,550, the typical annual income was about $11,800, a new car cost about $3,400, and gas cost $0.55 per gallon. There was the Munich Olympics terrorist attack, the Watergate scandal, and Equal Rights Amendment, which provides legal equality of the sexes. The popular television shows were: "Monty Python's Flying Circus", "Sesame Street", "The Benny Hill Show", "The Brady Bunch", "Hawaii Five-O", and "Here's Lucy".

CONDUCTING GLASS and HIGH-ENERGY PLASMA

"What are you doing down there?" Mom called from the top of the basement stairs. "The lights in the kitchen are flickering."

I called back saying, timidly, "Nothing... much...We're just playing with 300 Volts!"

Just then a brilliant light cast dancing shadows onto the staircase where Mom could easily see it. It was accompanied with a noticeable electrical hum that soon turned into loud tearing sound. Knowing that we did lots of unusual experiments with electricity, she just replied, "Alright...as long as it's only 300V. Just be careful!" She, of course, had no concept of just how lethal 300V could be!

"We will!" I called out sincerely.

We may have played with lethal voltages often when we were kids, but we were *never* careless about it. We were always very well aware of the danger and we respected it. Accordingly, we took reasonable precautions. After all, we had great plans for the future, and the terminal inconvenience of death simply wasn't in the equation!

"Can you believe this?" I exclaimed to Bill in reference to the piece of glass in front of me still glowing a dull red. "I'm drawing 3-inch long, yellow, furry arcs off of GLASS!"

"I always thought that glass was supposed to be one of the best electrical insulators." Bill replied accurately.

"I guess its properties change when it's molten." I speculated.

In fact, if we'd taken the well-established fact that glass *doesn't* conduct electricity at face value, then we might have missed the opportunity to create an intense plasma field – a staple of high-energy physics research – when we were fourteen... and I cannot imagine who'd would want to miss that!

By this time, we'd scavenged quite an assortment of spare parts from old TVs that were too far-gone to repair and re-sell. One such part was a large, heavy, power transformer. This high-power, 20-pound chunk of copper and iron transformed the standard 120 Volt wall current into a variety of different output voltages, including 300 Volts. I should mention that 300V would "normally" only jump an air gap of about 1/64th of an inch (See Education Alert #8), based upon certain physical and electrical standards. Not very impressive!

Now, remember one of our prime objectives with our experiments; to create big sparks and arcs (See Education Alert #9)!

Let's summarize here. We want to create big arcs, so obviously we connected this deficient power source up to a perfect insulator! Seems perfectly logical! Well, it really does when you consider the technique we used in our experiments.

We'd fashioned a crude probe-style electrode from a large nail inside of a wooden dowel. One wire from the 300 Volt output of the transformer was connected to the head of the nail, while the pointy end protruded from the far end of the dowel. An alligator clip was used to connect the other side of the 300 Volt output onto a piece of glass. Once everything was in place, and we were certain we weren't touching any of the high voltage leads, one of us would turn on the power and proceed to make very, very tiny sparks from the alligator clip to the nail, across the glass. Eventually, a small accumulation of carbon would be deposited on the surface of the glass, allowing current to flow through it. When this occurred, the glass beneath would heat up and start to glow a dull red-orange from the current now flowing *through* it. At the same time, the growing arcs would begin to favor the glass instead of the clip...and they got longer – a LOT longer! Soon, the gooey, molten yellow-to-white-hot glass was conducting the electric current entirely through it. At this stage, we could draw upwards of a *three-inch* long, fat, snapping, flaming, furry, caterpillar-like arc directly from the glass! This was possible because the super-heated air around and above the liquid glass had become ionized (electrically charged), thus creating a high-energy plasma field. At fourteen years old, making glass conduct using high-energy plasma fields is called FUN!

YELLOW SMOKE

This same transformer also had a very low voltage tap. It would put out about 1.5 Volts, but it could provide an enormous amount of current (like very high-pressure water). Because we were 14, we would, naturally, short these leads together and watch them heat up. Of course, we didn't want the transformer to burn out, so it made more sense to connect a thinner piece of wire to it instead. This would allow this other wire to glow brightly and then vaporize fairly quickly, without causing internal damage to the transformer. One kind of wire that we'd used for this had thick blue insulation on it. Amusingly, when the power was applied to such a length, the insulation would instantly go up in a flash of thick, noxious, yellow smoke. Without any thought or concern of the likely toxicity of this pastel vapor, we substantially avoided it simply because of its rather foul odor. This avoidance probably contributed substantially to our survival beyond 14!

THE SCALER

At another hamfest, we picked up a particularly huge piece of equipment. The name on the front said it was a "Scaler", but, to this day, I cannot understand why. By all appearances and functionality, it was nothing more than a simple pulse counter. By that time, Bill and I were most adept at building square wave digital pulse generators using a common integrated circuit called the "555 Timer". We could vary the frequency (speed) of the pulses coming from this timer, and would feed that signal into the Scaler. It had three stages of counters. The first two were electronic. The third was electro-mechanical. Although the electronic stages could accept a pulse train of up to 30,000 pulses per second (or 30 kiloHertz), it is this mechanical counter that limited the top input frequency to less than 500 Hertz. The thing that was novel about this device was the method used to display the first two digits.

Today, most people are used to seeing fully formed numbers on displays such as our computer monitors and Smart Phones, as they're usually presented as a picture of that number, but this wasn't always the case. Many will be familiar with seven-segment LED (usually red) or fluorescent (bluish-white) numerical displays. Illuminating the appropriate combination of these seven segments could represent any number from zero to nine. Some may even remember the old (red-orange) nixie tube numerical displays. Ten separate number-shaped cathodes would be energized, thus illuminated, as needed inside of a narrow vacuum tube. Their odd name came from Burroughs' "**N**umeric **I**ndicator e**X**perimental number **I**". The electronic displays on this

Scaler were none of these. It used a pair of "Bi-Directional Beam Deflection Decade Counter" tubes made by E1T/Mullard.

It amused us to watch the little "I"-shaped beam progress up and down their respective bands while moving consistently towards the right side of the tubes, and then we'd hear the solid "clunk" of the mechanical counter's electromagnetic solenoid pull in once the left-most tube returned to "0". Okay. We were easily amused.

You're probably wondering why we bought this Scaler device, if its function made no sense, and it was so severely limited in the input frequency that it could handle. Well, I think it was mostly the combination of a really small price, and the really large power transformer in it. Plus, you have to admit; these display tubes *are* pretty neat!

THE JACOB'S LADDER

Even if you don't know the name of this next item, you've probably seen it. The Jacob's Ladder...and I'm not referring to the Biblical version... is in every Frankenstein movie, and just about every other film involving a mad scientist. In fact, there's probably one setting in the corner of some scene in *most* of the movies made during the 1930s! Hollywood, during that era, seemed to be in love with them. It's that loud buzzing/snapping device where a bright electrical arc crawls up a pair of wires, and then snaps back to the bottom once it reaches the top. It continues this cyclic action as long as power is applied. It's a neat, attention-getting device that's great for special effects, but has very little, if any, practical purpose, and I *wanted* one in the worst way!

Now, the ideal setup would have been to use a neon sign transformer. This would supply a nice 10,000 – 20,000 Volt AC output, with enough current to create a hot, fast-rising arc. Of course, we didn't have a neon sign transformer, nor were we likely to be getting one anytime soon. They just were not in our budget, so we had to use the next best thing...a TV.

The older TVs generated upwards of about 25,000 Volts internally to accelerate the electron beam inside the picture tube, but there's very little current behind it. Low current means a lower temperature arc, and a cooler arc won't climb the ladder as well as a hot one – it's basic Thermodynamics

101! Still, since it was my first Jacob's Ladder project, I was willing to accept the less-than-optimal performance just as long as it worked at all – and that it did!

DEFLECTING HIGH-ENERGY PARTICLES

For this next story, let's consider an analogy. A fast-moving vehicle cannot turn on a dime. It's simple physics. Inertia is the product of mass and velocity. Now, consider how difficult it would be to turn if that vehicle was traveling along at a fair percentage of the speed of light – like 50%! Such is the case with the electron beam inside of a Cathode Ray Tube (CRT, or picture tube) in old TVs and monitors. Ordinarily, the beam of high-velocity electrons is deflected with electromagnets in a raster pattern across the phosphor-coated screen, thus producing a picture. Using the vehicle analogy, consider what might happen if the same magnetic energy was put into "steering" the beam, but the electrons were moving *much* more slowly. It should be clear that the beam will be deflected quite a bit more. We learned, by experimentation, that when this happens – as when the high voltage accelerator system is reduced – the resulting image appears to be significantly zoomed in. In reality, the beam is being deflected much wider than the TV screen, so the portion that remains on it is stretched out in both the horizontal and vertical dimensions, thus making the image appear much larger. In doing these experiments with the intentional reduction of high voltage to the CRT in a TV, we were unwittingly demonstrating a concept known as "blooming"... whose symptom was a zooming effect of the picture, and whose solution was to fix a deficient high-voltage system! Unbeknownst to us, our experiments, based purely upon our own curiosity, were providing us both with a highly accelerated course in advanced TV repair, and electronics along the way!

CONDITIONING OUR REFLEXES

When you work around electricity long enough, its unmistakable sting will become an all too familiar sensation. Most people will develop a healthy hatred for it. As one who's received his fair share of electrical zaps as I was growing up, I was certainly no exception. But, hating these nasty neural interrupters or not, they *did* help me to condition my reflexes to react in a far less severe action than I might have otherwise. Now why would I want to do this? The continuation of life is one rather good reason to me.

Reflexes are, without a doubt, an important part of the survival instinct. But there are certain conditions in which the typical, wild reflexive throwing of one's hand away from the source of a potential electrocution hazard can cause *more* harm than the brief electrical bite! For us, this usually involved a CRT in the vicinity! To re-cap this peril, a CRT picture tube is a huge, funnel-shaped, glass display device with an astoundingly high vacuum within. If it should break, it would hurl large, sharp chunks of glass in all directions, thus causing severe injury, if not death, to anyone within about a 100-foot radius. You might argue this, but for us, breaking the CRT was a *much* greater concern than the quick, deep-burning pinch from a meager 350V boost supply off of the exposed plate cap of a horizontal output tube!

Therefore, instead of the unrestrained reflexive reaction that most people might have when receiving an unexpected electrical shock, we were able to "train" ourselves to withdraw only an inch or so. This was always sufficient to remove ourselves from the immediate threat, without creating a new one that might be much, *much* worse!

BUILDING THE BETTER...Uh, Well... AN ANT TRAP

During this particular springtime the basement was quickly being overrun with huge carpenter ants. While not quite 25 feet long like they were in the classic 1954 movie "Them!", these ants were enormous! They averaged about ¾ inch in length. Our parents put out a number of ant traps, but Bill and I felt that we could "build the better ant trap" in our lab.

Bill set out to convert an old plastic Xacto knife case into a tiny lethal ant hotel. It used a photocell to detect when an ant crossed the threshold, thus activating the 20,000 Volt power supply, which would effectively zap the ant in its tracks. The concept was sound, but the problem was getting any ant to enter it! They seemed to know what awaited them inside! Either that, or they just didn't see any reason to go inside.

I decided to work this problem from a slightly different angle. I built a crude printed circuit board with a pair of copper traces spiraling from the perimeter of this 3-inch by 3-inch board, in towards the center. The trace pair was spaced just under one ant-length, which, oddly, never seemed to have made it into the International System of Units. I soldered a wire to the end of each trace at the edge of the board and connected them to our 300 Volt transformer. In retrospect, my foresight for a protective measure during the initial test was probably most prudent, even though, in theory, this trap wouldn't actually need it "in the field". I placed the 3x3 board into the bottom of a large tin can (about 6 inches in diameter, and 8 inches deep). Making sure that no part of the 300 Volt supply was touching the can, I turned on the power. My "volunteer" ant was crawling all about my hand as I held it precipitously over the opening. Very little could have prepared me for what happened next.

Bill said, "That thing won't work as good as mine!"

I replied, "Just you wait and see! You couldn't even get the ants *interested* in YOURS!"

Bill seemed to challenge me just by the smirk on his face.

If you've ever tried it, you'll know that it's very nearly impossible to *hold* an ant in your fingertips without damaging it. You'll either crush it, or tear off a leg or two, and I really didn't want to hurt the poor little guy. Therefore, I just let my tiny testing assistant come to me.

He climbed unsteadily up onto my hand, apparently from having hit the sugar stores in the root cellar a bit too much. Once I brought my hand up towards the apparatus that I was about test, he gazed down and started a zigzag path back to the edge, and I imagine that he would have said, "I think this is the way back to the sugar bar!"

Suddenly, my little ant friend executed a beautiful swan dive – really a bit more like a clumsy ant dive, but hey, this is my story! – and headed straight for the death spiral below. Now, I'd expected a quick little crackle or zapping sound as the experimental subject came across a copper pair. Instead, a brilliant white fireball erupted from the can, shooting up toward the ceiling. See the illustration titled Building the Better Ant Trap at the top of this chapter. It was accompanied by a loud, 60 Hertz rumble as the transformer struggled in an attempt to supply theoretically infinite current! Once I removed power and the smoke cleared, I was amazed to find only the charred remains of the perimeter of the circuit board, while a large hole now occupied that which used to be the center. The ant was nowhere to be found! No body, no crime!

And that's when our mother called down from the kitchen. "What just happened? All of the lights up here just dimmed!"

I replied diminutively, "Nothing…"

Technically, not a lie. It was just another experiment…a little bit better.

Technically, the tests of both ant traps were "successful". Both basically functioned, even if not quite as intended. They got rid of ants when poured directly into them. With a few minor tweaks I could see them in homes all around the world! Or not.

USING OZONE CREATIVELY

Okay…I've talked quite a lot about high voltage here. It was fascinating to us partially due to the huge sparks and arcs we could get from it, but also because it did some things that just seemed like nothing short of magic to us as kids. One of these concepts was corona discharge, which creates ozone. Basically, this is a bluish, glowing "spray" of positive ions shooting off of the sharpened end of a small gauge wire fed by a very high positive voltage – above about 5,000V.

Of course, we weren't going to mess around with anything as trivial as 5kV when we had 25kV sources available to us from the various cannibalized TVs that we had laying around! Corona discharge will occur at sharp points on any conductor fed with a voltage of sufficiently high potential as to ionize the surrounding air, combining with oxygen (O_2), and converting it into ozone (O_3). As we'd demonstrated with the conducting glass experiments, ionized air is *strongly* conductive. Therefore, if another conductor, connected to the negative supply, were to enter the corona region, a complete conductive path is created, thus causing a spark or arc to jump through the ionized air to the other conductor. If such an opposite-polarity lead weren't in the vicinity, we'd get just the blue spray of ions.

The most notable attribute of high voltage corona discharge is the unmistakable, sharp smell of ozone. Interestingly, the Greek origin for ozone, or "ozein", means "to smell". The books describe this smell as chlorine-like, but I've always thought of it more as that sweet, cool, fresh smell of a clear spring day after an electrical storm...or from the office copy machine, but I prefer the healthy outdoor visual, personally. Ozone is produced from the ionization of the air in a corona region. This liberation of electrons into the air creates ultraviolet radiation (See Education Alert #10). Ozone is also highly corrosive to malleable materials like rubber, plastic, latex, etc. and will cause them to harden and crack within a tiny fraction of the time it would take without such exposure. I can't tell you how many crystallized rubber grommets or rubber bands I'd found in various parts of TV high voltage cages. Ozone is also an irritant to mucus membranes. Just thought I'd throw that in. As such, using special precautions like making sure we did NOT put high voltage electrodes in our mouths, we would use this ozone spray to "blow" ping-pong balls across the table – something like a fan with no moving parts! To us, this was rather neat. What appeared to be a "wind" blowing the ball away from the wire tip was, in reality, a repulsion effect caused by the ions imparting their charge onto the surface of the Ping-Pong ball. Remember, while opposites attract, like charges repel.

MORTAL MOMENT #1

Our father traveled quite a bit for his industrial sales job, and the early 1970s was a ripe time for a new kind of short-distance radio communication which allowed him to get local traffic condition updates and such while driving. It was called Citizen's Band radio, but most commonly referred to simply as "CB". Because of legal power restrictions, and the carrier-based technology it used, CB was effectively limited to between 5 and 10 miles, voice communication. While CB radios could support Morse code, virtually nobody used it on the CB frequencies.

What made CB radio so popular with the non-technical populace, and SO overrun with WAY too many people trying to use the same channels in the same local areas, is that the radios were cheap, and there was no exam required! Licensure – yes, at one time a license *was* actually required to use a CB radio – was obtained by sending in $20 with your name and address. BAM! You had a CB license! Later, once EVERYBODY seemed to be on the CB channels – seemingly all at the very same time – the Federal Communications Commission (FCC) basically threw up their hands in frustration and gave up trying to issue licenses, or even police the usage, and just let total anarchy reign. And it *was* complete anarchy on the airwaves!

In fact, a lot of CB operators just picked up a microphone and, despite the large monetary fine and long prison sentence the FCC *could* impose (up to ten years and $10,000 fine) for the use of profanity over the air, these people just started swearing up a storm without the slightest concern or respect for anybody else. This certainly is NOT to say that there weren't decent people using CB radios. There absolutely were, and still are! But they represent a significant minority. Our father was, of course, one of this small group.

So, Bill and I were into ham radio, and Dad was into CB. The astute reader will, by now, have sensed a bit of tension there from my description of the "typical" CB person. Yes. It is true. Like oil and water, ham radio operators and CB people don't often mix! We, as hams, believe that the ability to broadcast over the air is a privilege that one earns, not a right that's given. If this sounds a bit stuck up, so be it. When we, as hams, put in a *significant* amount of time and effort to learn all of the technical aspects of radio circuits, we study the FCC rules and regulations to ensure proper and respectable use, and we become proficient in the Morse code that's used frequently as an alternate to voice, we respect the privilege that's been bestowed upon us in the form of an FCC license. Any time you work hard to earn something, you'll be far more inclined to work hard to keep it. In the context of radio broadcasting, it means that ham radio operators will follow the rules and be respectful of others, thereby maintaining a far more organized and useful communication media.

Now, since Bill and I loved to climb things, and we had no concept of our own mortality at that time, we thought nothing at all of climbing onto the roof of our parents' house to install or adjust Dad's big CB radio antenna. In fact, we'd almost beg to head up to the roof! This, however, was a cakewalk in comparison to another antenna we helped to install. As was his natural way with people he'd meet, Dad made lots of close friends among the CB community, as well. One of these, whose "handle" (CB alias) was "Fire Truck Doctor", had just come into the possession of a brand new, HUGE antenna for his radio, but it did him no good until it was installed. Unlike our parents' 2-story house, FTD's house was a 3-story structure, and the antenna was about 25 feet long, and 10 feet wide! I remember walking freely upon the crest of his roof some 30 feet above the ground with Bill and three adults, all holding this gargantuan antenna over our heads to put it into place. This is when I had my first "mortal moment". I suddenly realized how easily I could have fallen from this precipice. The mental picture I created of this event wasn't pretty. It didn't end well! Therefore, as soon as we set the antenna down for a bit, I actually requested a rope to tie between the chimney and myself, thereby lessening any damage if I should fall. I can't recall precisely, but I think Bill did, too. Once secured by a liberal length of rope, my regular sense of immortality returned, and we got the antenna installed without further concern.

THE BULLY UMBRELLA

This was the year that we began high school. Bullies had picked on us incessantly throughout junior high (7th & 8th grades), and, of course, they followed us to high school. Nobody likes bullies…except for their ever-present minions, and *maybe* other bullies. I truly hated those who'd bullied me, and I really wanted to put them in their place, but I was not prone to violence or physical altercations. Instead, using uncommon foresight, I chose to channel that hatred into making myself the most educated and successful person I could. How does this avenge the bullies? By their very nature, bullies are stupid people with no ambition or motivation. Their entire lifestyle revolves around the humiliation of others for the entertainment of their dim-witted minions. They never think of the future. They seem to believe, through their shroud of ignorance, that further education is a waste of time, so they remain stupid. By my soaring far, far above them in all aspects of my very successful life and career, while they're stuck still living in their parents' homes, working minimum wage jobs, I get the sweet satisfaction to see them wallow in their own self-made purgatory!

Once Bill and I got to high school we'd noticed that the bullies weren't as effective there. I'm quite convinced that a significant part of that difference was Dewey! We knew Linda Van Nuys by her nickname, "Dewey". She was in our homeroom class, and she was a girl on a mission! Bill and I were painfully shy, and hardly ever talked to anyone – *especially* a girl! This was, in fact, a trait that the bullies had exploited mercilessly. But Dewey had made it her personal goal to "get us to talk". To do that, she talked with us as much as possible during homeroom each morning, which actually did help build our confidence, and open us up some, but it was her affiliation with the bullies that really made the biggest difference. She was the girlfriend of one of the guys who'd bullied us. Her influence over him, to our benefit, was clear and immediate. I think she withheld affection from him when he'd consider picking on one or both of us. All I know is that he never picked on us again, but what's more, *other* bullies didn't bother us either! Our knowing Dewey seemed to provide us with some sort of protective "bully umbrella", which kept them away.

CHAPTER 11 – 1973; AGE FIFTEEN

Holograms, AC Electromagnet, The Flagpole, Car Alarms, & Calculators

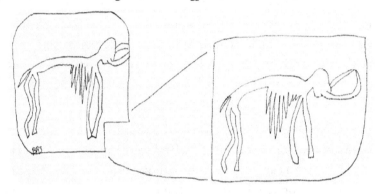

A Mammoth Hologram

In 1973, the average house cost $32,500; the typical annual income was about $12,900; a new car cost about $3,900; and gas cost $0.40 per gallon. US troops were withdrawn from Vietnam and peace treaty signed; Organization of Petroleum Exporting Countries (OPEC) began restriction of crude oil to countries supporting Israel, resulting in increasing oil prices. The World Trade Center in NY became tallest building in the world. Skylab is launched, and the personal watercraft is invented.

THE MAGIC OF REAL HOLOGRAMS

Our mother took Bill and me to the local museum of history many times, but I specifically recall the time when they had an exhibit of holography. A true hologram is a 3-dimensional representation of an object, which allows the viewer to check out a wide range of perspectives, including looking "around" portions of the main subject to see items in the background. Another most fascinating attribute of holograms we'd learned was that the entire image is contained in *every* part of the transparent film upon which the subject is captured.

A hologram is created with a LASER. I expect you're wondering why I've capitalized the word here. Most younger people will have only seen it as a single, lower-case word, but some who are older will recall that it is actually an acronym of five separate words: Light Amplification by the Stimulated Emission of Radiation. Acronyms are always capitalized. Ferrets are not!

After we'd checked out the entire exhibit, we headed to the gift shop where they were selling genuine holograms of various sizes and subjects. A true hologram, under normal illumination, just looks like a clear sheet of plastic with some wavy distortion on it. It doesn't reveal its image until it's illuminated either with another LASER, or by regular, incoherent (random, disorderly, as from a regular light bulb), monochromatic (single-color) light, and you look *through* it as if looking out a small window.

The hologram we chose – the one we could afford – was a small 3-inch by 3-inch representation of a model of a skeletal wooly mammoth. Most people today are familiar with the popular dichroic holograms used in a huge number of products, namely on credit cards, and, most recently, driver's licenses and the new $100 bills. These are readily visible under regular, ambient light, and require no special viewing technique to see the images contained therein. The original holograms, however, were created with the monochromatic, coherent (orderly; all wave peaks are aligned) light produced from a LASER, and, therefore, the use of monochromatic, coherent light would be the best method to view them. Now, since we were a bit short on LASERs at the house at that time, we chose the filtered incoherent light method to view it.

As I sit here typing this now with a pair of 99-cent LASER pointers setting on my desk, I expect that the sarcasm of the prior sentence might be lost on many. Here's a bit of helpful perspective. In 1973, *nobody* could afford a LASER in their home! The very cheapest LASER available at the time was a helium-neon laser with a brilliant red beam. It was about the 24-inches long, 4-inches square, and cost about $400 – which is equivalent to paying $2,200 today! As long as we're talking about ridiculous – yet true – LASER facts, the very first fully self-contained, commercially available LASER "pointer" was 13-inches long, weighed 10-lbs, had to be plugged into the wall, and cost $1,525…in 1963. This would be equivalent to nearly $12,000 today… for a LASER pointer!

We now return to our regularly scheduled program… Conveniently included with the hologram, was a green filter fit into a standard 35mm photographic slide mount. We placed this filter in a slide projector and used the brilliant green light that it threw into the darkened room to view the image trapped inside the clear acetate.

Well aware of the entire-image concept where you're supposed to be able to see the full subject in any and every tiny piece of the hologram film, and most eager to test it out, we cut a small chunk, out of one corner of our hologram. Back in dark, with the green filter in place on our light source, we peered intently through this tiny, ½ inch by ½ inch section of clear acetate until we could see something. Deep, down inside, as if peering through a very small keyhole, there was, in fact, the *entire* mammoth! See the illustration titled Mammoth Hologram at the top of this chapter. This sort of really blew our minds!

BUILDING BIGGER ELECTROMAGNETS

Who out there has taken apart a power transformer? Anybody? Anyone at all? Anyone? Well then.... If you had, you'd know that they're comprised of at least two huge coils of wire, wound around a core-form whose squared hollow center is, ultimately, populated by an alternating series of lacquer-coated "I"-shaped and "E"-shaped metal laminations. With this insight, and continuing my earlier interest in electromagnetism, I decided to wind a coil of wire that I could actually plug into the wall outlet – without burning out. I wound it on a square formed piece of cardboard that took its shape around a stack of "I"-shaped metal laminations from one of these power transformers. Once wound, I removed the ¾" x ¾" by 6" metal core. This provided an open area in the center of the coil which, when energized, was quite good at sucking up nails, screws, and other ferrous, metal odds and ends we had laying around. They'd become suspended in mid-air, inside the hollow core of this long electromagnet. We both thought this was really neat!

I also wound another coil, with far fewer windings, that would fit loosely around the same stack of "I"-shaped metal pieces. Connecting a light bulb up to the two wires coming from this second coil, I could make it light up by moving this secondary coil near one end of the primary coil once it was plugged into the wall. It went much brighter when there was metal in the core, and, of course diminished further as I moved the secondary coil away from the energized primary. This effectively demonstrated the precise action of a variable output transformer, or a Variac. Of course, to us, it seemed almost like magic to watch the light bulb light up when all it was connected to was a coil of wire that was placed near a bigger coil!

FLAG-TAG and THE FLAGPOLE LIGHT

The side yard of our parents' property had a small, round garden, perhaps 15 feet in diameter. A 50-foot-tall flagpole sprouted from the very center. There was a light bulb mounted at the very top of this pole. Despite the fact that we were directly in the flight path of aircraft taking off from, and landing at the Buffalo International Airport, this light wasn't red or flashing like most high structures near an airport require. Perhaps it wasn't quite tall enough to make this a necessity, or, more likely, we just didn't get the memo. On many a warm summer night, Bill and I would play a game of what we called "flag tag" with our then-best-friend David Fairlie. Being located relatively close to Lake Erie, we almost always had a fair breeze blowing through. This, of course, caused the flag, high up on the pole, to flap all about in random directions. Since it was up near the light, it cast a huge shadow down on the ground all around the garden. Once again, engaging our imaginations, we treated the shadow of the flapping flag coming over us to be a "tag". We had to remain close to the perimeter of the garden, while avoiding being tagged by the flag's shadow. We could either jump over the shadow on the ground, or we could momentarily run away from the garden to avoid a tag. Running away, however, counted as a "partial tag" – three such maneuvers would be equal to a full tag. Therefore, jumping was the preferred avoidance technique...except when the flag's shadow dwelled beneath us longer than it took for us to return to Earth! You see, as much as we wanted to fly, we still hadn't yet figured out how to hover for long durations unassisted! Being tagged meant we'd have to sit out until everyone else got tagged. Considering the frenetic activity of the flag, and the difficulty of avoiding its shadow, the wait usually wasn't very long. All of this was an exceptionally good aerobic activity.

Of course, in order to continue to play this game, to say nothing of its intended use of illuminating the yard around it, the bulb had to be replaced on occasion. Apparently, this bulb had only gone out once before while we'd owned the property, and our parents had the local fire company come by with a ladder truck or a cherry picker to replace it. This year, they didn't.

Our parents had inherited our grandparents' Winnebago motor home after they'd used it only once for an extended trip down to Florida and back. I guess Grandma and Grandpa weren't exactly the camping type, while our family camped all of the time. Therefore, once they returned from their Florida trip, they figured we'd get far greater use from it, and parked it in our driveway. So, we had this 23-foot-long camper. It was about 10 feet tall and had all of the aerodynamics of the proverbial brick! There wasn't a curved surface to be found on the thing! It was all flat, square angles, and the roof was no exception; totally flat. Why is this important? It was about to be put to use in an odd chain of increasing elevation required to help us replace the flagpole light, 50 feet above the ground.

Our father's extension ladder would go up to 32 feet – far short of reaching the top of the flagpole. He drove the "Winnie" over to the perimeter of the garden, and then Bill, Craig and I helped him heft the ladder up to the roof. With the combined height of the motor home and the fully extended ladder, the top rung reached about 40 vertical feet (when subtracting about 2 feet due to the angle of the ladder). The top of the ladder was still 10 feet short of the top.

The next thing that Bill and I had to do was very difficult for us. One of us was going to have to make this very dangerous climb, so it was necessary to determine which of us would be going up, and which was to remain on the ground. Knowing that it would be a tough decision, Mom had brought out a couple of toothpicks, and broken one in half. She held them such that we couldn't determine which was the short one, and then asked one of us each to select one. Bill made the selection. I saw his face drop as he pulled out the full-size toothpick. By simple process of elimination, it was obvious that I had the short stick. This meant that I'd be going up the pole. I sensed Bill's disappointment, but I was too excited to let it affect me too much.

After securing the new bulb inside my light jacket, and a screwdriver in my back pocket, I climbed to the roof of the camper, and then began to climb the ladder – which was being held by both Craig and Dad. Since the high end was only being supported by the very narrow pole, it had a nasty tendency to twist. It was, therefore, a tenuous ascent to the top of the ladder. This was just stage-2 in my journey!

Once I reached the pole where the top of the ladder was resting, I hesitated for a moment while holding onto both the ladder and the pole, as I considered the next part. Stage-3 consisted of me shinnying up the remaining ten or so feet of the narrow pole to the top where the light resided. While I could easily climb most ropes to the top with very little effort, and trees were even easier, this pole had neither the flexibility of a rope, nor the roughness of a tree's bark to give me adequate grip. Despite some amount of rust, the smooth pole and the 50-foot height made for a most challenging climb!

Naturally, the height didn't affect my *physical* ability to climb, but it *did* affect my psychological ability to climb *efficiently*, as I was being far more cautious than I'd be otherwise.

"Be careful!" Mom called up quite unnecessarily from the ground beside the camper.

"Well thanks, Mom!" I thought. "That had never occurred to me!"

"Only a few more feet to go!" Dad called up from the top of the camper. "You can do it!"

While I did appreciate their words of concern and encouragement, it was hard to take them to heart when I knew that they had a fully functional "spare me" standing on the ground right next to them in the form of my identical twin brother.

After what seemed like an eternity, with this pole – my only lifeline – clutched tightly against me, shinnying just inches at a time, I finally reached the top! With my legs wrapped tightly around the pole at this point, I had a fair amount of freedom with my hands. Unlike most outdoor lamps that require the removal of a couple of screws to get the clear protective glass cover off, this one was more like an inverted mason jar. It was threaded into the pole. As it'd been untouched for many years, it took a fair amount of tapping with the handle of the screwdriver I had with me, and a lot of hard twisting to get it to budge. Once opened up, I unscrewed the old bulb, placed it in my jacket, and installed the new one.

Bill ran inside and flipped the switch on for a quick test. Seeing that it worked, I screwed the cover back in place, and prepared to begin my descent. As the most dangerous part would be getting back onto the ladder, I chose, instead, to have Craig and Dad lift it away from the pole, allowing me a completely clear path to slide down the entire pole, unimpeded, to the safety of the ground. The pole was larger in diameter at the bottom than it was at the top, but it didn't taper smoothly. It did so in discrete sections with a hard ridge at each seam. Sliding down, I hit a couple of these ridges as I gained speed. They were becoming increasingly unpleasant, so, once I was about 15-20 feet from the ground, I decided to just push off to avoid the rest. This was the closest I'd ever come to actually flying...that is, until my rather awkward meeting with the ground in the middle of Mom's garden! I'd succeeded not only in replacing the light bulb, but I also got some much-desired airtime! I'd call that mission accomplished!

HOME-BUILT CAR ALARMS

I'm not sure why we started building car alarms. I think it was simply a natural progression once we'd experienced the latching characteristic of the SCR from prior projects. We, therefore, designed, built, and installed a car alarm into our father's car. Why wouldn't we just install an off-the-shelf car alarm? No such thing existed in 1973 – at least not at a price that mere mortals could afford! In retrospect, it was exceptionally crude, but, at the time, it was sufficiently unique that any would-be thief certainly wouldn't expect it, and the noise would catch *someone's* attention. This would be enough to deter one from completing their despicable act.

Our early alarms were little more than a high-power solid-state switch (the SCR of prior stories) going between the battery and the car's horn, with a small toggle switch mounted in an inconspicuous location to arm and disarm it. Basically, once armed, it would cause the horn to blare if any door was opened. I said it was crude! Eventually, we installed another into Craig's car, and even our mother's. In later years, once commercial car alarms had become far more common, we noted that most people simply ignored a static noise like a continuous blast from a horn. It just became part of the background sounds. This brought about the warbling siren-like alarms.

Much later on – once I'd graduated from college and bought my own first car – I designed, built and installed a far superior alarm for it. This one, mounted inside on the main console, had a 10-digit keyboard. When I'd get out of the car and lock the door, I'd also turn a special key switch next to the door lock to arm the system. When I was ready to re-enter my car, I'd turn off the key switch first, then unlock the door. This would establish a 20-second countdown, during which I'd have to sit down and enter the 4-digit code to deactivate it.

There was also a pair of magnetic proximity switches installed surreptitiously just beneath the dashboard that could be used as a secondary method of deactivating it if I'd forgotten the code. By simultaneously applying a magnet to each location on the surface of the dash, this would also disarm the system. And, naturally, something else DID go wrong. I hadn't anticipated the thermal instability of a specific component in my timer circuitry when it got very warm – as the very hot Southern California summers often would! This caused my 20-second disarming delay to count down in about 5-seconds! This didn't give me nearly enough time to tap out the code, so I had to resort to the proximity switches! Eventually, I started not arming it during excessively hot days. Live and learn!

THE FIRST ELECTRONIC CALCULATORS

Today, most people don't even think twice about electronic calculators. They're everywhere. They last nearly forever on a set of batteries, or just a solar panel, and they're really cheap! You can even find a basic 7-function calculator, with memory, for just about a dollar right now. There are even calculator applications on most computers and cell phones these days. They are truly ubiquitous! But this wasn't always the case.

Sanyo developed one of the very first "portable" calculators in 1970. It was a 4-function device that cost $425. In today's dollars, that's more than $2,600! Clearly, this high cost didn't make these calculators exactly appealing to very many people back then. It'd take a few more years before prices, and the size, of calculators dropped to where they'd start to interest some consumers.

It was in 1973 when I saw my very first electronic pocket calculator! Dad liked gadgets. As such, it was no huge surprise when he came home one day with one of the very first commercially available *pocket* calculators. It had eight red LED digits with a fixed, two-digit decimal place, and three standard functions, and an unusual form of subtraction. It could add, multiply, and divide in a normal manner for a standard algebraic notation calculator, but to subtract, you had to enter the numbers in a way that was far more consistent with Reverse Polish Notation (RPN). To subtract, you had to enter the numbers like this: 6 + 4 -, read 2. The four AA batteries lasted for about 15-20 minutes of continuous use, and they weren't rechargeable. Oh, and the best part; this amazing calculator cost *just* $99...in 1973! Today, that would be like spending $540 on a 4-function calculator...IF you could even find such a basic calculator these days!

I remember asking my 9th grade science teacher if I could use it on the final exam. He was hesitant, as there was no established policy for electronic calculators yet, but, after conferring with the other teachers, he finally allowed it, but only to "check" my answers. Conversely, the message was VERY clear when it came to the *math* finals! No computing device, whatsoever, would be allowed on those finals! This included electronic calculators, adding machines, slide rules, and even abacuses!

Perhaps it would be appropriate, at this point, to mention something about the two methods available to enter computations into calculators. It seems with technology that there are frequently two very different systems competing for the market share. It happened with Sony's Betamax versus JVC's VHS videocassette systems. It's still happening with PC versus Mac, and it happened with calculators in the 1970s.

While the very first calculators operated in a manner very similar to RPN, it wasn't long before the best-selling calculators were those that accepted standard algebraic entry (i.e., 6 - 4 = 2). For simple calculations, this is very straightforward and intuitive; enter the numbers just as you'd write them on paper. But not everybody does only simple calculations. Hewlett Packard (HP) catered to scientists, engineers and technicians with their variety of electronic test equipment, so it wasn't a stretch for them to offer scientific calculators using the true RPN system (i.e., 6 enter 4 -, read 2) for these technically inclined consumers, beginning in the 1970s.

Consider this example equation: ((15 - (5 x ((8-2)/3)))) x (8/(9-5)) = 10

Robert C. Trautman

Keystrokes
Algebraic (31) RPN (23)

Parenthesis One

Parenthesis Five

One Enter

Five Minus

Minus Five

Parenthesis Enter

Five Times

Times Eight

Parenthesis Enter

Parenthesis Two

Eight Minus

Minus Three

Two Divide

Parenthesis Times

Divide Minus

Three Eight

Parenthesis Enter

Parenthesis Nine

Parenthesis Enter

Parenthesis Five

Times Minus

Parenthesis Divide

Eight Times

Divide

Parenthesis

Nine

Minus

Five

Parenthesis

Parenthesis

Equals

Using RPN, there are eight fewer keystrokes, but more importantly you don't have to mentally plan opening parentheses, count them as you go, and then count closing parenthesis, closing them only at the proper times. With RPN you can also start the computation at ANY point within the equation, never worrying about parentheses. Doing a very long computation like this example equation with an algebraic entry calculator is just inviting errors. I've used RPN calculators ever since I got my very first one (an HP41-CV) in 1981. Even the calculator app on my cell phone is an RPN calculator; the HP48GX

CHAPTER 12 – 1974; AGE SIXTEEN

Accidental Binary Addition, Driver's Ed, "The K", Seeing in the Dark, Harkness Center, Slide Rules, The Test Box, Amplifier Class, TV Cameras, Our First Oscilloscope, Our First Color TV, The Voicewriter, and Our "Radio" Shows

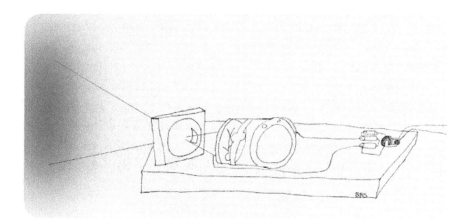

Night Vision Apparatus

In 1974, the average house cost $34,900, the typical annual income was about $13,900, a new car cost about $3,750, and gas cost $0.55 per gallon. President Nixon resigned after the Watergate scandal, the 55MPH speed limit was imposed to preserve gas usage in US, pocket calculators started being sold, and the Magnetic Resonance Imaging (MRI) scanner was developed; interestingly, this was originally called NMR imaging for Nuclear Magnetic Resonance, but they had to remove "Nuclear" from the name due to public fear.

ACCIDENTAL BINARY ADDITION

Earlier, we talked briefly about 7-segment LED displays. I'd recently bought an 8-digit, 7-segment red LED display from our then favorite electronics mail-order store, James Electronics. Decades later, they're still in business and now called "Jameco Electronics", but they still sell pretty neat stuff for the hobbyist. This was a "multiplexed" display, meaning that with just

17 connections, any numerical value in any or all of the eight digits could be produced in what would appear as simultaneous, while using only as much power as a single digit. Without multiplexing, it would require 64 connections, and would consume *eight times* the power!

I discovered something most interesting when I would push two buttons on the keyboard I'd connected to this display, at the same time. There are 16 unique combinations on a 10-digit keyboard that cause the resulting displayed number to equal the sum of the two digits I'd simultaneously pressed! After working out the binary equivalents of the decimal numbers on the keyboard, it became obvious why this happened, but at first I was very surprised to see an apparent (accidental?) addition function without using any physical adder circuitry.

Example 1: 1 decimal = 0001 binary (this number is pressed)

2 decimal = 0010 binary (this number is also pressed)

3 decimal = 0011 binary (the two bits from the two numbers displays 3)

Example 2: 3 decimal = 0011 binary (this number is pressed)

4 decimal = 0100 binary (this number is also pressed)

7 decimal = 0111 binary (the three bits from the two numbers equals 7)

Example 3: 5 decimal = 0101 binary (this number is pressed)

8 decimal = 1000 binary (this number is also pressed)

13 decimal = 1101 binary (the three bits from the two numbers equals 13)

There are, of course, many combinations that *don't* work like this. One such combination is 4+5, which simply comes out as 5, not 9. This is because it's just an "accidental" binary adder. But for the combinations that do work, it seemed pretty neat to us at the time.

DRIVER'S ED

Bill and I both got our driving permits in February on the afternoon of our 16ᵗʰ birthday. I should mention that driving wasn't exactly a novel concept to either of us, as we'd been driving our stick shift riding lawn tractor to mow our lawns and plow our driveways since we were 10 or 11. Therefore, with the exception of speed, traffic, and road signs, we pretty much had the concept of controlling a vehicle down. Once we had our permits, though, our mother would ride with each of us as Bill and I took turns in the driver's seat of her stick shift 1967 Volkswagen camper for the next several months. We'd enrolled into the Driver's Education class that year, too, but it wouldn't begin until July.

The first thing they did in Driver's Ed was to show the entire class a film that was designed to shock us all into driving safely – or get sick to our stomachs, as some did from the gruesome images. Showing pictures of real accident scenes, it was easily the goriest thing we'd ever seen at the time. You'll recall that we were just 16, and the only movies that contained such images at the theaters at that time (or so we'd heard, since we'd never seen them) were rated "R" – Restricted to 17 and over. We could only get into movies rated either "G", for General audiences, or "GP" for General audiences WITH a Parent present to help kids deal with the profanity these films contained. That was before they changed "GP" to "PG" for "Parental Guidance"…removing the need for a parent to accompany the child, so long as the parent counseled the child after what they'd just viewed. There was no "PG-13" at that time!

This gory cautionary film was shown in black & white, of course, and was a precursor to the infamous "Red Asphalt" that I would hear about many years later. After the classroom instruction that first day, we were all divided up into groups of four, and shown to our cars and instructors. Our group had just three; Bill, myself, and a girl named Emily. All three of us had driven other types of vehicles for years prior, so for the next week or two, we simply chauffeured our driving instructor all about town, while executing each maneuver he'd requested with accomplished precision. Apparently, this wasn't sufficiently exciting for our teacher. Perhaps he was falling asleep from boredom. I don't know. Either way, the administration decided to shake things up a bit. They moved Emily to another car and brought two other girls into our car. I can't recall their names, but even if I could, I feel that I should withhold them to save them from any embarrassment.

Well, if our instructor had wanted to be more on the edge of his seat, then he certainly got his wish with these two! It was as though they'd never even seen a vehicle of any kind before, and they truly seemed to have no concept of cause and effect! It took weeks for them to correlate the accelerator with going faster, and the brake pedal with stopping! It really seemed that they'd just randomly press either pedal without any concept of what might happen with that action.

While there were far too many incidents with these girls in the driver's seat to recall them all, one was forever burnt into my memory. I recall that we were coming up to a line of traffic at a red light. We were in the right-most lane of the multi-lane road. Despite the instructor's urgent pleas to slow down, we were still flying past cars stopped in the next lane over, and Bill and I had already found ourselves standing hard on imaginary brake pedals from the back seat! Finally, at the very last moment, the car did a nosedive, and we nearly screeched to a halt, about a foot from the stopped car in front of us. I was relieved that we were stopped. But something still didn't seem right. The engine was making a loud noise, as if revving. Finally, after sitting there for several seconds, the instructor looked over to the girl in the driver's seat, who was still holding the wheel at the 10 and 2 positions and looking out in front of her as if just sailing down the highway, and asked her, "Do you mind?!" While he had his foot mashed on his secondary brake pedal, her foot was still pushed down on the accelerator!!! After a moment, I guess she finally figured out what he meant, and she released her foot from the gas, but *still* didn't bother to place it onto the brake pedal, allowing the car to creep forward a bit when the instructor released his pedal…and then had to re-jam it down! I'm certain that they didn't pass Driver's Ed, and, therefore, the driver's test at the DMV, but I don't know if they ever did actually learn how to drive or get a license. The roads would be a far safer place if they didn't!

We got our licenses immediately after successfully completing Driver's Ed with some of the highest grades ever given. In NY State, a license issued at age 16 was only a "day license". That is, we weren't allowed to drive past sunset or before sunrise. Since we'd completed Driver's Ed, our license became a full, unrestricted license once we turned 17. Those who didn't take or complete the class couldn't drive at night until they were 18, even if they got their license at 16.

THE CHRYSLER 300K

A few years prior, our older brother, Craig, had bought a very special car. It was a 1964 Chrysler 300K, convertible. This was part of the limited edition "letter series" of stock, high-performance cars that Chrysler sold from 1955 (with the 300A), to 1965 (300L), skipping "I". There were only 625 of the 300K convertible ever made, so, despite being just ten years old, it was already considered something of a collector's item. It sported a 413 cubic inch V8 engine, with a 4-barrel carburetor, and was rated at 390 horsepower. An option was to have dual-quads (two 4-barrel carbs) connected with cross-ram induction air intakes. The steering wheel was oddly rectangular, and it had a heavy-duty 3-speed, TorqueFlite automatic transmission, commonly used in trucks, or used for drag racing. There was also a large vacuum gauge built into the center console. It was calibrated both in inches of mercury, and Miles Per Gallon (MPG).

We'd heard stories of Craig racing "The K", as we came to call this unique vehicle, against our family dentist driving his Jaguar XKE…and The K won! The Jag was a nimble little sports car weighing in at just over a ton, while The K was a beast at 2-tons, but The K simply out-muscled the Jag.

About a year before Bill and I got our licenses Craig had bought another Chrysler 300. This was a standard New Yorker. It had much more luxury, and much less performance. Because he couldn't afford to insure two cars, he'd put "The K" up on blocks. Once we had our licenses, it was a natural progression to use his "hand-me-down" once again. We replaced a broken torsion bar, replaced a faulty alternator, patched the exhaust system, put on a couple new(er) tires, and began paying our parents for the added insurance to put it back on the road again.

Not only did the intoxication of power and speed that it so effortlessly provided take us in, but we also learned that it was a considerable gas-hog! Even at just $0.55 per gallon, it took both of our combined meager incomes from our first job just to keep the gas tank filled. The MPG-calibrated vacuum gauge gave us an indication of how much gas we were using as it sat there hovering around 20 MPG at an idle. It'd quickly drop to about 12MPG the instant we'd touch the accelerator and would peg the needle to just 2 – 3 MPG each time we'd "punch it" (floor the accelerator). The allure of power didn't affect only us, though. One time, when our mother's car was in the shop, she drove "The K" for a few days. I remember being most amused to see her burning rubber – and not just once or twice by accident, but often with apparent intent!

One time a bunch of guys from school in a supped-up car challenged us to a race on our way home. Jim Miesner, an "occasional friend" (he was also into electronics, but we didn't always get along well back then) asked to ride with us for this race. The course was a 1-mile straightaway on the 4-lane (2-lanes each direction) Sheridan Drive, just past the light at Main Street.

The light had just changed to green as we approached, so both vehicles rolled through at about 20 MPH, side-by-side. With the transmission in Drive, Bill punched it as soon as we entered Sheridan, pinning Jim hard into the back seat. The transmission automatically downshifted to 1st gear. I watched the speedometer reach 55 MPH before the gearbox took us to 2nd gear seconds later, chirping the tires as it shifted. A few seconds later, we hit 95, and the TorqueFlite automatically shifted into 3rd gear! Seeing the speedometer reading 110 MPH, I noticed that the telephone poles whizzed by as if a picket fence! We dropped to just 100 as we went into the curve – still side-by-side. Coming out of the curve, Bill put his foot down once more, and the engine put out an explosive growl as the transmission downshifted to 2nd gear for a moment, propelling us forward, well beyond our competitor. Stopping at the next light half a mile away, the other car finally caught up with us. One of them called out the window, saying, "All we heard was an explosion, and you guys were gone!" And that was The K.

SEEING IN THE DARK

Ever since we'd begun ordering electronic parts from James Electronics, we'd started receiving a couple of other catalogs in the mail. These dealt mostly with military surplus equipment, but no ferrets. Since we just didn't have quite enough space to accommodate a surplus P51 Mustang airplane, an M60 tank with low mileage, or an old Messerschmitt ME262 fighter jet, we turned to the pages near the back that contained the small electronic parts. There, we discovered an amazing device. With it, we would be able to see in the dark! What kid wouldn't want that? All of those monsters that come out from under the bed after the lights go out wouldn't have a chance!

I should mention that these were not complete night-vision goggles. It was ONLY a converter tube. More specifically, it was a CV148 Infra-Red Image Converter Tube that was popular in early military night-vision devices. We called it an IRICT, for short. They were unexpectedly inexpensive, and remarkably simple to use. They required just 5,000 to 7,000 Volts across their two terminals (an anode and a transparent photocathode) to function. We HAD to get a couple to play with!

These tubes worked by way of a concept known as "secondary emission". That is, when energized, the negatively charged transparent photocathode on the front would respond to the photon energy from an infrared image focused upon it. That would then knock out electrons, charged proportionally to each portion of the image, off towards the back of the tube, to the positively charged, phosphor-coated anode screen. The "electron image" would cause the phosphor screen to glow green in proportion to the charge density about the image, thus producing a visible, rendition of the invisible, infrared image. Pretty neat and conceptually simple enough for even our young teenaged minds to easily grasp!

We were, of course, no strangers to high voltage. We were surrounded by it in all of the TVs that we'd repair and experiment with in the basement. But they would each generate somewhere between 20,000 and 25,000 Volts – *way* too much for our 5kV IRICTs that had only a 3mm space between the cesium silver oxide photocathode and the platinum grid covered phosphor screen. This meant we'd have to build our own "lower high-voltage" power supplies, preferably operated from a battery so we could make our night-vision systems portable.

We found that we could generate the required potential using a 9 Volt battery, a simple oscillator, a power transistor, and an audio output transformer connected in reverse orientation. As these tubes would operate on either AC or DC, we just applied the AC output from the transformer directly to it. This method was simple and crude, but it worked.

Next, we got a ceramic light socket and a standard floodlight, and installed them inside of a large tin can, facing the open end. The intent, once we received the 6-inch infrared filter that we'd also ordered with the tubes, was to cover the open end of the can with this filter, thus producing a brilliant infrared source that would nicely illuminate dark scenes in a way that was undetectable with the naked eye.

In a couple of weeks the mailman delivered to us a pair of these amazing tubes, along with the infrared filter.

With the IR filter installed over the floodlight, and before connecting up our image converter tubes, the only way we could tell whether or not the floodlight was turned on was by the heat coming from it. No visible light could be seen coming from our crude-yet-effective IR-illuminator!

With all of the individual assemblies mounted onto a chunk of wood and ready to go, we just had to wait for nighttime to arrive before we could do a true test to see if we could really see in the dark! See the illustration titled Night Vision Apparatus at the top of this chapter.

And then night fell…

"Lights out!" I said.

"The floodlight is on," Bill said.

Yes, he actually had to announce it, because, even in the completely dark basement, we couldn't see any light at all coming from the tin can floodlight apparatus.

He then said, "Apply power to the tubes."

We each turned on our portable power supplies connected to our individual image converter tubes that we'd mounted crudely onto blocks of wood, with a large magnifying glass in front of each tube to focus the image.

"Wow!" I exclaimed as I peered at the green image. "I can clearly see everything I look at!"

"Yeah, I can too!" Bill agreed.

It was almost magical to us to see things in the completely darkened room as if all of the room lights were on!

Later on we headed outside into our darkened back yard. We used one of Dad's long extension cords to plug in our filtered floodlight. Okay, so our clumsy blocks of wood with the large magnifying glass and glass tube upon it, combined with the sizzle of high voltage, might not have exactly been

SEAL quality night vision goggles, but we were pretty sure that we were the only 16-year-olds in our town who had the ability to see in the dark!

VALUABLE VOCATIONAL EDUCATION

Concurrent with our junior and senior years in high school, Bill and I attended a 2-year certificate course called "Technical Electronics" at a nearby vocational school by the name of Harkness Center. This center, a member of BOCES (Board Of Cooperative Educational Services), serviced more than a dozen local high schools by offering nearly the equivalent of a 2-year college education in dozens of vocational subjects.

Considering our intent of studying electronics engineering in college, and subsequently making it our careers, this course provided us an excellent head start – well, in addition to our own very early head starts! Attending Harkness also introduced me to Terri Sterling, who, by some striking coincidence, was from our very own high school! She was studying a different subject – dental hygiene – there, but she rode on the same bus going between the center and our high school. She was cute, blonde, and fun to talk with. Our friend Dean Russell also attended Harkness. He was studying criminal justice there. Altogether, Bill, Dean, Terri and I had a great deal of fun on these bus rides, and, once we were driving, on our car rides back to school. Little did I know where this would lead… (See Chapter 14)

SLIDE RULES

While electronic pocket calculators had been available to the public for about two years by this point, and the prices had dropped significantly, the curriculum for this Technical Electronics course specifically indicated that students were to use slide rules to perform the often very complex calculations associated with electronic circuit analysis. Once again, the administration hadn't kept up with the technology of the time. Our instructor for both years was Mr. Crosley – a crusty old guy with a wry sense of humor, an incredibly deep understanding of electronics clearly gathered from decades in the industry, and no tolerance at all for students who acted up! He ran a "tight ship" and we learned well from him! He, unlike the administration, was well aware of the newer calculators coming onto the market and would allow those who could afford one of the new scientific calculators to use that instead of a slide rule. That one person ended up trying to figure out how to use his new calculator on his own while Mr. Crosley taught the remaining 29 of us how to use our slide rules very effectively and efficiently.

What IS a slide rule, you may ask? It's an amazingly versatile and accurate handheld computing device with most of the functions found on some of the most advanced scientific calculators made today, but with no batteries to go dead in the middle of an exam! With a slide rule, you can easily multiply, divide, compute all of the trigonometric functions and their inverse functions, raise numbers to any power and find their roots. You can determine any natural, or base-10 logarithm, and its inverse. Speaking of inverses, many slide rules would also provide 1/x values very conveniently. You can compute directly with pi, as so many formulas require. While not made to do addition and subtraction, it can be done in a rather roundabout fashion in a pinch. All of this can all be done with between 3 and 5 digits of accuracy beyond the decimal point! What a slide rule is NOT, is a ruler! Do not attempt to measure things with it – EVER! First of all, it simply isn't calibrated for this function, but mostly, it would enrage Mr. Crosley if anyone tried to call it a ruler.

Speaking of rulers, a significant portion of our classes there involved learning electronic, and mechanical drafting – drawing schematic diagrams of electronic circuits, and the chassis they'll go into. For this, we were required to use three-sided, graduated "scales". Each of the three sides had two linear scales inscribed upon it, providing a total of six scale-drawing ratios along the length. Basically, they'd allow us to make a scaled down drawing of mechanical objects without having to compute each measurement. Mr. Crosley reminded us frequently during the first week of our drafting classes, "This is a *scale*, not a ruler! King Henry is a ruler!" But...I digress, again.

So, the best slide rules are – uh, *were* – made from bamboo, since this material is extremely dimensionally stable. That means that it won't warp, bend, expand or contract significantly with moisture. It's also very strong, and self-lubricating. This is a considerable benefit when sliding two interlocking pieces of wood along each other.

Bill and I each got a bamboo Log-Log-Deci-Trig slide rule. Our parents paid $40 for each one, which translates to $220 in today's dollars! Later in the year, as more and more people started getting scientific calculators at our high school, we occasionally engaged in something that might make us the envy of all the jocks – or probably not; a contest between calculators and slide rules, of course! About 75% of the time those of us wielding the slide rules would win by getting the correct answer more quickly over those with the calculators! Oh…and ferrets aren't good with either, just in case you were wondering!

MY GENERAL-PURPOSE TEST DEVICE

With all of the electronic apparatus troubleshooting that we did, I decided that I needed a single, portable piece of test equipment that performed a number of different useful functions. This was the concept that propelled me to building my multi-function test box. It had a variable-frequency oscillator that I could use to inject audio tones into amplifier circuits. It had a high-gain amplifier that I could use to detect the smallest signals in a circuit, making them audible, allowing me to trace those signals. It also had a variable-output power supply that could be used to power specific circuit elements at up to 12 Volts DC. This was all built in (and on) a small plastic box about 6" x 2" x 2". Because of the three slide controls I decided to use for the variable functions, and our interest in the original "Star Trek" series in the 1960s, it was difficult not to make a comparison of this device to the control panel used for Star Trek's personnel transporter system. We had very good imaginations, and we knew how to use them!

WORKING AT PENNEY'S SERVICE CENTER

Just before our February birthday, we got word, through Mr. Crosley, that the local JC Penney Service Center was in need of one or two electronics technicians. This was a regional repair facility where many of Penney's electronic products were serviced. They were offering $3.60/hour – almost twice minimum wage ($1.85/hr) at the time, and equal to nearly $20/hr in today's dollars! Bill and I both applied. They had us take a very technical written exam as part of the employee consideration process. We both scored 100% on our exams and were hired on the spot. It was billed as "temporary employment" – and defined as a 3-month job with the specific intent of helping the other half-dozen techs get out from under a huge backlog of new color TVs. These were recalled for a modification to their high voltage regulation circuitry. The new components would reduce the possibility of x-ray production in the event of a certain type of circuit failure.

Well, by early May, between the two of us, we'd installed this change into 1,100 color TVs, signifying the end of the defined task. But the management seemed to like our work, so they started giving us other items to repair, including faulty TVs, radios, cassette, 8-track, and reel-to-reel tape decks, stereo systems, turntables, mechanical digital clocks, etc. The problems with most of these devices were almost laughably simple to diagnose and repair, leading to yet another problem; we'd worked ourselves out of a job…again. Once the repair shelves were completely bare, we were no longer needed!

About a month before this, though, our manager called down to the workshop where Bill and I did our repairs alongside the other technicians, asking us to come up to the break room. Oddly, there were no other techs in the repair area that night. We soon found out why. With the fairly recent popularity in CB radios, the facility started getting a lot of units in need of repair. The problem with this is that radio transmitters of this type could only be legally repaired by a technician who possessed an FCC 2ⁿᵈ Class Commercial Radiotelephone Operator's License.

None of these old techs were so-licensed! Therefore, the manager was holding study classes for about an hour each evening with them with the intent of having them all become licensed. He'd provided them each with a thick study guide and was encouraging each of them to help out the others anyplace they could – basically the blind leading the blind.

He asked us if we knew anything about the various classes of amplifiers (A, B, AB, & C). Quite by chance, we'd just recently finished studying these amplifier classes in our classes, so we had an in-depth understanding at that time. We'd only just turned 17, and we were now standing in front of this class of crusty old techs who were each easily more than three times our age, teaching them all about amplifiers!

Less than a year later, I took the same very rigorous technical examination for which these techs were studying and received my own 2ⁿᵈ Class (now General) Commercial Radiotelephone Operator License.

OUR VIDEO QUEST

We wanted to put pictures on the TV! Back then, if we'd said this to my parents, they'd have gathered up several small, framed photographs from various shelves around the house, and placed them on top of the TV set! This, of course, was *not* what I meant. What I was referring to would require one of two things: A TV (video) camera, or a videotape recorder/player – neither one of which we had, or were very likely to have anytime soon. At that time, TV cameras and Video Tape Recorders (VTRs) were only found in broadcast studios. The cameras would usually go for about $50,000 a piece, and a common VTR was around $75,000 in 1974, and each weighed nearly 200 lbs! Added together, a video camera and a means to record the image would cost the equivalent of $640,000 in today's currency! This meant we'd have to figure out some other way.

We'd begun to make new connections and acquaintances throughout the ham radio community, and some of these people were into "Slow-Scan TV" connected through their radios. This meant that some of them would have parts to build a TV camera, or at very least a flying-spot scanner (See Education Alert 11).

One ham gave us a pair of vidicon image pickup tubes, which were the heart of cheaper (i.e. lower-quality) TV cameras (i.e. not typically used in the larger broadcast studios) at that time. Of course, even with the "heart", we'd still need the "brain", and other support structure to make it function! Our Aunt Nancy had worked at a company that made many electronic devices, including lower-cost TV cameras, such as those used in bank security systems and manufacturing processes. She sent us a circuit board and deflection yoke assembly that had both been discarded after being rejected by her company's quality control. This board was basically the "brain", or controller of the camera, and the yoke was the remaining support structure! With all of the parts finally all together, now we only had to wire it, assemble it, and figure out what problem had made them reject the various parts…all without any documentation, of course!

This was actually pretty much par for the course, as it were. That is, throughout the prior several years, many people had asked us to repair their TVs and other electronic equipment…AFTER a professional repairman had failed to repair the items… and, of course, we'd be doing it all without *any* of the detailed service manuals or schematic diagrams to guide us! In every case we were able to diagnose the problem, but a few times the parts for the repair would simply be more expensive than the person wanted to spend, so they'd just "donate" the device to us for our hobby use. This helped us develop the ability to troubleshoot intuitively.

It wasn't until we were about 13 before we'd learned of the existence of "Sam's Photofacts". These are booklets containing incredibly detailed schematic diagrams for virtually every television, radio, tape recorder, and many other electronic products made since 1946. They also provide signal waveforms and voltage readings throughout the circuits right on the schematic, as well as mechanical assembly instructions. This was meant to assist technicians repair the devices. While Photofacts are now widely available on the Internet, there actually was a time when the Internet didn't exist. That's when we went to our local library to make a copy of any Photofact that we needed.

It seems, however, that we'd finally met our match with the TV camera controller circuit board and yoke assembly. It was the first circuit that we couldn't deduce intuitively without a schematic diagram, as it was just too dense with unfamiliar circuits. We literally tried every possible combination of connections between the eight unlabeled wires coming out of the yoke assembly and the circuit board, with our best guess for power, but we never could get anything even remotely resembling a video signal from it. While this might have been seen as a failure by most, to us it was just something to drive us harder to understand video circuits better. It's all about your attitude!

OUR FIRST OSCILLOSCOPE

How could we tell what sort of a signal it produced, you ask? I seem to have neglected to mention that Bill and I had picked up a 7-inch oscilloscope from a local surplus store called "Salvage Sam" a year or so prior. What is an oscilloscope? Again, I refer you to the movies. This time, we're talking about films made during the 1950s. The atomic bomb ended World War II in 1945, but it also started an entirely new genre of entertainment featuring new technological developments. Many movies at the time were cautionary tales about the awesome power that mankind then possessed, and its adverse effects if misused. They frequently included scenes of scientists working in military labs equipped with all sorts of fancy electronic equipment. These apparatus ALWAYS included one, if not several, oscilloscopes in gray metal racks.

They were the devices with a tiny round picture tube-like screen, displaying a bright dot moving from left to right. It could be made to sweep very slowly across the display surface, or move so fast that it would produce what appeared to be a solid bright line. Most oscilloscope displays at that time were green, but, of course, they'd appear white in black & white films. In these sci-fi flicks they ALWAYS displayed one of two basic waveforms; a sine wave (serpentine pattern), or a Lissajous pattern (a free-rotating ellipse). Unlike the Jacob's Ladder device often found in the movies of the 1930s, both the sine wave and Lissajous patterns actually provided useful information to engineers and good technicians about a circuit's function. Of course, this isn't why Hollywood had these patterns displayed on oscilloscopes for a decade and a half after WWII; They were remarkably simple to produce, *and* they grabbed peoples' attention...and it is this attribute that makes them similar to the Jacob's Ladder in the earlier movies.

In addition to displaying simple patterns on their screen, an oscilloscope is, perhaps, one of the most useful pieces of test equipment that a scientist, engineer, or technician will ever use. Useful patterns are produced by deflecting an electron beam up and down in response to the amplitude (strength) of a varying signal being tested, while moving from left-to-right at a very precise speed. The beam strikes a phosphor-coated screen, thereby illuminating bright green. By doing this, it produces a very accurate representation of the signal's changing amplitude over time. Most oscilloscopes today are fully solid-state, using a large, full-color, Liquid Crystal Display (LCD), but the general concept remains the same. We'd used our oscilloscope to look at video signals in TV circuits many times prior, so we had a very good idea of what it should look like. The signals we observed coming out of that TV camera's control board never looked right to us. Ultimately, we ended up abandoning further work on it. This, of course, only intensified our desire to somehow build, buy or use a TV camera.

OUR FIRST COLOR TV

So far, we didn't have a color TV in our home. In fact, Bill and I had only ever seen brief portions of TV shows in color when we'd test the new color sets coming through the JC Penney Service Center after we'd done the high-voltage modification on them. Our parents seemed to have no interest in getting a color TV. At about $800 (equivalent to $4,000 today!), I suppose I could understand this. Therefore, we did what we do best; we built our own. Actually, technically, we didn't really "build" this one, even though it *was* a kit (Heathkit), but we *did* pull it from the curb after somebody else had built it, and subsequently discarded it, and then we repaired it until we had a functioning color television...well, sort of. Okay, sepia is a color, I think.

Everything displayed on this TV came out in shades of this brownish tint. Well, at least people's faces looked more or less natural next to brown cherries, grass, sky, sunsets and such! This "sort-of-color" TV served us well for a few years

OLD-STYLE RADIO SHOW and THE EDISON VOICEWRITER

Another item that Bill and I had picked up at a local hamfest flea market was an original Edison Voicewriter. No, this wasn't one of Thomas Edison's cylindrical wax gramophone recording devices. It was actually a Dictaphone sold to businesses in the 1950s. It recorded whatever was spoken into the microphone onto a very thin, floppy plastic disk about the size of a 78-RPM record, or for those too young to relate to those, think of something like an over-sized CD (Compact Disk) or DVD (Digital Video Disk)...only it's not rigid. This was *not* a magnetic disk. The Voicewriter scratched a modulated groove into the spinning plastic in accordance with the intensity of the sound signal received. In many ways, it was a miniature record maker with very limited fidelity. Since this device was intended exclusively for use in the office place where managers would dictate a memorandum into the device, and their secretaries would then play it back and type up the memo for distribution as directed, the manufacturer didn't put much effort into either fidelity or noise-reduction.

These audio shortcomings actually worked in our favor for the use we found for it. Once again, Bill and I got together with our good friend Dave Fairlie and used our collective imaginations to entertain ourselves. We decided to create amusing "radio shows" on audiocassette tapes. We were inspired by the infamous "War of the Worlds" story by H. G. Wells, which was directed, narrated, and broadcast over the radio by *Orson* Welles in 1938. It was, therefore, no great coincidence that the theme for one of our more notable recordings was a conglomeration of invading aliens, space travel and time travel. The "small" voice that came out of the Voicewriter, along with the strong static and popping from the crude recording mechanism, lent itself well to sounding very much like a long-distance radio signal. We'd pre-recorded responses to questions that one of us would ask over the "interstellar link", as part of the audio play so that when we played the Voicewriter recording back during the live audio play, it would sound like a real-time dialogue over an actual short-wave radio. Since we had just one audiocassette recorder, however, we didn't have the luxury of post-production editing. This meant that everything had to be performed live. If we messed up our lines, we'd have to back up the tape and record over the previous one.

Ultimately, we ended up with a most amusing "space epic" that made liberal use of Einstein's "twin paradox" thought experiment, the delays of radio signals traveling at the speed of light, and other physical elements that interested us deeply at that time.

CHAPTER 13 – 1975; AGE SEVENTEEN

Operating the Portable Video System for Sports, The Slime Creature

Portable TV Camera and Video Tape Recorder

In 1975, the average house cost $39,300; the typical annual income was about $14,100, a new car cost about $4,250, and gas cost $0.44 per gallon. Jimmy Hoffa, ex teamsters boss, disappeared, never to be seen again; Patti Hearst became Most Wanted for armed robbery. Motorola patented first portable mobile phone; Seymour Cray developed the Cray-1, the first commercially available "super-computer", and the Altair 8800 microcomputer was released; "Microsoft" (for microcomputer software) became a registered trademark; NASA launched Viking 1 planetary probe to Mars; Sony Betamax and Matsushita/JVC VHS videotapes are introduced for home video recorder use.

SHOOTING VIDEO OF FOOTBALL GAMES

As Bill and I were just finishing up our junior year in high school, Mr. Corrigan, a history teacher, approached us for a special assignment. By this time, we were well established as the most noted "techno- geeks" in our high school (yeah…the jocks really admired us. Not!), so it was little surprise that this assignment was technically related. In a remarkably ironic twist of fate, it was, in fact, the athletic department who needed our talents! They'd just purchased a brand new "portable" video camera and video tape recorder with the intention of recording football games for review by the coaches and players...but nobody in that department or on the teams knew anything about operating such a system – but we did. Rather, we understood video, and, while we'd never used such a system yet, we virtually lusted over the opportunity to do so! This would partially satisfy our TV camera interests from earlier.

Mr. Corrigan showed us this enormous metal suitcase – about twice the length, height, and thickness of the largest piece of standard luggage available. Inside this huge case was a portable (i.e. battery-powered) B&W TV camera with a built-in 1-inch viewfinder in the back, a compact reel-to-reel ½-inch video tape recorder (VTR), and a large power/charger unit – all resting in cutouts in the thick foam rubber padding. He showed us how to connect it all up, operate it, and keep it charged. We provided the phone number to our house so that they could get in touch with us over the summer when the football team would start practicing.

I still remember the excitement I felt when August rolled around, and we got that first phone call to come down to the school to videotape the football team's first practice game. We met Mr. Corrigan there, and he opened up the room where the equipment was stored. We talked briefly about the setup again for a refresher. He left, and then Bill and I hefted this huge case out to the football field, and up the bleachers to the box at the top. We had to crawl through a trap door in the bottom and pass the equipment (once removed from the case) through so we could set up inside. We had three or four reels of videotape. Each one would last 30-minutes. Once we got everything connected up, and the tape threaded around the head-drum assembly, through the capstan, and onto the take-up reel at a level lower than the supply reel, we were ready to shoot. See the illustration titled Portable TV Camera and Video Tape Recorder at the top of this chapter.

When zoomed out wide, despite the magnifying lens on the back of the viewfinder, the players resembled ants on the field. Hmmm...Ants and a magnifying glass...once again, I digress. Anyway, unlike football games on broadcast TV where they have half a dozen (or more) cameras following all of the action in full-screen, colorful close-ups, we were instructed to maintain a fairly wide-angle view so the coaches could see all of the action on the field. Eventually, since the zoom lens would actually allow us to get pretty close up to the action, we'd begin a set zoomed in until the ball was in motion, and then we'd go wide until we could locate the ball. Of course, this was no simple feat on the 1-inch B&W viewfinder monitor! Once the practice was over, or when we ran out of tape, we'd pack up the equipment, carry it back to the room where we locked the door as we exited, and delivered the tape reels to the coach.

With Mr. Corrigan's assistance to set up the VTR with a TV monitor, the coaches would then play the tapes back for the players at a later date to study their plays. This went on through the end of football season in the fall, capturing not just their practices, but the games, as well.

THE SLIME CREATURE

I remember, one day, thinking about the state of most of our experiments in the basement. They were almost always in a constant state of flux...in progress...always room for improvement, therefore never *quite* done. Now, I'm not saying that we didn't complete anything. In fact, we did, constantly. What I mean is that we were never quite satisfied with them performing just the basic function intended. We'd always make an improvement here, a tweak there, and ultimately make it operate more efficiently, more spectacularly, or in a more user-friendly manner. So, it occurred to me this one time that I was glad that I wasn't thinking of becoming a doctor or biochemist (read: mad scientist), as the chances are, I'd leave cultures out, unattended, and, ultimately come down to the basement someday and find some kind of a slime creature slowly taking over the ping-pong table.

CHAPTER 14 – 1976; AGE EIGHTEEN

Pong, Gypsy Miss Electra Costume, Wilson Greatbatch, The Microcalorimeter Chamber, 555 Timer Circuit and The New Engineer, Helium-3/Helium-3 Fusion Reactor, "The Film", Crystal Beach with Terri

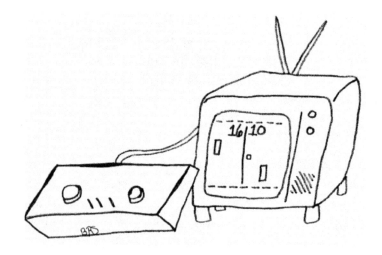

Pong – The First Video Game

In 1976 the average house cost $43,400, the typical annual income was about $16,000, a new car cost about $3,200, and gas cost $0.59 per gallon. The US celebrated bicentennial independence from British rule; In NY City, the "Son of Sam" began a series of gun attacks that terrorized the city for a full year; The $2.00 bill is introduced. Apple Computer Company is formed; NASA unveils fist space shuttle, Enterprise; Matsushita introduces the VHS home video cassette recorder (VCR); the first laser printer is introduced by IBM.

PONG! THE FIRST VIDEO GAME

This year marked the date of the very first video game: Pong!

For Bill and I, the game itself held our interest for only about 2 minutes, but the virtually inconceivable concept of being able to *control* something appearing on a TV set (which is where Pong was most often played), was nearly beyond our grasp! We found this to be exceptionally fascinating, and we HAD to build one for ourselves to, uh, study the technique much further! Yeah…we'll go with that…to *study* the technique!

Younger people, growing up with movies always available either on videocassette, DVD, or, more recently streaming online via the Internet, the multitude of video games played 'round the clock, and DVR (Digital Video Recorder) systems with the ability to record and play back all of your favorite TV shows any time you wish, might find the concept of *not* controlling what's on TV equally inconceivable. You have to remember that prior to Pong in 1976, TV was a *completely passive* experience. It was controlled entirely by big television networks and local broadcasting stations.

There was no way for the average person to record or play back a TV show or feature movie in the home. If you wanted to see a particular show or movie on TV, you had to scour the weekly "TV Guide" publication to see if and when it was listed to air. If it was scheduled for a time when you couldn't be home, well, that was just too bad. You'd just have to wait a few months, or a year for it to be repeated. Many movies would be repeated a couple of times a year, and for regular shows, many would come around eventually in re-runs. You also had to sit through all of the commercials, and if you took a somewhat longer bathroom break during a commercial, the show would resume without you. There were no second chances…that is, until reruns came about years later. Therefore, with the exception of getting up to change the channel to one of our three local stations (most TVs didn't have remotes), fiddling with the horizontal or vertical hold controls when the TV would invariably lose sync, or turning the set off occasionally, we had absolutely no control of what happened on the TV screen. Therefore, the idea of actually controlling what the TV displayed, as with the Pong game, was nothing short of magical to us!

We mailed in an order for the appropriate chipset, sold by Texas Instruments, and we were soon building our very own Pong game! Of course, this would be no ordinary game console. Bill was the primary designer of this system, and he chose to build the enclosure out of ¼ inch Plexiglas, stained a transparent, electric blue. This control unit looked, to us, about as futuristic as the entire idea of controlling what was shown on the TV. See the illustration titled Pong – The First Video Game at the top of this chapter.

General Instruments made the AY-3-8500-1 chip. It was a 6-game version, including tennis/ping-pong, hockey/football, squash, practice, and two shooting games, target 1 & target 2.

The concept used in the shooting games inspired us to build a novel "light pen" a couple of years later (Chapter 18). This allowed us to draw lines, shapes and squiggles of light directly onto the TV screen.

GYPSY

Our school put on one or two big musical plays each year. The play they put on in March 1976, during our senior year of high school, was "Gypsy". This was the story of Louise Hovick, who, as Gypsy Rose Lee, became the most famous striptease artist of the 1930s.

It presents the hard times they face in the early years as Louise's mother, Rose, who is the epitome of the typical overbearing stage-mother, takes Louise and her little sister June to one burlesque house after another trying to sell the girls' singing and dancing act. Burlesque, at that time, didn't involve stripping at all. It was a live stage show very similar to vaudeville featuring singing, dancing and comedic performances, usually designed to mock more serious performances, and even literature. Burlesque was the variety show of the early 1900s and is distinguished from cleaner vaudeville by many of its acts being more crude, lowbrow, or raunchy.

Due to an unexpected costume failure, where a strap broke, causing her dress to fall off during a performance, Louise discovered how to capture an audience. Ultimately, her sister left the act, Louise changed her name to Gypsy Rose Lee, and she made her act focus on planned costume removal. Gypsy was the ultimate classy stripper, whose witty remarks during her act were a main feature.

Once again, the reputation that Bill and I had around the school of being very capable in all things electronic was well known. One day in late February, while Bill and I were studying in the library, two teachers approached us with a challenge. I knew Mr. Conover from the one music and choral class I'd taken as a freshman, but I'd never had a class with Mr. Pappas, who I knew only as the faculty adviser of the Drama Club. They asked us to build a costume for the play, "Gypsy"!

When we looked confused about this, they told us that one of the strippers in the play, "Miss Electra", had to light up during her performance, and they'd been told that we could do this! They gave us a couple of standard plug-in strings of tiny Christmas tree lights and told us it had to run from a battery hidden in her costume. It was fortunate that they'd selected sets of series-connected bulbs – the ones where all of the lights in the string go out if just one bulb is bad. For a string of 20 lights that plug into the wall (120 Volts AC), each bulb would be rated at 6 Volts (6 x 20 = 120). This meant that we could power the string – after we'd re-wired it, of course – with a simple 6 Volt battery. Well, that was the theory, anyway.

At home we completed the rewiring task, connected up a couple of micro-switches we had laying around, and tested it with a standard 6 Volt lantern battery. It worked, of course, but the lights weren't nearly as bright as we'd expected. This meant that we'd have to use two batteries connected in parallel to get more current into the bulbs! Now, I'd like to point out that a single lantern battery at that time was no tiny or inconspicuous thing, especially to hide into a girl's clothing. Now, we had to use TWO! We took the reworked string back to school the next day and gave it to Mr. Pappas at one of the after-school practices. He gave it to one of the girls who'd be sewing it into the fabric of the main costume.

When they had their next practice, Bill and I showed up to show Betsy Bittar, the girl who'd be playing Miss Electra, how to activate her costume. When she put the costume on we noticed that they'd worked the two big batteries into the costume in a position just above her buttocks – in the small of her back. To completely cover them, the costume girls had placed a huge bow on the back of her bodice. Each of the micro-switches hung just beyond the ends of each sleeve, where she could palm the switches easily, thus turning on one arm and half of her torso, the other side, or both.

We were asked to attend each performance just in case we were needed for a last-minute technical issue with the costume, but it worked flawlessly during each performance. The best part was the audience's reaction when the stage lights were dimmed, and her costume would light up! This was very satisfying!

Dr. WILSON GREATBATCH

In April of our senior year at high school, Bill and I got jobs at Wilson Greatbatch Ltd. (WGL) as electronics technicians. We made $2.35 an hour and worked there until September that year when we went away to college. The company manufactured lithium-iodide batteries for use in pacemakers, and they needed experienced technicians to design and build equipment to test the batteries in life-like environments. Dr. Wilson Greatbatch – the founder of this company, as well as another in town called Mennen-Greatbatch (which manufactured electronic medical monitors such as heart monitors) – was an exceptionally humble and reserved individual. In fact, despite the nearly six months that Bill and I worked with him, and the decades that we've known him from around town, at church gatherings and other places, it wasn't until sometime around 2005 when I visited Dr. Greatbatch's latest research facility with my two young sons that I heard people calling him "Dr. Greatbatch". He got his PhD in 1970, yet in 1976 everybody, including Bill and I, just called him "Mr. Greatbatch". We just didn't know otherwise!

Dr. Greatbatch was not only a successful business owner, but a prolific inventor, a university professor, and a Sunday school teacher. But he also had some eccentricities. Most people who meet or know of Dr. Greatbatch will note his ever-present bowtie, but few will mention his long line of Karmann Ghias. This car, made by Volkswagen, was small yet somewhat sporty looking. He seemed to favor his cars in a ghastly pumpkin orange color.

While he held more than 325 patents, the one item that most people associate with Dr. Greatbatch is the implantable cardiac pacemaker. He patented this invention – his first – in 1962. Since that time, he started a medical monitoring equipment company, a pacemaker battery company, dabbled in plant cloning research, was interested in rapidly healing broken bones through electrical stimulation, contributed to AIDS research by proposing the use of a particular nucleotide to keep the AIDS virus from replicating, and, finally, was a strong proponent of alternate energy production – specifically clean nuclear fusion using He3 (Helium-3) fuel.

Once again, Dr. Greatbatch wasn't like so many other owners, founders and CEOs of companies who typically remain fully isolated up in their ivory towers, away from all of their common employees and communicating only through their boards of directors and other upper executive management. During that summer when Bill and I worked at WGL there was a total of 15 people in the entire company. Dr. Greatbatch joined the entire population of the company in a conference room to celebrate every employee's birthday. Everybody also gathered at the Town Park, which was just a short drive from the company, a couple of times that summer to have a leisurely picnic lunch in the park – Dr. Greatbatch always joined us!

Since Wilson Greatbatch Ltd. manufactured pacemaker batteries, they had to be rigorously tested in life-like conditions, and their discharge characteristics had to be well understood. To bring the batteries up to body temperature (37 degrees C [98.6F]) in some of the smaller test chambers, we used a simple light bulb connected to a thermal control unit to regulate the temperature. As there were so many in use in the facility, Bill and I became quite expert at installing and repairing these electronic temperature controllers.

THE MICROCALORIMETER CHAMBER

The chief chemist at the facility had built a prototype micro-calorimeter chamber to test the heat lost from a battery when discharged with a load equivalent to a pacemaker. Due to the incredibly tiny amount of heat they were looking for, this apparatus needed exceptionally stable thermal isolation. He built a very small thermally controlled chamber set at 37C, and installed that inside of a somewhat modified chest freezer, taking the temperature around the small chamber well below zero. This produced a well-isolated thermal environment.

One day, my supervisor asked me to repair the thermal controller on this prototype micro- calorimeter chamber. It was the sole piece of equipment setting right in the middle of an otherwise completely bare, huge room intended for manufacturing apparatus to be installed later in the summer. There was no furniture nearby, so I just sat on the floor to do the repair. I was the only person in that cavernous room. Soon I heard a door open far behind me. As I was focused on the repair, I didn't bother to turn to see who it was. A good 30-seconds later, while the echoing footsteps approached, Dr. Greatbatch appeared beside me, and promptly plopped himself down on the floor next to me! He went into "professor mode", like he was apt to do. He began telling me all about the original concept for this chamber, what it did, how it did it, and how it's the only functioning micro-calorimeter chamber in the entire world. They'd contracted a Swiss company to build a production version of the chamber, but they'd yet to be able to get it to function properly. This is just how he is. Very personable, and not beneath associating with the common employee, sitting on the floor, as if peer-to-peer!

While Bill's and my tasks at WGL were initially centered around the assembly of battery test racks, our supervisor, Mike Bakos, soon learned that we were far more capable. Apparently not wanting to waste our talents – or perhaps to exploit them while paying us just minimum wage – we soon found ourselves doing engineering drafting and circuit design work for the company. There were just two engineers at WGL at that time: Dr. Greatbatch, the owner of the company, and Bill Holmes, the chief engineer. Therefore, by having Bill and me take on some of the basic test equipment design work, it freed them up to do more complex engineering work.

A VERY GREEN ENGINEER

Sometime in mid-summertime, they'd hired a fresh engineering graduate from a noted engineering school in NY State. This was the first, but certainly not the last, time that Bill and I would clearly see what a huge difference experience makes in an engineer's capabilities. Both to save him any humiliation, and because I truly cannot remember his name, I shall call this very green engineering graduate John Ferret.

John was assigned to design a tiny thermal chamber to test a single pacemaker battery. As before, he used the standard thyristor-based temperature control circuit we'd been working with and repairing for months prior. That circuit made a small light bulb inside the box go on and off to regulate the temperature to 37C. Simple enough...except that there was a huge thermal gradient throughout the little box. It was really hot near the bulb, and much cooler on the side opposite, where the sensor was positioned, making the battery – in the center – somewhere near the middle of this range. This was not acceptable.

We recommended that he mount a small fan inside to circulate the heat, thus evening it out. He did this. When he tested it, he found that the light only came on for a few seconds before the controller shut it off...yet the temperature continued to rise! It turned out that the fan motor actually generated so much heat that the controller never turned the bulb back on after it initially got up to temperature! John was, once again, at a loss. All of the theory he'd learned in his engineering classes never prepared him for this! Once again, Bill and I made the suggestion that he cycle the motor on and off. We also happened to have a fair amount of experience with motors, so we knew that they'll actually heat up a lot *more* if they're turned on and off at a rapid rate due to a phenomenon called hysteresis. We suggested that he build a simple controller that would cycle the fan at a 40% duty cycle – that is, on for 40-seconds, off for 60-seconds. Because it's off longer than it's on, it won't heat up through hysteresis, and it's also not on long enough to generate much heat from just running.

The simplest solution was to use the single-most common and basic timer device ever made. Known as the 555 Timer, this chip was developed in 1971, and is *still* widely used today because it's so elegantly simple, yet diverse in its capabilities. There was also a reed relay involved, but for the sake of this discussion, this isn't important. John wasn't aware of this amazing circuit, so we had to introduce him to it. He went off and looked it up in a data book and soon presented us with his design. For those who might not be aware, the electronic circuit development food chain goes like this: Engineers design new electronic circuits, and technicians build them. Since he was the engineer in this situation, and Bill and I were technicians before we became engineers ourselves a few years later, we were expected to build what he'd designed.

Those who become engineers without ever working as a technician will often look down on techs because of the disparity between their respective levels of education. John was one of those engineers. While he'd gone through four years of rigorous engineering classes touching upon all sorts of theory and complicated mathematical formulas, he'd never actually designed a circuit, and, what's more, he'd only ever handled electronic parts for a few lab classes. He had no real-world experience, intuition, or capability in the area of practical electronic circuit design. He could probably derive the set of poles and zeroes of a Laplace transform that describes an electronic filter in the complex plane using both real and imaginary numbers for an exam, but he had no concept of how to apply this information to an actual, physical circuit.

It took no more than a momentary glance at the schematic diagram representing his design for us to know that his circuit wouldn't work as he'd intended, and we told him so. Because he felt superior, however, he didn't believe us and insisted that we just build the circuit as he'd designed it. Not wanting to rock the boat, but more wanting to prove that he was wrong, we did as we were told...and it functioned precisely as WE had predicted – which was not how HE had expected it to work!

Bill and I had been playing with the 555 Timer chip in dozens of circuits for as long as John had been in college! We knew this circuit inside and out and didn't even need to use the formulas to achieve an output frequency within a ballpark region of interest. It was totally intuitive to us. Of course, for fine frequency selection, we'd do the computations, but because we had a very good idea of what component values should produce what results, we'd know immediately if we'd made an error with the math. He did not.

At that point, he was clueless. He threw up his arms and asked us how it could be fixed. We immediately gave him a capacitor value that we *felt* would be close. He asked us to install that value and retest it. We did, and, as predicted, it worked perfectly as was originally intended. After that, the freshly humbled John asked us to review all of his subsequent designs for practicality before attempting to build them. Had he taken his designs to the chief engineer for review, he probably wouldn't have been there very much longer.

In September that year, Bill and I headed to Columbus, Ohio to begin our own college level engineering education. We'd stop by WGL occasionally during Christmas breaks, or catch up with Dr. Greatbatch during some of the frequent times that his Presbyterian church and our parents' United Methodist church held combined services.

THE HELIUM-3/HELIUM-3 FUSION REACTOR IN THE GARAGE

Many, many years later – around 2005 – during a visit to my parents' house with my teenage sons, Drew and Bryce, I decided to visit Dr. Greatbatch at his latest company. This was a new one located in Clarence Hollow, where he was doing research into alternative energy. I brought my sons along so they might get the opportunity to meet Dr. Greatbatch – my former engineering mentor. He'd written a book called, "Making Of The Pacemaker: Celebrating A Lifesaving Invention", and gave each of my kids an autographed copy. I already had one.

Any time I'd visit, Dr. Greatbatch would always enjoy showing me his latest projects, but he especially relished the opportunity to interest children in the engineering sciences. Unfortunately, he had an important meeting that morning, so he asked the chief engineer of his new research company to show us his latest work in nuclear fusion. This engineer got into his classic MG and asked us to follow him. We drove out to Clarence's farmland region and pulled into a parking area just outside of what amounted to a large, rented garage.

Inside, it was like we'd walked into another world. Scattered all about nearly every square inch of floor space were many dozen large capacitors and ancient voltmeters in their original wooden enclosures. There was also a large apparatus constructed substantially of PVC tubing and metal connected to the capacitors. But what commanded our attention was the rather odd-looking structure occupying about a quarter of the garage space. The chief engineer told us that this huge stainless-steel cube setting upon four stout cylindrical metal legs, looking very much like something you'd land on the moon, was, in fact, a Helium-3, Helium-3 Fusion Reactor! The PVC apparatus, he told us, was a huge "contactor" whose purpose was to put all of the parallel-charged capacitors into a series configuration, thus providing a very high voltage – more than 1 million Volts. This "excitation voltage" was then fed into the chamber of the hollow steel cube after pressurizing it with Helium-3 gas. This would produce a high-energy plasma region inside, which would fuse the He-3 gas. During the conversion from He-3 to He-4, an atomic-level charge disparity occurs. This difference in charge results in the production of a very high voltage Direct Current (DC) which is collected from grids inside the reactor, and brought outside of the device where it can be converted down to useful power.

The engineer went on to tell us that this fusion reactor is both clean and efficient. There is no radioactive material used in the device, and the only byproduct produced through the fusion process is Helium-4 – the common lighter-than-air gas used in children's balloons. All nuclear reactors that I'm aware of, *except* the Helium-3/Helium-3 fusion reactor, produce electricity by making steam from the heat put out by the nuclear process inside the reactor. The steam turns turbines connected to generators, which create electricity. This process, called the "Carnot Cycle", is only about 40% efficient, due to heat loss, friction, and many other factors. Put another way, 60% of the energy produced in a typical nuclear reactor is wasted by the time it becomes useable electricity.

The He-3/He-3 fusion reactor is nearly 100% efficient. It creates electricity directly from the fusion process, with no conversion into heat, then heating water to steam, and then pushing a turbine around to mechanically produce electricity. If all of this sounds too good to be true, well, there is one tiny little catch. Helium-3 is not plentiful here on Earth, but it is extremely prevalent on the moon! Dr. Greatbatch has estimated that there's enough He-3 in the ilmenite mineral found in the regolith (like "topsoil") portion of the moon to provide helium-3 fusion produced electricity for the entire world for about 10,000 years. He's even done serious work into determining the feasibility of setting up a mining operation on the moon, and the cost of the extraction and purification of He-3, as well as the transportation back to Earth. With all of these factors considered, electricity produced in a He-3/He-3 fusion reactor would cost less than what we pay for electricity now! He's met with US presidents and had convinced them to fund NASA to start new lunar exploration specifically for the extraction of Helium-3. Due to ongoing wars, government budget cuts, and changes of administration, however, this ambitious yet extremely important project was cut!

MAKING "THE FILM"

The summer of '76 not only marked the bicentennial anniversary of the United States, but, at least equally important (well, to us!), it was also the start of a series of short films that Bill and I would create with our good friends David Fairlie and Dean Russell. We'd picked up an old Bell & Howell Director Series Zoomatic model 414PD 8mm movie camera at a garage sale, so we were compelled to put it to good use. I think we paid $5 for it. This precise model of movie camera was most notable as it was on November 22, 1963, when 28-seconds of film from just such a camera captured the moment that John F. Kennedy was assassinated. This model camera had originally sold in 1961 for about $200 through Sears Roebucks. In today's dollars, that'd be just short of $1,600.

It was completely mechanical and had to be wound up before shooting a short segment. The film it used was a bit unique. It took 16mm film, but only exposed one 8mm strip at a time – which required us to turn it over halfway through. This meant that we could get three minutes on a side, or six minutes for the entire reel. This wasn't the only uncommon feature of this camera. It also had the unique capability of capturing individual frames – to create animation – by pushing *up* on the lever that would otherwise cause standard motion capture when pushed down one level, or slow-motion if pushed two levels down. It also had an automatic zoom lens.

We'd all been long term fans of the late 1960's BBC show "Monty Python's Flying Circus", which had finally made it to US TV stations in the early-mid-'70s, so it was no surprise that our short films would be substantially influenced by the silly antics of their skits…only ours were silent. Something we'd seen on "Monty Python" was a stop-motion technique called "pixilation" – not to be confused with "pixelation", which is a blocking-up artifact observed when digital images are enlarged beyond their visual fusion size. Using pixilation, they would sometimes show people moving about in a standing position without moving their legs. To do this, they'd take a single frame, then the subject would move very slightly, then take another frame, and so on. It let them do some things that couldn't otherwise be done, as the special effects technology available at the time was extremely expensive and didn't fit a tight budget. As we had no money to spend on special effects, either, we fully embraced this capability.

Over the next two years, the four of us would complete five short films during the short periods we'd be home from school. Each movie was heavily infused with pixilated scenarios such as the "Lawn Chair Races", "The Standing Race", "Hovering" (or hopping, as one set turned out!), and a much more refined "Space Epic" done entirely on a chalkboard. Because of the nature of these films, we had to mentally pre-visualize the end result of each scene based upon our understanding of the technique, and the frame rate once the film was developed and viewed. Because our editing equipment was quite limited, each scene had to be fully thought out and filmed in sequence, with no re-takes. It sometimes took several hours to produce a 30-second scene. Despite the extremely poor image quality of 8mm film with poor optics (a cheap lens), these films actually turned out exceptionally well.

By April 1978, we'd completed the following films. They were titled, in this order, "The Film", "The Film III", "The Film V", "The Film IV ½ ", "The Film IX", and a couple of untitled fillers. Sometime within the following year, we spliced all of the films together onto one big reel and played the full set in chronological order at a special screening on April 17, 1979. As Bill and I would soon be accepting our brand-new engineering jobs in California, this screening would mark the last time that all four of us (Dave, Dean, Bill and I) would all be together with an opportunity to view "The Film Series", for a very long time. Since these movies were silent, Dave and Dean took it upon themselves to add their own sound effects, live, as the film played. Fortunately, I'd had the foresight to set up an audiocassette recorder during this screening to capture all of these sounds and commentary.

Twenty years later, while I was living in Virginia, I took the large reel of film to a local shop that specializes in 8mm film to videotape transfers. Once I had the movies on VHS (Video Home System) videotape, I used the audio-dub feature of my VCR (Video Cassette Recorder) and the audiocassette recorded 20-years prior to add the soundtrack. I got a few copies of this completed videocassette made and sent one to each of the participants. Seven years later (2006) David surprised me by creating a DVD from the VHS tape containing "The Film Series", only now it had active chapter selection, animated titles, pictures of Bill, Dean, Dave and myself from our

1976 yearbook and some additional musical accompaniment! I then took some of those pictures and generated a graphic in Photoshop to produce a printed cover image on a printable DVD copy. I then sent out copies of the DVD that David had created, only with professional looking cover art to the rest of the group! The overall process to get this film series to its current state of completion took a total of 27 years!

CRYSTAL BEACH AMUSEMENT PARK

Shortly after we graduated high school in June 1976, Bill and I wanted to head up to the Crystal Beach amusement park in Ontario, Canada with a couple of friends from school. I was solidly involved with Terri – the girl I'd met on the bus from Harkness Center during our junior year (Chapter 12) – but Bill didn't have anyone specific at that time. He called up a couple of girls, but they weren't available. I think one had to paint her couch, and the other had to feed her cat, or some silliness like that. Finally, Terri suggested her friend Anne Bathory. Because this would be very much like a blind date, Bill decided to invite Dean, to make it seem less like a date for Anne. Also, Dean already knew Terri from Harkness.

Once we got to Crystal Beach, Bill, Dean and Anne went one direction, and Terri and I went our own way. This was not only my very first *real* date, but it also resulted in my very first real *kiss* (kissing our cousin doesn't count as a "real kiss"!). Terri and I went on a large variety of rides, but it was those that took us through dark tunnels that evoked the kissing! For some odd reason I enjoyed those rides the most!

Regrettably, due to differing schedules and commitments, or maybe she just had to feed the cat, Terri and I weren't able to get together again throughout the summer, and then Bill and I left the area for college in the fall. Well, that, and ferrets are weasels.

REAL-LIFE ADVENTURES
SECTION 5 – THE COLLEGE YEARS

CHAPTER 15 – STILL 1976; STILL AGE 18

Starting College, Troubleshooting By Proxy, Amateur Radio Licenses, The Eternal Chess Game, Working in the School Lab, The Electrostatic Motor

The Electrostatic Motor

STARTING OUR COLLEGE EDUCATION

In September 1976, Bill and I left home to start our engineering education at the Ohio Institute of Technology in Columbus, Ohio. It's changed names at least twice since then; I believe it's now called "DeVry Institute of Technology" or "DeVry University". This school was a pure technical school. There were no liberal arts degrees, no athletic or sports opportunities, no general science degrees, and, regrettably, virtually no women! They offered an Associate and a Bachelor of Science degree in Electronics Engineering Technology, and also a Technician Certificate... only. The school was wholly focused on electronics, and very well equipped for the best balance between practical labs and theory classes. Bill and I graduated with our bachelor's degrees in just three years by attending school, full-time, through the summers.

Now for the prior six years we'd been repairing all types of electronic equipment for people in our community – charging very little more than the cost of parts. This made us the cheapest, as well as the most effective, repair service in the area. People heard about us. Therefore, even though we'd left the area to attend school, they continued to come by our parents' house with televisions, radios, tape decks, and other items to get repaired. While our parents would tell them honestly that Bill and I were no longer living there, and weren't expected back until the next holiday break, many of them were more than willing to wait. As a result, each time we'd come home for a holiday, we'd end up spending all of our time repairing stuff! This wasn't exactly the way we'd prefer to spend our holidays.

Remember, this is 1976. There were no cell phones, no personal computers, and no developed Internet that would support e-mail to most people yet. When we needed to contact our parents from our location some 350 miles distant, we could either write a letter and wait two weeks for a response, or we'd have to make a long-distance, collect, phone call. Back then, long-distance phone calls were for emergencies only. Collect calls were even more expensive, so they were for even more dire situations – somebody had better have died, because if we'd made such a call and it wasn't the case, then we'd surely be next in line! This simply wasn't an option.

Being a technical school, they had an amateur radio club (with the call sign WB8PEN), as well as a well-equipped radio room at one end of the main building. Also, you'll recall, Ralph Endres, the neighbor across the street from our parents' house, was an avid amateur (ham) radio operator with an impressive radio room, himself. His official call sign was WA2RGR. Therefore, we worked out a method to communicate with home instantaneously every week without costing anybody anything.

Because we only had our Novice amateur radio licenses, we could only communicate via Morse code without supervision. Despite our mother's earlier demonstrated proficiency when *sending* Morse code, she was very rusty in *receiving* it, so it made more sense to communicate via voice. But, for voice communication, we needed a properly licensed ham in the room while we used the radio in voice mode. This was no problem most of the time for us, and our mother would either run across the street for our weekly scheduled call, or Ralph would set up a phone patch to our parents' house.

TROUBLESHOOTING BY PROXY

So, there were times when someone would bring their TV by our parents' house, and we'd want to get an idea of what the problem is, so we'd be better prepared once we were home on a break. That way, we might be able to reduce the amount of time troubleshooting and enjoy our breaks more. This meant that our mother was our eyes and ears. This would help us diagnose the problem over the radio. Now, I should mention that our mother had absolutely *no* technical capability, whatsoever. She was a wonderful person and mother, who'd accomplished more in her life than most women, and many men, but she just didn't understand anything technical, i.e. electronic. This is why it was so amazing, after a few of these "troubleshooting-by-proxy" situations, when she actually accurately diagnosed a problem with a TV just by listening to the sounds it made when first turned on, observing what, if anything, was displayed on the screen, and then recalling what we'd concluded from prior discussions! Perhaps, at that point, we should have let her take care of all of the repairs up there, so we could just enjoy our vacations.

OUR AMATEUR RADIO LICENSES

Once Bill and I had built up our Morse code speed, we drove to the downtown federal exam center again and took both the written technical exam and the code receiving test with the intent of getting our General amateur radio operator licenses, those which would allow us to communicate on the radio using voice without supervision. We both passed the technical exam with nearly perfect scores, but I still faltered with the code reception. I didn't quite make the full 13 words per minute required for the General class ham radio license, but I was well above the 5 WPM required for the Technician class ham license when associated with the General license technical exam.

This class of license would allow me to communicate with voice over a fairly short-distance (50 miles or so) via a radio medium called 2-meter FM. This was in reference to the wavelength of the designated frequencies, and the modulation technique. Bill got his General license, allowing voice communication on most of the short wave bands, including 2-meter, and the very popular, long-distance (thousands of miles), 40-meter band. Bill and I were subsequently issued our new licenses with the following call signs: WB2JTQ and WB2KWD, respectively. In addition to the privilege of being able to communicate around the world with a radio, it was very well organized. Most hams respected the airwaves, since they'd invested so much time and effort into learning the technical material and building the Morse code speed that was required to become licensed. With that investment, they/we didn't want to lose it, so it was self-regulating and self-policing...for the most part people were very polite and respectable. We still didn't have a radio transmitter of our own, but at least we were licensed to use the school's radio, or in the future if we ever got our own radios.

THE CHESS GAME

When Bill and I went off to college, we went with a plan to keep in touch with our good friend, David Fairlie, who remained in Clarence, NY. Our plan was to play chess with him through the mail. Due to the periodic need for new chess moves, this encouraged continued writing. This actually worked, but only for about 25 years. Ironically, as we progressed to faster and more efficient means of communication – from handwritten letters sent through the mail, to typed letters, also through the mail, to e-mail letters, to a website dedicated to the ongoing chess games – the response time, therefore, the games themselves, actually became longer and longer! One game, I recall, lasted 11-years and 10-months! This is not what I'd call speed-chess!

THE SCHOOL LAB

Bill and I both worked 25 hours every week in the school lab from soon after we started school there, until we graduated. This was in addition to the 18 – 21 credit hours of engineering classes we took each term. We also continued our classes (and work) through each summer, allowing us to graduate with bachelor's degrees in just three years. I started working in the school lab first, while Bill was working at TeleCinema, a local cable TV service. The standard procedure for those who worked in the lab was to first put in time up front in the stockroom portion, and then migrate to the back where we'd repair the lab equipment. Therefore, for the first two or three months that I worked there, I was relegated to the front where I'd interact with students checking out equipment and selling them parts to do their labs.

The lab stockroom had just about everything you could imagine for a lab experiment. A student could check out tools and equipment ranging from screwdrivers and hammers, to CB radios, digital circuit trainers, and even analog computers, servomotors, and a tiny-yet-pricy spectrum analyzer. It also had an impressive stock of electronic components such as resistors, capacitors, LEDs, switches, and transistors, which could be purchased for a lab or a project for just pennies a piece.

Our school provided a high-quality education. The classes were as tough as those of any other school's engineering curricula, but it seemed that they'd accept *anybody* who applied. It wasn't at all unusual to have 300 new students in a first-term class. That number, however, would drop precipitously with each subsequent term. Ultimately, only about a dozen students would make it through the full bachelor's degree program. We liked to think that we were the "best of the best" …the most determined…or maybe just the most obstinate!

Working in the lab stockroom essentially gave me a front row seat to observe these first-term students close-up. It was a bit like an anthropologist observing apes in the wild. This is when I began to truly grasp just how *badly* the education system had failed a huge segment of our population. Most of these education-challenged individuals had come from the Detroit, Michigan area. These were college students, and yet many of them couldn't even figure out how to write their name on a line at the top of a very basic checkout form, much less compose a coherent list of parts that they'd need for their lab! Trying to decipher their atrocious spelling presented a new challenge with each checkout form I'd be given! It really was quite pathetic.

Calculators had been out for about three years by this time, and Bill and I had relegated our trusty slide rules to the bottom of a dresser drawer in favor of a pair of TI-30 scientific calculators. While we both used these calculators extensively during our classes and homework, it just wasn't the best solution when having to add up prices for a dozen small parts, and then making change when there was a huge line of people waiting at the window for their parts. It just took too long. This is the first time that I'd had to do such a huge volume of mental addition and subtraction for such an extended period, and I feel that it really helped me out in the future. Remember in Chapter 1 when I'd said that I was really bad at making change? After this brief stint doing a large volume of mental change making under pressure, it's caused me to be able to figure out change from any purchase I make now almost instantaneously. It helps to know what amount of change you should expect back so that you're not a penny short when your mother makes you balance your books!

Finally, our supervisor hired another student to handle the front, allowing me to move to the back where I'd be doing what I really wanted to do at that time: Repairing electronic equipment! A short while later, Bill had applied at the lab. Because the supervisor was impressed with my repair work, instead of making Bill "pay his dues" up front, he was hired directly for repair work in the back. We were scheduled on opposite shifts. One of us would work in the morning, while the other had classes. Then, the other would work in the lab in the afternoon, while doing classes in the morning. Because we looked very similar back then, some people thought that we were actually just one person who worked there all day!

THE SPINNING PEANUT

What do Styrofoam packing peanuts have to do with motors? Actually, quite a bit, when positioned within a high voltage electric field! As you've, undoubtedly gathered by now, Bill and I were fascinated with high voltage, particularly when we could make it do spectacular things for us like sparking, arcing or blowing things around from ozone emission. It was, therefore, no great stretch when we strung a knotted thread through the center of one piece of packing material, causing it to be held about an inch above a table, positioned between the two terminals of a 50,000 Volt source on either end of it. Once the high voltage field was activated, the foam legume would begin to spin, and spin, and spin! It spun very fast until we turned off the power. What we'd built was something called an electrostatic motor. To understand how such a motor can work, I'll first have to provide a little information about charges.

Just about everybody's heard that opposites attract. No, this wasn't derived from the dating scene. It was about electricity and magnetism. What it means is that positive charges attract negative charges, and like charges repel. Therefore, if you build up a charge of static electricity of a particular polarity onto an insulator such as the suspended Styrofoam material, that charge will soon become strong enough to push the movable insulating peanut away from the terminal that's charged it. Then, as the insulator rotates, the charged ends will soon feel the attraction of the opposite terminals, pulling that charge to them, and soon replacing the stored charge with a new charge from the nearest terminal. This, again, pushes it away. It continues this sequence cyclically, thus making the Styrofoam rotate like a motor's rotor. See the illustration titled Electrostatic Motor at the top of this chapter.

CHAPTER 16 – 1977; AGE NINETEEN

Eckel's Lake, Hang Gliding, Flying a Cessna 172 Airplane, Programmable Digital Sequencer, Building a Degaussing Coil

The Traveling Rings at Eckel's Lake

In 1977, the average house cost $49,300, the typical annual income was about $15,000, a new car cost about $4,300, and gas cost $0.65 per gallon. There was the NY City Blackout, where lightning strikes caused city-wide power outage for 25 hours, resulting in looting and rioting. The US returned the Panama Canal back to Panama. The Apple II Computer went on sale, the Trans-Alaskan Oil Pipeline opens, and NAVSTAR Global Positioning System (GPS) is inaugurated by US DoD.

ECKEL'S LAKE

Partway through our first summer (1977) at school in Columbus, Ohio, we discovered an amazing swimming hole called Eckel's Lake. It was billed as a "water gymnasium". The lake, fed by the nearby Olentangy River, spanned nearly three quarters of an acre in a roughly triangular shape. The apparatus area occupied just over half an acre. As it was just 30 minutes north of our apartment, we headed up there nearly every weekend when the weather was good during the remainder of that first summer. The following two summers we purchased season passes!

The attraction of Eckel's Lake went way beyond the sandy beach area, two large rafts anchored in the middle of the lake, a low- and very high-diving board, and a high slide with water running down it – most swimming holes had these, or similar apparatus, as it was pretty much standard fare at the time. What set Eckel's Lake apart from the rest, and made it truly a water gym, were three specific devices on and over the water: The Flying Rings, The Traveling Rings, and The Barrel!

THE FLYING RINGS

The Flying Rings were essentially two sets of standard gymnastic rings suspended side-by-side on a bar that was supported by a pair of stout telephone poles jutting out towards the water from the bank on a 45-degree angle. There was a wooden ramp that sloped down the bank, allowing people to hold the rings while running down the ramp to gain momentum, propelling them out into the lake. Now most people seemed to just run right down the ramp, and straight into the water, with little or no swing from the rings. They'd just reach the bottom of the ramp, and then their arms would straighten suddenly by their body weight pulling them down, ripping their hands right off of the rings. This is *not* how it was supposed to be done!

While we'd never had formal gymnastics training, Bill and I were always climbing trees and ropes, and had a set of very crude gymnastics rings hanging from one tree at our parents' house. Therefore, we had significant upper body strength. As such, we took the Flying Rings at Eckel's Lake to a new level. When we first started using these flying rings, we did a very basic maneuver. We'd just hold ourselves up to the rings like a chin-up while swinging through the full arc over the water, releasing into a forward dive at the apex of the swing and into the water. As we got more comfortable with them, we then started doing the "double-leg cutoff" gymnastics move I'd first described in Chapter 8. Unlike the "croissant roll" rings we had when we were twelve, the flying rings were the proper diameter, were made of wood, and they swung out over the water!

To execute the double-leg cutoff maneuver on the Flying Rings, I'd begin by bringing the rings back to the top of the ramp, then I'd throw my legs up and around the top with my crotch just touching the rings, and my feet facing behind me. At this point, I'd be swinging down over the ramp with my legs over my head, quite inverted. With this move, timing was important. About halfway through the swing, I'd throw my legs forward, straightening out my body, and swinging backward on the rings as they're still swinging forward. If timed right, I'd reach the apex of the swing just as my legs were swinging forward again. I'd go into a wide straddle position and release my hands from the rings, doing a back tuck high in the air, and then dropping into the water far from shore.

Another favorite move on the Flying Rings was the "L-Hold". In this case, Bill or I'd, again, draw the rings all of the way to the top of the ramp. Then, I'd jump while pressing down on the rings, thereby positioning my body above the rings where I'd go into an "L-Hold" position. Holding this position through the full swing of the rings allowed me to do a forward dive from above the rings. This gave me lots of extra height and distance.

THE TRAVELING RINGS

The Traveling Rings consisted of a set of about twenty gymnastics rings, each suspended from a 10-foot cable, each spaced about every 10-feet along a 200-foot long cable about 20 feet in the air. The idea was for people to swing along from ring to ring, like Tarzan, traveling from one side of the lake to the other, without ever touching the water. See the illustration titled Traveling Rings at Eckel's Lake at the top of this chapter. There were four things that made this just a bit tougher than it might at first seem. 1) You had to be able to hold nearly twice your own body weight with one hand (due to G-forces) while swinging, 2) The rings were always wet – therefore, slippery – from people ahead of us who'd just come out of the water, 3) The rings were spaced far enough apart that you could not reach an adjacent one unless either you, or it, was swinging, and, finally, 4) This was a *2-way system*; people would travel in *both* directions on these rings, simultaneously!

The optimal technique, once stepping off of the platform onto the Traveling Rings, was to swing on the first ring to the second, but hold onto the first.

Then, I'd pump up my momentum by pulling on each ring in turn. Once I had a good amount of momentum, I'd proceed on to the third ring, and then, with a subtle pump before leaving the second, I'd swing onto the fourth, and so on. If I ever lost momentum, and couldn't reach another ring, I'd have just two options; Drop into the water, or wait for another person to come along, bringing with them the next ring. Because we both traveled these rings numerous times during each visit there, we frequently got "rips". A rip occurs after you've developed fairly substantial calluses on the palm of your hand from an activity such as working the rings, and then that thick callus will tear off such as once it's softened by the water while gripping the rings. Such a rip exposes a half-inch or so diameter raw spot on the palm that stings severely when you enter the water. With this sort of incentive, it wasn't at all unreasonable to think of the water as if it were molten lava – because that's just what your rip would feel like as soon as you hit the water! This was, of course, just part and parcel with the enjoyment of the Traveling Rings. Sometimes we'd tape our hands before going across, to minimize the possibility of ripping.

CROSSING OVER

How, you're likely wondering, is it possible to sustain two-way traffic on these rings? When another person is coming towards you from the opposite direction, you have to hope for one of two things to happen; 1) Either they're so intimidated that they just drop before getting to you, which usually happened, or 2) They're experienced at crossing over. If they don't fall into *either* of these categories, then they'll hold onto the rings and attempt the crossing, but, ultimately, they'll lose the rhythm, and the next ring, leaving you both stuck there hanging from a single, stationary ring, with just one way out; drop into the lava!

In order to successfully cross over, I'd time my swing to align with his or hers. Then, ideally, both would grasp a common ring, while each was still holding onto a second ring. While the two of us are holding three rings (one in common), we'd then begin a coordinated pumping action to build the momentum that had been totally cancelled out by the meeting in the middle. Once enough momentum was built up, one of us would have to release the far ring, placing both people on two rings. More pumping. Then, the other person would move on to his or her next ring, and the transfer would be done. Ferrets cannot do this!

GOING DOUBLE

There was still another interesting way to cross the Traveling Rings; Double! This is where two people travel as one – making all of the same grabs and pumping in sync with the other – as if you're both of one mind. We'd heard rumors of some of the locals going double on these rings, but it was so very rarely ever executed, that it basically seemed like an urban legend… until that day *I* did it. Every hour all public swimming areas in Ohio had a mandatory 15-minute break, during which no one could be in the water. Presumably, it was intended to let the water settle enough so that anyone who might have drowned might rise to the surface. Well, that's what they'd told us! Or it might have just been to give the lifeguards a break. I really don't know for sure. Anyway, one very attractive guard – Heather – was in her chair at the far side of the Traveling Rings and wanted to get back to the other side. Normally, the guards would just head across the Traveling Rings on their own, or they'd take the long, circuitous route through the woods around the perimeter of the lake. The rings were *much* quicker and most of the lifeguards were quite good on them. This one time, after all of the guards gave their long blow on their whistles indicating the break, I was next up in line at the Traveling Rings, standing right next to where Heather sat. By this time, we'd become quite well known by the lifeguards there, so it wasn't really a huge surprise when she asked me if I'd like to head across the rings, going double with her! Not only was she incredibly cute in her bikini and short-cropped dark hair, but I also knew that she was quite strong. With the line completely clear, we'd have absolutely no problem getting across efficiently. Now, while it's probably of no consequence, I should mention that all of the female lifeguards normally wore the standard red-orange one-piece bathing suits. Heather was in a tiny blue and white floral print bikini. It's possible that, since she was already there clearly relaxing earlier, as if taking a day off, she might have been asked to work when another guard apparently didn't show up. Just speculating there.

So, without further delay, she and I both grabbed onto the first ring, and swung out to the second – as one entity – where we had to pump to get our momentum. Once we'd reached the second ring, she'd positioned herself with her front against my back. We pumped three times, and, intuitively, without having to speak a word, we both released from the first ring at precisely the same time and sailed on to the third. We kept our momentum up as we proceeded along the full set of rings during the most silent trip I'd ever known across the expanse! Everybody on the beach, on the rafts, and on the banks, waiting for the break to end, was silently staring at us in rapt fascination! As we approached the far side of the travel, the silent spectators began to chant, "Go! Go! Go!" all in unison. It was really quite surreal…to say nothing of being exceptionally fun!

Had we not made it across, or tripped up along the way, it would have been incredibly embarrassing; but, of course, we didn't. We got across with barely any effort, arriving at the other end to cheers that erupted from the chanting crowd! It was only then that I'd actually noticed that they were all staring at us. Before that moment, I was totally focused on the task at hand.

The most accomplished regular at Eckel's Lake was a guy known only by his initials, "P.I." He'd developed his own very aggressive style on the Traveling Rings. Instead of just swinging in-line with the cable suspending the set of rings, he also got a substantial amount of lateral momentum, forming wide, sprawling arcs, while traveling along the rings. Usually, when P.I. was on the rings, people would just drop off before they got anywhere near him, but occasionally, they'd remain in place, creating a possible collision concern. I can recall, more than once, hearing one of the lifeguards cautioning P.I. to tone it down some.

RUNNING THE BARREL

There was also a large floating barrel held in place in a narrow portion of the lake with a long cable on either end attached to bearing plates. This allowed it to turn freely. The barrel itself was about nine feet long, and three feet in diameter. In order to provide some traction on the otherwise slick, wet metal surface, the barrel was coated with thick grit, like very coarse sandpaper. There was a wooden board walkway leading up to it from the shore on one end. People would stand in line and walk onto the barrel from there.

Because the barrel turned freely, it was necessary, when walking onto it, to either counter the motion by stepping on the opposite side with your other foot, or just to walk in the opposite direction that it's already turning to stay on the top. The guards and regulars, such as Bill and I, had not just mastered mounting the barrel, but we could also stand on it all day, keeping it stable with almost no effort. Therefore, when someone new would try to step onto it, we'd try to keep the barrel stable as they mounted it, and then we'd start it turning very slowly, which usually resulted in them literally just falling off of it in the direction of rotation, within seconds.

We also learned, VERY quickly, that frequent running of the barrel would cause severe blisters on our bare feet. Therefore, you could always tell the experienced barrel runners, because we'd all walk onto it wearing old sneakers! There were frequent times when four expert barrel runners – usually consisting of lifeguards on break, locals, or regulars such as ourselves – would get the barrel turning so fast that we'd all be in a full-out run, with white water coming up the backside of the barrel, creating a thicker film of water on the top, making it much slicker. Ultimately, we'd all run ourselves off and into the water, but it was extremely fun to go that fast!

I remember at least a couple of times when an inexperienced person would get onto the barrel and actually get some speed going. Then, they'd trip and end up straddling the top of the barrel. Of course, the massive barrel has a lot of momentum, so now that sandpaper finish I'd referred to earlier is tearing into this person's thighs and legs until they finally rotated off and into the water! Lava!

FIRST FLIGHT

With the exception of the fleeting periods that we'd been airborne when jumping from a tree, swinging out on a rope into water, or jumping off of the high dive at Eckel's Lake, Bill and I had never been off of the ground. That's right, we were 19 years old, and we'd never, ever flown before, and yet, we'd yearned to be airborne our entire lives! Well, this was about to change.

Our school's student population was painfully short on women. There were just two women who graduated from the bachelor's degree engineering program while we were attending, and a couple of others a year or so behind us. But there were a few – and by "a few", I mean that literally; maybe three

– young women in the Technician's Certificate program. We were, of course, friendly with all of the women in the school, so it wasn't at all odd when this one female Tech student told Bill and me that she was planning to go skydiving with a few friends and wondered if we'd be interested in joining her.

Now, you have to remember that back in the late 1970's, and "tandem jumping" had only just been conceived. It'd take the better part of another decade in the "experimental" phase before it would become widely available as a viable method for first-time skydiving enthusiasts to experience freefall while strapped to an experienced skydiver. This allows the newbie to experience up to about 60-seconds of freefall before the expert diver pulls the ripcord and the pair sails gracefully to the Earth. Back in the '70s, you were on your own, and, because the ripcord was connected to a static line – which guaranteed that the chute would open – it opened *immediately* as you exited the plane – ensuring *no freefall*, at all.

Remember my philosophy when it comes to risk? Never take a *careless* risk. Therefore, Bill and I carefully considered the benefits along with the risks to skydiving and concluded that the reward simply wasn't worth the risk. Basically, we wanted to experience freefall, but, at that time, this wouldn't happen until a person had completed a number of lessons, and finally had enough jumps that an instructor felt they were competent enough to be allowed to jump without being connected to the static line. It could take hundreds of jumps before we might achieve this. Also, of course, there was the simple fact that jumping out of a perfectly good airplane was a one-shot deal. If *anything* at all went wrong, you'd soon be little more than a stain on the ground! There were no second-chances.

At the very same time, we'd also learned about a local guy who was giving lessons in hang-gliding. To us, this would not only satisfy our initial need to become airborne, but it also seemed to be far safer. We met up at a farmhouse in a hilly rural area where the instructor had permission to use their land to give lessons. He had two rolled-up gliders mounted on top of his truck when we got there. We helped him get them down, and we all walked over to the top of a long, rolling set of hills. There, we helped him assemble the Rogallo wing glider, while setting the other glider aside. A Rogallo wing glider is the commonly known triangle-shaped, flexible-wing device.

Once the glider was assembled, and I was strapped into the harness beneath it, I started to run down the gentle hill. Gaining speed, I moved the nose up just a bit, and it caught the air, lifting me off of the ground! At that moment, I was suddenly whisked back to when I was five and I ran into the wind in my parents' back yard with cardboard wings strapped under my arms! Only this time, I actually did become airborne, even if for only a moment. This was a sensation like none I'd *ever* felt before! It might have been only for just 20 or 30 feet, but I was airborne! Of course, I'd end up stalling it, and, invariably, come to back to terra firma, thrusting the back of the main mast into the ground! But I flew, and it was incredible! Bill went next, and reported a similar feeling, and abrupt stop. We took turns doing several more runs down this hill, while trying to fine-adjust the pitch of the wing so we could get a farther flight, but it was clear that it'd take much more training for that.

Once our collective lessons were done for that time, the instructor had us help him roll up the Rogallo glider, and carry it back to his truck, and then we helped him carry the second glider up a very steep hill. Once at the top, we helped the instructor assemble his "fixed-wing" glider. He wanted to demonstrate a more advanced form of hang gliding by sailing off of the precipice at which we were now standing. After waiting quite a while for the wind to be just right, suddenly he ran towards the cliff, went out a few feet, and then headed straight down! It seemed that he dropped for a solid ten seconds – with the trees below coming ever closer – before he pulled up and narrowly avoided scraping the treetops below! After we climbed back down the steep hill, and met the instructor back at his truck, we asked him if that flight profile was what he'd intended, as it seemed very risky. He said, in fact, that it wasn't, but the wind just changed suddenly, and he lost lift until he got enough speed from the steep descent!

The hang-gliding fun served to whet our appetite for flight, so some while later we got in touch with a local flight school and set up what they called an "Introductory Lesson" for each of us in a Cessna 152. This fixed-wing aircraft is just a 2-seater. This meant that one of us would have to remain

Earthbound while the other went up with the pilot/instructor. The lesson began with some brief ground-school instruction. After that, we both headed out to the tarmac where we participated in a preflight check. Once done there each of us went up in the plane, in turn, with the instructor for about 30-minutes. It was exceptionally exciting, and it felt like we'd finally achieved our childhood goal of flying – except that we'd have a lot more work in front of us if we were going to achieve the "full control" part of our vision of flying. That meant much more money than what we could part with just then. After all, we *were* still in school.

We'd also gotten to know another female Tech student who was interested in flying. Kelly worked in the school cafeteria opposite her class schedule. When she'd heard about our Intro flights, she got all excited and asked if she could do one, too. Never ones to turn down a pretty face, to say nothing of an intelligent young woman interested in both electronics *and* flying, it wasn't long before we were on our way back to the flight school, only this time, with Kelly along. Because there were the three of us, and Bill and I wanted to see the thrill in Kelly's eyes when she took the controls, we opted to rent a Cessna 172 – a 4-seater – this time, with, of course, the instructor pilot taking one of the two front seats.

A while after Kelly's flight, once Bill and I'd saved up a bit more money, we went back for another lesson. Despite my strong desire to fly more, I was bothered at how...well...dull it was.

Once the engine was going, we'd taxi to the end of the runway and wait for the tower to grant permission to take off. He'd set the flaps, throttle up, and have only the lightest touch to the control yoke (the steering wheel-like control). Once we reached about 60-knots (69mph), the plane easily began to rise from the runway, barely pulling back on the yoke. So, basically, you give it some power, point it in a direction least likely to run into something, and essentially take your hands off – you're flying!

Since I'd spent most of my life lusting over the day that I'd fly on my own, I have to say I was more than a little bit disappointed by this recent revelation. We both decided to put off further flight lessons for a while...until we could find another form of flight that truly gave us both the satisfaction that we'd sought all of our lives!

THE PROGRAMMABLE DIGITAL SEQUENCER

While I was in high school, I'd designed a very elaborate electronic device, but, at that time, I didn't have a sufficient, steady income to be able to afford the parts to build it. Once I was working at the school, I was finally able to buy the required components – many from the lab stockroom. I also had the tools available to wire it and build the case. This device, in retrospect, was substantially similar to the early microprocessors that would soon come out and change computing forever.

I called my device, a "Programmable Digital Sequencer" because...well... that's what it did. It consisted of 256 bytes of solid state, static Random-Access Memory (RAM), and an 8-bit up-down address counter that could be loaded to any address to start. Once a location was set from a group of eight toggle switches beneath eight LEDs, then data could be entered into that location via the same switches. Once all 256 memory locations were loaded with a unique data byte, then the memory would be changed from write mode to read mode, and the clock feeding the address counter could be increased in speed to fuse the played-back data patterns into a smooth-looking series of sequencing LEDs.

I had also connected each nibble (one nibble is four bits) of the output to one of two one-of-sixteen binary decoders. These were each, in turn, connected to sixteen ten-turn potentiometers, which created a single variable-voltage output from each 4-bit "channel". These two analog signals were fed into a pair of Voltage Controlled Oscillators (VCOs), which output a trio of waveforms – sine, triangle, and square waves. Connected such, I was able to play stereophonic music in a variety of "voices" (wave-shapes), whose tones were selected by the binary value programmed into the memory during the writing process. Because it could create programmed music, some called it a programmable music box.

BUILDING A DEGAUSSING COIL

Wouldn't you know it...just as soon as Bill and I were out of the house, our parents bought a color TV for their living room! Of course, we didn't find this out until the next time we'd visited – probably Christmas that year (1977). The first thing I'd noticed, when I saw the new TV, was a pink-to-green "smudge" on one corner. Mom and Dad didn't seem to notice it, but it was all I could see when I looked at the screen. Both from working at the JC Penney Service Center when we were 16 and working in the school lab where we had to service color TVs when the Tech classes messed them up during their lab experiments, we knew that it just needed to be degaussed; a very simple operation, if you have a degaussing coil. Apparently, someone had brought a magnet, or something containing a magnet, like a speaker, too close to the screen, thus magnetizing the metallic shadow-mask behind the phosphor enough to deflect the electron beam to the incorrect colors.

The only thing standing between the smudge and a proper display was a basic degaussing coil...which, of course we didn't have! We looked at buying one, but they were going for around $50 or $60. Now, if this was something we'd need to use often, then it would be a good investment, and we wouldn't hesitate to buy one, but it was most likely to be just a one-shot deal. Finally, we decided to just do what we've always done before; build our own! I'd estimated that 400-feet of 24-gauge, lacquer-coated magnet wire would serve the purpose, so we headed to Olsen Electronics in downtown Buffalo, as the local Radio Shack stores didn't have it. We also picked up a fairly heavy-duty, momentary-contact switch and a power cord to plug it in. One last thing, we needed a good quantity of electrical tape to hold it all together.

Now, while they come in some variety of sizes, generally a degaussing coil's diameter needs to be fairly large so as not to introduce a concentrated electromagnetic field on any one part of the TV screen. It should, therefore, cover a significant portion of the screen so as to apply a gentle, overall field, thus removing any stray magnetism from specific areas, which will cause changes in hue. Once we'd picked up the parts, the first thing we had to do was to find something with a large enough area to use it as a rudimentary "coil form". After scouring the basement for any wooden boards wide enough, with no luck, we suddenly caught sight of an old phone book. This would serve our purpose nicely.

After scribing a crude circle upon the cover of the book, we hammered in several long nails along the circle. This provided an ideal coil-winding form with a good diameter. After tying one end of the first of four 100-foot coils of wire to one of the nails, it was simple work to wind the entire length around

YOUR SUCCESS - YOUR CHOICE

the circular shape, layer upon layer. Because we couldn't find 400-feet of magnet wire in a single spool, we had to splice four 100-foot lengths together as we wound it – insulating the soldered splice, of course. Eventually, we'd used up all 400-feet of wire, so we removed the nails, allowing the large, loose coil to be picked up off of the telephone book. At this stage, it needed two things: Structural integrity, and additional insulation for handling. The roll of electrical tape would do both. We wrapped the tape tightly around the entire coil, overlapping the width of the prior tape wrap with each new wrap. Once taped up, it felt very solid, and was also safe to handle once power is applied. Of course, to get power to it safely, we still had to install the switch and power cord.

Now, understand that 400-feet was nothing more than a total gutfeel guess. While we were well aware that the inductance of coils driven by an Alternating Current (AC, as from the wall socket) increased its impedance (AC resistance) well above its Direct Current (DC, as from a battery) resistance, we didn't have the applicable formulas with us to derive a precise value, so we just winged it! Therefore, there was a great amount of trepidation after I'd plugged it in and was about to switch it on! As neither Bill nor I yet had any credit cards or ATM (Automated Teller Machines) cards, because ATMs were extremely rare in 1977, we didn't have to remove our wallets and place them a good distance from the magnetic field this coil would generate. I assumed the classic pose – outstretched arm, face shielded but turned enough so that I could see any resulting fireworks – and I hit the switch! It didn't explode, or even burst into flames! It just sat there emitting a healthy buzz! After it'd been on for more than a few seconds, the coil did get noticeably warm, but that's why we'd installed a momentary-contact switch. It seemed to operate just like any commercial degaussing coil we'd used before.

After this initial, successful trial, we let it cool down a bit, since the process of degaussing the TV would require up to 30-seconds of continuous operation. Turning off a degaussing coil while it's still close to a color TV will result in an extremely colorful record of the magnetic field on the screen. While Bill and I would have found it rather fascinating, I suspect that our parents wouldn't have been quite as enthusiastic about it. I think they'd have noticed *that much* color distortion! I held the cooled coil a fair distance away from the operating TV when I switched it on. Despite this precaution, I still saw the display instantly distort slightly. I began the familiar circular motion about the screen as I approached until nearly touching it. Then, while continuing the same motion, I moved back away from the screen until I could see no further affect from the field. Switching off the now rather warm coil, I noted that the color TV screen was completely proper now; no more pinkish-green smudge! This cobbled together, makeshift degaussing coil had done its job.

CHAPTER 17 – 1978; AGE TWENTY

The Dayton Hamfest, The 3,000 Volt Shock of My Life, Importing Women From Local College for Party, New Women at Our College, Flashing Mice, Computer Programming, F009 Error Code, The First Minicomputer, American Liquitronics, The TV Studio

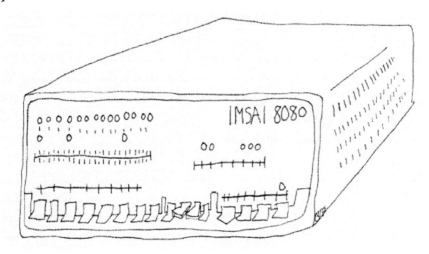

Early Minicomputer

In 1978, the average house cost $54,800, the typical annual income was about $17,000, a new car cost about $4,600, and gas cost $0.77 per gallon. Serial killer David Berkowitz, the "Son of Sam" is sentenced to 25 years to life. In the Jonestown massacre, 900 people commit suicide with cult leader Jim Jones at the "People's Temple" in Guyana. The first *cellular* mobile phone system was introduced by Illinois Bell; "Space Invaders" video game was introduced in arcades. 98% of American homes had a television; the first computer bulletin board system (BBS) was created.

THE DAYTON HAMFEST

In May of this year, while Bill and I were still attending school in Columbus, Ohio, we drove to Dayton to attend the Hamfest of all Hamfests! The Dayton Hamfest was infamous for being the biggest gathering of amateur radio operators, aficionados, hobbyists, and commercial electronic parts vendors in the country, and we were virtually drooling over the possible bargains we'd find there! We were definitely not disappointed. Spending less than $150 total ($565 today), which we split, of course, we left with an ancient television camera, a smaller, portable TV camera, a ½-inch reel-to-reel Video Tape Recorder (VTR), and innumerable small electronic parts for our various on-going projects. We were told that all of these items functioned, but of course, to what degree, we couldn't know until we got them home.

The old TV camera was one of many built in 1947 for use in remote-guided missiles. It used the original image pickup tube, the Iconoscope. Vladimir K. Zworykin of RCA developed this type of tube for the very first electronic television systems ever built. Ferrets aren't known for their inventions. The camera itself was remarkably streamlined in its physical design for a device of that vintage, but even so, it was quite heavy and bulky, and it also required a power supply that was heavier still! These cameras were put onto the surplus market once it became apparent that a human operator sitting at a desk several miles away from such a missile simply didn't have the required reaction time to successfully guide it to a target. This vacuum tube filled camera came with a 1957 issue of CQ magazine in which a conversion from 28V operation to wall power was detailed. It included a complete schematic of the camera, and, of course, featured the new power supply. True to the word of the guy who'd sold it to us, it did, in fact, still function, but, like all TV cameras of that era, it required A LOT of light to produce its clear Black & White (B&W) picture on a monitor!

From yet another vendor, we picked up both a smaller TV camera, and a reel-to-reel B&W Video Tape Recorder (VTR). This small camera used the then-current video image pickup tube, the Vidicon, and the whole camera was just about the size of a loaf of bread. This home-built device came with an issue of the Popular Electronics magazine in which the camera project was featured. The schematic of this solid-state (except for the vidicon), B&W camera was also included in the article. This camera required *far* less light to produce an image on a monitor than the old camera, but it was prone to "smearing". That is, bright spots, such as lights or reflections of the sun, would leave a long streak across the image when panned. But this was not a defect. It was common to all television cameras of the time that used the Vidicon image pickup tube.

Now that we we'd picked up all of these video cameras, it made sense to get something that would let us record and play back the images. This VTR came with one full 6- or 8-inch diameter reel of tape, plus, of course, the empty take-up reel. With its single, scanning video head, a recorded image would often have some "flag-waving" at the bottom when the tape is stopped for a still-frame, but it was a solid image otherwise. This machine also had an interesting special feature – not unlike our 8mm movie camera. It had a recording mode where it would lay down a video track once every 1/3rd second, instead of the normal rate of sixty per second. When such a recording was played back it provided the effect of time-lapse; very slow-moving things, like a growing flower, would suddenly become quite animated.

Over the span of the next year or so, Bill and I used these cameras and recorder frequently to record many short productions. Unlike the hours of video capable on DVDs today or VHS tapes of the recent past, a full reel of tape on our VTR would last just 30-minutes on playback. In the time-lapse recording mode, it would take 48-hours to fill the reel. It seems logical that this VTR was built for surveillance, such as in a bank.

MY WORST ELECTRICAL SHOCK EVER

If I didn't religiously practice the "one-hand-rule" whenever working on energized equipment with high voltage inside like television receivers and oscilloscopes, I'd be sitting here dead now, and you wouldn't be reading any of this!

I was in the back area of the lab stockroom/repair area working on one of the brand-new dual-trace oscilloscopes made by Leader, after a student had managed to damage it out in the lab. Any device containing a Cathode Ray Tube (CRT) requires high voltage to accelerate the electron beam needed to paint a trace or image onto the phosphor screen. Television receivers generate around 25,000 Volts with a very low-current flyback power supply system. An oscilloscope, however, having a much smaller screen, requires only around 3,000 Volts, so it's stepped up using a standard power transformer right off of the line. The resulting output, therefore, has the capability to supply a *lot* of current.

I was making a measurement deep inside the circuitry, when I suddenly feel the sharpest, deepest, most searing, strongly vibrating pinch I've ever known, across my right hand. In order to get the test probes into position, I'd carelessly let my hand come across the 3,000 Volt DC accelerator supply! As I'd conditioned myself years earlier, my instinctive reaction jerked my hand just far enough to remove it from the offending connections, but not so far as to cause further damage or injury. As I took a step back, I suddenly felt a strong wave of adrenaline course through my body. And then the worst part…I felt like I was about to lose bladder control! I didn't, but it was the closest I'd ever come to that, and the shock was easily the most severe I'd ever experienced.

What kept me alive was the one-hand-rule. This is a technique where one hand – my left, since I'm right-handed – will be placed firmly in my back pocket, or on an insulated tabletop, while the dominant hand is used to enter the hostile environment. This absolutely ensures that high current voltage sources will never travel through my chest, therefore, my heart, as it would if it were to pass from one hand to the other. The very worst it can do is startle and burn a small portion of one hand – and maybe make a wet spot on the floor.

FETCHING WOMEN for PARTIES

Our college had a substantially male student population. It wasn't intentional. It just seemed to work out that way because, prior to the 1990s, women just weren't encouraged to go into engineering, thus perpetuating millennia-old stereotypes. As such, when the school had parties, there'd have been a very strong preponderance of guys there if we didn't "import women" from some of the surrounding schools. Since Columbus was considered a "college town", with something like a dozen colleges and universities within perhaps a ten-mile radius, it wasn't difficult to find women wanting to attend a party on a Friday night!

At one of the parties, some of us were asked to head to various school dorms where women had already expressed an interest in attending, but

YOUR SUCCESS - YOUR CHOICE

needed a ride. I was asked to go to a local "school of beauty", apparently one specializing in cosmetology. At that time, Bill and I were sharing a 1978 Pontiac Sunbird – a small 2-door hatchback with proper seating for three passengers comfortably, or four tightly if one sat in the middle of the back seat without a seatbelt. I managed to squeeze NINE of these young women into the car that night! They were doubled up all around. Three girls sat on the laps of the three sitting in the back seats. Another sat on the lap of the girl sitting in my passenger seat, and one sat in MY lap! Mine sat sideways to allow me to steer, see through the windshield just a bit, and shift the car. It might not have been the most legal thing, but I was sure that everyone was safe, and it sure was fun! Now, in retrospect, this is what I'd call a bad decision. But I'd had nothing to drink, and I *had* considered the ramifications of a worst-case scenario. As such, I was sure to drive slowly and carefully, and I'd asked the girls to keep me apprised of the presence of any vehicles around us in case I found a blind spot – such as from the boob that kept smacking me in the face each time I'd turn my head!

FEMALE ENGINEERING STUDENTS

As a result of an active push by the school's administration to interest more women in the field of electronics engineering, the fall term in 1978 produced four brand new female students in the bachelor's degree program. We met them at the incoming student mixer party held at the school. They were Sarah Beth Delaney, Stephanie Hale, Julie Warfel, and another whose name I can't recall. These three became very good friends, and significant to us both in our remaining time at the school. Bill and I "shared" Sarah – just as a good friend – in the beginning, until she started dating another guy about three months later. But that was okay, as, by then, I'd actually begun dating Stephanie, and Bill was getting interested in Julie.

Backing up just a bit...Sarah Beth was incredibly good-looking, and very intelligent, but when all of that was combined with her quaint, colloquial southern accent she absolutely pegged the cuteness meter! One weekend in the early fall, Sarah, Bill and I decided to have a picnic lunch at a local park. Sarah had made a Quiche Lorraine from scratch as a special picnic treat for us. After an idyllic picnic upon a standard picnic blanket covering a small patch of the warm, sun-drenched grass with a very beautiful young woman,

207

we packed up and took one of the scenic trails back to the car. The wind had picked up just a little and was gently blowing falling leaves about. I recall thinking, at the time, that it was just like that one line in Dan & John Ford Coley's "I'd Really Love to See You Tonight", where they say, "We could go walking through a windy park..." It was a magical, light, fun, and very satisfying day.

Later on, Bill and I had decided to return the favor of Sarah's quiche by building her something special that she might find cute. We'd designed a small "mouse" made entirely of electronic parts. No, this is not like the computer mouse that didn't even come into existence for another 10 – 15 years. This had a surprisingly similar appearance to a real mouse, only in a really cute way. We wired up a 555 Timer circuit to a red LED, and shoved it all inside a large, red, rubber alligator test clip boot, without the clip of course. After adding three thin strands of wire near the LED fashioned in a bit of a "bowtie" shape, which looked remarkably like whiskers, and a pair of ceramic disc capacitors for big mouse-like ears, we wrapped it in long, brown, furry fabric – probably from one of the all-too-popular shag rugs of the time. Adding a wire "tail" out the back it finished off the look. Of course, we also had to accommodate a 9 Volt battery and a power switch, but they were easily hidden inside the main body. We used a folded computer punch card as a sleeve to hold the battery. Shortly after we presented this cute, flashing electronic mouse to Sarah, her roommates, Julie and their other friend both wanted "mice" of their own. Stephanie was in another apartment with other roommates.

To accommodate their request, Bill and I went to their apartment the following weekend with the parts and tools needed to construct a new pair of electronic flashing mice. Julie helped us solder the components together and fit the parts into the boot and body. Her mouse substantially resembled Sarah's, but their other roommate chose to apply cotton balls around the circuitry to form something like an albino mouse body! Either way, both were functional and very cute. They loved them! To this day, I'm not sure if they also like ferrets.

THE F009 ERROR CODE

Many people today – specifically those born after about 1985 – will probably have a tough time visualizing the computers that we had to use for our classes in the late 1970s; they might even find it quite ludicrous that I'd never even SEEN a computer up close until I was 20! Now, I'm not talking about calculators that had come a long way, such as exhibiting many computer-like characteristics, since they'd first been introduced about four years prior. I'm talking about something that has a standard alphanumeric keyboard for input, and an output device with more than just eight numeric digits.

The first real computer that I'd ever seen was a huge IBM 1130, model 4B. It, and its needed peripherals (such as the IBM punch card reader, and a line printer), occupied a substantial portion of a large glass-enclosed room in the school. Such a computer would have cost around $35,000 in 1971, shortly after the school was established. This is equivalent to more than $205,000 in today's dollars! It's not exactly what you'd call a "personal computer"!

Just outside of this hallowed chamber, where only a trained operator was allowed entry, was a row of three or four "keypunch" machines. This was as close as us mere mortals were normally allowed to approach the sacred computer. We'd sit at one of the keypunch machines and type out our FORTRAN IV programs. Each line of code was encoded onto a single IBM punch card. Therefore, a program with 100 lines of code would require 100 punch cards. They were called punch cards because the machine literally punched small rectangular holes into the card to numerically represent the line of code that was also printed on the top of the card.

Once we'd completed the arduous task of typing out a stack of punch cards, we'd place that "job" into a cubbyhole just outside of the computer room. Then, sometime overnight, the operator would mysteriously intercept the cards, run the program, and then re-deposit the finished job, now wrapped in a printout of the results, back into the same cubbyhole for us to pick up the next morning. We never actually saw the computer operate. It was like a purely mythical, nocturnal creature, being fed and coming to life only at night! The only evidence that anything at all had occurred was the new presence of the wide green and white fanfold paper encircling our cards, which included a full listing of the program, the printed results, and, if it didn't work as you'd expected, which it usually didn't, an error code in extremely large letters across the entire printout!

This error code could have signified any of hundreds of syntax, formatting, or other kinds of simple errors. But the error code that was not tolerated by our instructors was F009! Pronounced, "Foo Nine". On this system, it represented an infinite loop. The instructors firmly believed that there was no acceptable excuse for writing a loop that would never exit in your program, thus locking up the system. Because the operator had to forcefully abort the program in such a case, the printout would consist only of the command listing done before it began executing the code, and it would have "F009" manually scrawled across it in thick marker, instead of the standard printed characters, making it seem like a much more personal affront.

Now, I was always very careful with my code, and took great pride in the fact that all of my loops had logical exits within the program. There would be no infinite loops associated with any of *my* programs! This is why I was so very surprised and really a bit upset when, this one morning when I went to the computer room and picked up my job, I saw it! The kiss of death! F009 was angrily etched into the front sheet of my printout in thick red marker! Hoping nobody else had noticed it, I made a hasty exit to one of the study tables in the Upper Commons area and started poring through each and every line of code associated with any loops.

After what seemed like hours, and I just couldn't find *any* problems with my code, I brought my job back into the computer room where I knocked on the glass surrounding the inner sanctum. I knew the operator from one of my classes, so I asked him if he could do me a huge favor and run my job while I stood there – that's right, in real time! Cue scary music! Just by making such a request, I felt certain that I was about to cause the implosion of the universe. I'd be violating one of the most holy rules of the computer room.

Anyway, he wasn't very busy at that moment, so he agreed. After what seemed like an eternity – literally three seconds to read *each* punch card! – it finally executed the program. We waited a bit, and then he brought my attention to the lights on the main console. They were all sort of half-illuminated, as if stuck in a loop. My program performed iterative complex computations to produce points in the form of "X"s on a graphical chart. The method I'd used to generate the outputs essentially cut the value by one half with each pass. Therefore, the value would never reach zero – just like Zeno's Paradox. But I wasn't testing for a zero value to kick it out of the loop. I was just looking for the change in values to be less than a certain value for just 1,000 iterations – something I'd expected that it'd run through in a small fraction of a second. I was, therefore, most surprised when I saw the console lights appear to lock up.

But, since I knew what was going on in my program, I told him just to wait a bit. After a solid 30-seconds had passed it DID, finally kick out, as designed! I hadn't realized just how lethargically S L O W this computer really was! After that, I reduced the test loop to just ten iterations, and re-submitted it for my grade, and it was, of course, a success!

THE MINICOMPUTER and THE FIRST VIRUS

Later in the year I took an Assembly Language Programming class. I was very excited about this class because the school had JUST purchased and installed a brand new "minicomputer" for the advanced programming classes. In order to boot up the machine, we had to flip eight address switches, and eight data switches in a specific sequence, while loading each location of memory with the selected data. It could take fifteen minutes to complete the fairly substantial boot-up sequence.

The manual boot sequence was definitely a headache, but the IMSAI-8080 minicomputer we used did have some great advantages. See the illustration titled Early Minicomputer at the top of this chapter. The most amazing feature of this minicomputer was that we could sit at any of perhaps a dozen monochrome Hazeltine video terminals with an attached keyboard, type in our programs, and then watch them run... while we sat there! Another nice aspect of this minicomputer was that it was SO much faster than the antiquated IBM 1130 machine! That 1,000-iteration loop in my previous FORTRAN program would take only a couple of milliseconds (thousandths of a second) to complete!

At the time, I never thought anything odd about this one task that we were assigned in the class, but now, as I look back, I see that it was the very basis of a computer virus! The class assignment required us to initially enter our programs – in Assembly Language – into a specific region in memory. The function of our program was to copy the contents of the memory in the specified locations, into a new location in memory, and then clear out the original code. That replication process is a classic virus, and could, if not properly limited, monopolize the entire memory, including important system locations, thus corrupting the operating system and shutting it down – not that we ever did that. Okay, maybe we did, but not a lot!

THE LARGEST LIQUID CRYSTAL DISPLAY EVER MADE

By this time Bill and I had built a reputation around the school administration and staff as being very competent with practical electronic projects. Basically, we just knew our stuff – probably the result of having worked with electronic circuits since we were about eight! I suppose, therefore, we shouldn't have been very surprised when Jim Wagoner, one of the administration people, contacted us with a proposal. He had started a small R&D (Research & Development) company on the side called American Liquitronics. He needed some technical assistance. One thing he was trying to do was to manufacture and sell electronic novelties, but he also had a fairly well-equipped chemistry lab set up where he had a chemist, Don Simmons, working on cutting-edge liquid crystal display technology.

The first project we designed for Jim W. was a sound-activated chirping ball of fur. He gave us this small (8-inch diameter) soft fabric ball covered with long, bright blue, soft feathery strands. We were to design and build the circuit to be installed inside this fur ball. We did, of course, and it worked nicely. If you clapped or made a loud enough sound near it, it would begin a brief serenade of chirps, and a pair of LEDs would make its eyes flash. Sally, Jim's wife, had affixed a rudimentary "face" onto the device, to make it look more like a pet than just a ball of fur. While not quite the same as the hugely popular "Furby" first sold in 1998, there were substantial similarities. Unfortunately, it seemed that the market just wasn't ready for something like that yet, so they never sold any.

We'd also discussed installing flexible circuit boards into T-shirts so that they could display various patterns with a matrix of LEDs. That project never got off of the ground as flexible circuit board material was very expensive and not very flexible back then. Also, the number of LEDs required drove the cost way up, as well. We figured there'd be very little market for a $200 (equal to $750 today!) T-shirt that would end up being very stiff and couldn't be washed. Its only real benefit was that it lit up!

These were apparently side projects that Jim was trying to sell in order to help finance the primary function of his R&D company. That was the development of novel liquid crystal displays. With Don Simmons' chemical expertise, and with Bill and me assisting, we succeeded in building the world's largest functional liquid crystal display...at the time. We helped Don photographically apply the photoresist to the front sheet of ¼ inch thick, indium-tin-oxide (ITO) coated glass, and then remove the unwanted, transparent ITO coating by pouring hydrochloric acid over it. After that, Don placed a number of microscopic plastic spacers all about the large plates of glass, and then dabbed a tiny drop of cholesteric liquid crystal into the middle before sealing them together.

Once the epoxy had cured, we applied an alternating current to the two wires now protruding from this heavy chunk of glass plates about 16 inches by 20 inches in size. The area beneath the remaining pattern of ITO turned a frosted white, clearly revealing the pattern. It worked! This was the largest liquid crystal display ever built, at that time.

THE TV STUDIO

There were a number of interesting clubs at the school. Well...for those who had technical interests, anyway. One such club was the TV Production Club. We joined this club because it was held in the glass-enclosed (fishbowl) TV studio, with big, studio TV cameras setting on hefty tripod-dollies, and an adjoining control room with big, professional 1-inch tape reel-to-reel VTRs. With our strong interest in all things video, the very sight of this accumulation of high-tech video equipment had us virtually drooling!

We were, naturally, most disappointed when we learned that none of the TV cameras actually worked! Apparently, several prior students, who didn't know what they were doing, had worked on the video circuitry inside the cameras for some reason, and ended up causing all three of them to become non-functional! Now, this wouldn't have been so bad, as we figured we could just repair them like we did with every other piece of broken electronic equipment we'd ever encountered. The problem was, after this incident with the prior students, the administration sent down an edict forbidding any student from touching the cameras!

Mike Wentz was the Teaching Assistant (TA) assigned to the defunct TV studio. He had a 1ˢᵗ class FCC Commercial Radiotelephone Operator License, which allowed him to, among other things, work on commercial broadcasting equipment and transmitters. Due to this, and the disappointing non-usability of the studio's video equipment, he re-defined the club, calling it the "Broadcasting Careers Club", or BCC for short. It had two purposes under that name: 1) Members would prepare for their own Commercial FCC Licenses (3ʳᵈ, 2ⁿᵈ, or 1ˢᵗ Class), and 2) Members would produce audio newscasts to be played through the school's PA system.

With this tutelage, I was successful in earning my 2ⁿᵈ-Class Commercial license, which allowed me to work on non-commercial transmitters such as amateur radios and CB radios, but not commercial broadcast transmitters. A couple of years later, the FCC combined the 2ⁿᵈ-Class and 1ˢᵗ-Class licenses into one, calling it the General Radiotelephone Operator License, thereby, upgrading my license to the privileges of the 1ˢᵗ-Class by default.

Knowing our strong interest and competence in video equipment, Mike asked Bill and me to stay a bit one evening after the BCC meeting was over. He told us of a proposition to bring new life to the club, but it would mean defying the administration. He needed our assistance to make it work, though, and we heartily agreed! So, the next evening, around 7 or 8pm when we'd expected that most of the administrators would have left, we convened at the studio and drew the curtains closed, just to be sure. We brought a couple of oscilloscopes down from the lab and started making measurements on the internal video circuit boards of these huge, ancient color TV cameras. That first evening, we succeeded in aligning the gain and offset controls of one of the three, color video channels in one of the three cameras, thus allowing it to produce a high-quality B&W picture! Over the next few nights, we got another camera aligned to produce a B&W image and aligned the circuits of the other two color video channels of the first camera, thus producing a full-color picture in that camera!

With this success, we made a deliberate decision to open up the curtains and start using the cameras during the day to actually produce a real *video* newscast! It didn't take long for the administration to notice that the cameras were actually being USED, and clearly functioning! We went on to get color functionality on the second camera, and B&W capability on the third, but we were now boldly doing these alignments during the day with the curtains *open*. We were more than a little bit surprised with the reaction from the administration.

Instead of admonishing Mike, Bill and me for going against their edict, they thanked us for getting the studio functional again! But that wasn't the best part. They also gave the club a check for $17,000 (equal to $64,000 today!), which they'd been withholding over the past few years basically as punishment to the prior club members for damaging the equipment. Now that the three of us had demonstrated to the administration that we were competent, and would take care of the equipment, they wanted us to use that money to buy all new equipment! With this money, the club was able to purchase three brand new, much smaller, state-of-the-art, studio-quality color JVC TV cameras, two brand new JVC Video Cassette Recorders (VCR) – both with full editing capability – and a completely self-contained video "port-a-pack", for remote newscasts! It was better than Christmas to us!!!

CHAPTER 18 – 1979; AGE TWENTY-ONE

The Lab Competition, The Video Frame Memory, Special Effects Generator, and Light pen, First Sex

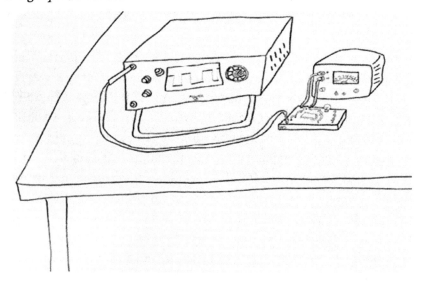

The Lab Competition

In 1979, the average house cost $58,100, the typical annual income was about $17,500, a new car cost about $5,000, and gas cost $0.86 per gallon. The Three Mile Island nuclear accident in Pennsylvania occurred, and 63 Americans were taken hostage in the American Embassy in Tehran. VisiCalc became the first spreadsheet program, and Sony introduced the Sony Walkman. Voyager I revealed Jupiter's rings, the snowboard is invented, and the first commercial cellular network (NTT) was established.

THE LAB COMPETITION

Having demonstrated our proficiency with designing, building and testing practical circuits in the lab, repairing lab equipment, making circuits for Jim Wagoner, and assisting Mike Wentz to repair all of the studio TV cameras, our capabilities hadn't gone unnoticed. Walter Hawkins, our supervisor in the lab, had even petitioned the administration to allow Bill and me to earn a wage equal to the TAs, due to our exceptional performance and capabilities…and it was granted!

It was, therefore, not a great surprise when Bill and I were selected by the school administration that spring to represent our entire school in a national lab practical competition! Student teams from each of about six or eight engineering schools nationwide convened at our school lab for this competition. Each team consisted of two or three students from their respective schools. Each team station in the lab had the same kit of parts, and a sheaf of papers describing each of the ten projects, showing schematic diagrams, and indicating the required measurements from the completed circuits that would confirm a satisfactory build.

The intent for this competition was for each school's team to build each described circuit on a proto board, apply power, take the applicable measurements and waveforms, get a faculty proctor to sign it off if correct, and move onto the next project, repeating the process, until done. See the illustration titled Lab Competition at the top of this chapter. There was a one- or two-hour time limit for the competition. We truly had no idea where any of the other teams were in the series of projects, as we were strongly concentrating fully upon our own projects. Once the proctors indicated that the competition was over, and Bill and I had only completed seven of the ten projects, we felt defeated – that is, until we learned that the next closest competitor had completed only *four* of the projects!

Our "prize" was the equivalent of getting an "A" in an additional class put in our respective transcripts.

THE LIGHT PEN

As my big project was the Programmable Digital Sequencer device I'd built the prior year, Bill's big project was a video frame memory and special effects generator. Coupled with this, we'd discovered that we could use a photocell to create a "light-pen" which allowed us to move a white box around the screen of a TV! Okay…we were easily amused.

EDUCATED, GRADUATED, DEGREED, EMPLOYED, and SATISFIED!

Bill and I would be graduating in the fall of 1979 with our engineering bachelor's degrees. We'd also both already accepted our very first professional engineering job offers at large defense contractors in California, where we'd begin earning eight to ten times what we had been while in school. This would, therefore, be the last summer that we'd spend at Eckel's Lake. By that time, we'd gotten to know many of the lifeguards and regulars there pretty well. Still, I was most surprised when Mandy (not her real name), one of the lifeguards, asked me to come with her as her date to a special end-of-season celebratory dinner with the rest of the Eckel's Lake staff. I thought it could be fun to socialize with her and some of the other guards.

Despite a bit of a fiasco with the dessert, I was actually somewhat pleased when she asked me to take her to a drive-in movie the following weekend. I suppose I shouldn't be surprised about what happened next – I mean, it *was* a drive-in, after all. Let's just say that we saw very little of the movie at first, and then even less when we headed back to her parent's farm after just a short while. They were gone for a couple of days, so we had the house to ourselves. This was, in fact, my very first time getting intimate with a woman, and it was quite nice. As I still had my grand plans yet to accomplish, I had no intention of getting her pregnant, which would derail those plans, so, of course, I practiced safe sex!

REAL-LIFE ADVENTURES
SECTION 6 – ACCOMPLISHED GOALS AND OTHER SELECTED STORIES AFTER COLLEGE

CHAPTER 19 – GYMNASTICS

Bob Doing a Back Handspring

STARTING GYMNASTICS AT 21

In 1979 Bill and I were both 21, we'd just graduated college, and moved to California to begin our engineering careers. I landed in Southern California, and Bill found Northern California. It was the very first time in our lives that we'd been apart from each other for more than a day or two, and we were definitely ready to establish our own individual identities and start dating women who liked each of us for our own individual attributes, and not just for the novelty of experiencing a twin.

In order to attract datable/marriageable women, I obviously wanted to present myself in the best manner possible. This meant that I couldn't let myself go physically, like so many other engineers I'd known in school had done after graduation. I was suddenly earning eight to ten times what I did while in school, so it was only natural to splurge a bit with meals that I could never have afforded previously. This meant that I had to find some sort of physical activity to keep me fit. I enrolled into gymnastics classes at a gym in Anaheim that offered such classes to adult students.

To briefly recap about how we stayed in shape previously, we'd run around our parents' yards with made-up games, climb trees, and ride our bikes everywhere when we were very young. Once we got into high school, we were still riding our bikes quite a bit, until we started to drive. At that point, our physical activity was reduced to just gym classes in school...that is, until we started skating regularly at the local roller rink. We found this to be a remarkably good aerobic activity, which we naturally continued when we went to college. In addition to the summers at Eckel's Lake's water gymnasium, the skating helped keep us fit throughout school.

Because I was already in good physical condition, and quite strong from staying very active, it wasn't very long before I became an accomplished gymnast. I did floor exercise routines, as well as my share of work on the rings, parallel bars, and high bar, but I really concentrated on the strength and flexibility aspects required for good, high-energy, tumbling routines on the floor.

Gymnastics is a very young sport. By that I don't mean that the *sport* itself is young – it's not. In fact, it was one of the few sports performed at the very first Olympic event held in Olympia, Greece around 700BC. When I say it's a young sport, what I mean is that, due to the physical rigors and flexibility required, most of the *participants* are very young. In fact, it's most unusual when you see a female gymnast in an Olympic competition, older than 18. Men generally top out at about 25. Of course, since I had no Olympic aspirations, I wasn't concerned about just *starting* my gymnastics fun at 21.

Why gymnastics? Well, for me, it was because I despise exercising, but I love doing fun physical activities that also happen to result in a great workout. There is no sport or activity other than gymnastics that naturally provides such a complete and intense workout by building strength, flexibility, and overall body fitness. Unlike the stiff, bulky, bulbous muscles of bodybuilders, gymnasts develop lean, functional muscles that enable us to be extremely strong while maintaining the considerable flexibility required to throw ourselves through the air gracefully and safely.

BACK HANDSPRINGS AND WHIP BACKS

Speaking of throwing my body through the air, I desperately wanted to do back handsprings like I'd seen the Olympic gymnasts do, but for more than a year I felt like I was just a sack of potatoes. I lacked power. I'd do a round off into a back handspring, but then I'd just barely get through it, and land just standing there – no power at all! Then, one day it occurred to me that I was holding back. I was being *too careful*. I guess I felt that I'd be safer if I didn't put too much power into it…kind of like not wanting to lose control. In fact, it was quite the opposite; adding power was actually safer! Finally realizing this, I decided, just before going into my next round-off back-handspring attempt, to literally throw caution to the wind, and simply go full out! All of a sudden I found myself flying through the air with height and distance like I'd never experienced before! Since I didn't know quite what to expect that very first time, I wasn't ready for the extreme spring I'd have at the end. Where I used to just come back to the ground at the end, and remain fixed there like a ton of bricks, this time I bounced strongly, ending up high in the air again, feeling like a feather, thus landing rather gracelessly upon my back.

The next time, however, I was ready for it, and, instead of ending it there with a single back handspring, I threw myself into another, and another, and then another! I had SO MUCH POWER suddenly that these flip-flops (multiple back handsprings are called "flip-flops") became virtually effortless (see the photo titled Bob Doing a Back Handspring at the top of this chapter showing me doing one such back handspring when I was 25)! And that's when I discovered the *whip back*. The more handsprings I'd do in my set of flip-flops, the more height I'd get with each one – eventually causing my hands to become superfluous! A whip back is very much like a back handspring, except your hands don't touch the ground (except in the round off) – I had enough power to go directly from my feet back to my feet. Before the whip back, I thought that flip-flops were amazingly fun. The whip back, however, makes flip-flops seem quite banal by comparison. Yeah…I really loved doing whip backs!

THE NEAR MISS...OR WAS IT A NEAR HIT?

Once everyone in our class started getting pretty good with flip-flops, our coach would have us throw fifty of them – ten sets of five – along one of the diagonals of the spring floor...*as a warm up!* Occasionally, we'd be sharing the floor with another class. I remember this one time when we were tumbling on adjacent diagonals with the advanced girls team. One of us in the adult class would signal to the person waiting on the other diagonal, and they'd throw their set of five flip-flops. Then, a team girl would signal our side that she'd be doing a set. It went back and forth just like that, alternately, for many passes. The signals were subtle – usually just a quick glance, making eye contact, and a slight nod of understanding from the other side.

This one time, I looked over to the next team girl in line – my signal that I'd be going next. Apparently, she didn't get the memo. Unbeknownst to me, she began her run at the very same moment that I did! We were both SO strongly focused on a spot on the floor immediately in front of us where we'd be setting our hands for the round off, that neither one saw the other heading on a collision course! I was into my second of five back handsprings when I felt something odd; like something had brushed up against me.

Now, gymnastics is an extremely mental activity. If your mind isn't prepared for a particular maneuver, you'll never accomplish it, no matter how strong or flexible you are. When you're flying through the air, you can't be *thinking* of what to do next. It HAS to be completely automatic. It's called "muscle memory". When it "feels right", you'll do well. But, if something feels "off" just a bit, then your body doesn't know what to do next, and your mind can't react in time. This will cause you to "freak". By "freaking", I mean that you just stop doing the automatic action you'd started – you freeze! That's what happened just after I'd entered my second back handspring in that particular run.

I freaked, froze, and fell, rather gracelessly onto the spring floor on my back! It wasn't until afterward that I learned that the team girl had done her flip-flop run at the very same time that I had. We had actually "meshed" together in our handsprings! What could have been a catastrophic side-on crash was, instead, a simple brushing of limbs. Had I been prepared for this, I could have finished my set without incident. Instead, my body aborted my continued flip-flops immediately! Of course, I wasn't at all hurt – just *very* much surprised.

HANDSPRINGS AND HILLS

Doing gymnastics well is nearly intoxicating! In fact, anytime I'd see a wide stretch of lawn, such as in a park, I was strongly compelled to throw a set of flip-flops with whip backs! Of course, the terrain in parks isn't always level like the tumbling spring floor in the gym. I soon learned that, despite the incredible ease of tumbling down a slight hill, there was one somewhat notable drawback; I couldn't stop! At first, I was reaching new heights in my tumbling, doing whip back after whip back with increasing altitude in each, and it felt incredible. When tumbling on a level floor, I know how much power to put into a back handspring or whip back to land properly on my feet and launch into the next. But, when tumbling downhill, my feet would consistently find the ground lower than where I'd launched, thus increasing the amount of rotation, thereby putting me on an ever-increasing backward angle each time I'd land. My only options were to try and stop, falling onto my back – not my most favored choice – or keep on tumbling! Tumbling is fun. Falling is not. I think the choice is obvious. Unfortunately, the advantage of Option #2 is only temporary since the landing angle is cumulative in this situation. Therefore, even that option soon turns into Option #1, because, at some point I'd invariably get so much height that I'd find my feet "missing the ground", and I'd *still* end up on my back! Moral; don't tumble downhill if you don't want to crash.

GIANT SWINGS ON HIGH BAR

I'm sure that just about every kid has tried to swing so high, on a swing set, that they feel like they might go around the top! I know I did when I was younger. I think this is why it was so fun when I learned how to do giant swings on the gymnastics high bar! I'd kick up to a handstand on top of the bar, and then allow gravity to pull my body over, as if I was falling forward. Once my feet had swung down, and started coming up behind the bar, I'd give a slight pull with my arms, to add the "nudge" of power needed to overcome friction, and not violate the conservation of energy, thus pushing me over the top. That is the giant swing, broken down.

223

Now I found giant swings to be extremely relaxing! I could swing around the bar for several minutes before having to stop to let my forearms have a break. Just for variety, I'd play around by pulling my legs in so that it was like I was basically "sitting" cross-legged as I swung around the bar. This reduction of my center-of-mass, of course, significantly increased the speed of my rotation like a spinning skater, which was, of course, great fun! I also tried different head positions. Normally, when doing giant swings on high bar, you'll be looking straight out in front of you, like when you're standing. Again, for variety, I'd either turn my head to the side, looking out at the gym spinning around in circles, or I'd look directly at the bar. I should mention that looking at the bar while doing giant swings will cause a psychophysical sensation that is not entirely unlike what you'd feel going down the big drop on a roller coaster! Yeah, I really liked giant swings on high bar!

THE OLD TIMER'S MEET

I continued to do gymnastics, off and on, until I was 41 years old. In fact, while I'd done a fair number of gymnastics exhibitions throughout the years, I'd never competed…until I was 40, and living in northern Virginia. In November 1998 I signed up to do a gymnastics competition called an "Old Timer's Meet" to be held in December! Now, "old timer" in gymnastics vernacular means anybody 25 and older. As a reminder, male gymnasts have just hit their prime at 25, so us *actual* old-timers would be competing against some very capable gymnasts in this meet. While I very much enjoyed doing individual floor exercise tumbling maneuvers, I'd never before put together an entire routine. My coach helped me assemble a number of strength moves in addition to several powerful tumbling runs. The first time I went through the entire series at one time, I started getting winded after just the second diagonal tumbling run, and when I started into my third, I was running across the spring floor about to enter a round off whip back set, when my legs just turned into jelly! I crumbled into the mat! I NEEDED to improve my endurance – FAST! I just kept doing the routine until I built up the needed endurance, in very short order. Finally, I was ready for the competition, which was the just the next weekend.

I performed my tumbling routine and *didn't* come in last place! This was very gratifying to me, considering the younger age of the other competitors.

After everybody had completed their routines on the various apparatus, the announcer indicated that there was to be one final competition: a stationary handstand contest. For this, the owner of the gym, who was also 40, joined in. The idea of this contest was for everyone to kick up to a handstand and remain stationary for as long as possible. We weren't allowed to make a single step. Our hands had to remain fixed in place the moment they hit the floor. Any hand movement, and we'd be disqualified and had to come down.

It was quite the sight in my peripheral vision as I kicked up with something like 30 others all around me, all in unison. Instead of seeing the gym going upside down like normal, it seemed that it remained normal since everybody else was inverted as well! That is, assuming that we were now all hanging onto the ceiling, as the floor had just apparently become! As I was concentrating on my own situation, I was somewhat oblivious of anything happening around me after first kicking up...until I heard the announcer call out saying, "All of you young guys should be ashamed of yourselves! The two oldest guys here have already beat you!" Another minute or two and my shoulders were absolutely burning, but I wasn't about to be the first of the two of us remaining, to come down! Finally, a cheer came up from the crowd that I took to mean that the gym owner had come down. Still, I held on for a bit more just to be sure. Finally, with jelly arms, I came down and found myself to be the recipient of the trophy for the stationary handstand contest!

Chapter 20 – PHOTOGRAPHING BEAUTIFUL MODELS

Michelle Modeling in the Mirror

MY FIRST REAL CAMERA

It was August 1980, soon after I'd bought my first car, when I purchased my very first good camera! All through high school, I'd seen the photographer kids. These were the ones who walked around all of the time with a beautiful 35mm camera hanging from their necks, and whose pictures made up much of the background material for each of the school yearbooks. They were the ones with nice cameras. I desperately wanted a nice camera with which I could preserve in photographs the scenes and people that I'd encountered, but I just couldn't afford one.

Our parents had heard Bill and me lamenting about a camera, so they did what they could for us. For our high school graduation, we each received a 110 Instamatic Kodak camera. Now, while I substantially appreciate the thought behind this, if you're at all familiar with the 110-size film medium and the camera that uses it, you'd know that it was really more of a taunt than a treat.

For those who don't have this familiarity, I'll explain. The problem was two-fold. The first issue was the film size. It was just 13x17mm (about half an inch by two thirds of an inch), or about one quarter of the area of 35mm film (at 24x36mm). The second problem was the "lens". It was a poor variant on the pinhole concept. As such, it was billed as having "everything in focus", but I'd contend that the more accurate descriptor would be "nothing in focus"! The best image we could get under the most optimal conditions like bright daylight would be a fuzzy shape that might be a dog, or it could be a mountain landscape. You really just couldn't be sure. Okay…I'll admit that it wasn't *quite* that bad, but a bit of hyperbole never hurt to get a point across! Again, I didn't have enough money during college to replace my awful camera with something useful, so I stuck it out until I'd graduated and had much more than enough disposable income to get a nice camera.

Knowing absolutely nothing at all about photography at the time, I headed to JC Penney and bought a Minolta XD-11 35mm Single-Lens Reflex (SLR) camera with a 50mm lens – based substantially on the recommendations of the salesperson. At the time, a department store like Penney's seemed like a reasonable place to get a good deal on a camera. Still, I recall it being the largest purchase I'd ever made, with the exception of my car. It was $250, which would be $760 today.

I took my beautiful, brand new 35mm Minolta camera home and set it aside, and then I actually read the operator's manual from front to back! For something this expensive, I wanted to be absolutely certain that I fully understood what I was doing. I started experimenting, shooting all sorts of simple still life scenes all around my apartment. The prints from those first few rolls of film were dismal at the very best! I desperately wanted better results from this very expensive machine, so I found a camera store, and asked for advice. They recommended that I use slide (transparency) film instead of the print (negative) film – well, that and a new lens that they were more than happy to sell me.

The reason for the slide film was so that I'd be able to see the precise results from each exposure directly on the film, instead of what some minimum wage mini-lab photo processor operator *thought* I wanted in a print! This made an *incredible* difference, and soon, a significant improvement in my results! The new lens was a 135mm lens of mediocre quality, but it was a very effective portrait lens…if only I had anyone to take portraits of!

Now, while I didn't know it then, the Minolta XD-11 was actually an exceptional camera body for its time. Sold as the "XD-7" outside of North America, and as just the "XD" in Japan, it sold from 1977 through 1984, and was Minolta's top of the line camera when it came out. It was distinguished from the competition by offering a most unique set of exposure and operating modes.

Nikon's F2, introduced in 1972, is ostensibly the first SLR that integrated an electronic light meter with the shutter control mechanism, thus creating the very first Aperture Priority auto-exposure system in a 35mm SLR. By 1974, Canon, Konica, Miranda, Petri, Ricoh and Topcon were sporting Shutter Priority auto-exposure modes, while Nikon, Minolta, Asahi, Pentax, Chinon, Cosina, Fujica, and Yashica offered Aperture Priority. It wasn't until 1977 when Minolta introduced the XD-11 that *both* auto-exposure modes were to be found in *one* camera: the XD-11. This camera also provided still another unique feature. Not seen in 35mm SLR cameras for many years by then, the XD-11 offered a completely *mechanical* operating mode!

Why would Minolta bring back this blast from the past? Backup! But how likely is this ever to happen? Well, let me give you an example that may or may not have actually happened.

Let's say you're shooting in a remote location on Kauai, like Hanakapiai Beach. All of a sudden, your camera battery dies, and the camera refuses to operate! You hadn't thought to pack extra batteries, since they normally last for years, and the closest civilization that might carry such batteries is about a 1.5-hour hike back to Ke'e Beach, and then about a 30-minute drive to Princeville. In reality, this is more like a 4.5-hour round trip when including shopping time. What will you do? What *will* you do?! You'll switch to the "O" mode, which obviously standing for "Mechanical"! Sure, you can't meter, but since you're shooting 100 ISO film and the shutter speed is fixed at $1/100^{th}$ second in this all-mechanical operating mode, and you just stop down the lens to f/16 and continue shooting, using the "sunny 16 rule"! This is precisely what may or may not have happened! (Based on two actual events, combined into one for brevity)

Having read the camera manual, I knew that I could set it to the "aperture priority" automatic mode, set the aperture where I wanted, and observe how the camera set the shutter speed. I took copious notes with each and every exposure and then compared those notes with the processed slide results. In doing so, I soon discovered a very interesting reciprocal relationship between the aperture setting and the shutter speed, which was linearly offset by the film speed. All three were interdependent upon each other, as well as the intensity of the light from the scene! This beautifully elegant mathematical relationship – all multiples of the square root of two – fascinated my engineer brain! I hadn't expected to find such beautiful science buried in an instrument meant to create beautiful art! THIS was the focal point I'd been unwittingly looking for; the place where science overlapped art! I also picked up a flash and my very first book about photography; "The Photographer's Handbook" by John Hedgecoe. This reference confirmed the concepts I'd already discovered on my own, plus it helped me understand composition and lighting.

I practiced shooting (photographically) everything I could find for the next couple of months, thirsty for any new opportunity to develop my newfound skills! As the local camera store had become like a second home to me by then, it would have been difficult for me not to notice a local rag publication called "Western Photographer Magazine" that they always had stacked up on the checkout counter.

SOUTHERN CALIFORNIA PHOTO DAYS

It was late October when I noted, in the current issue of WP magazine, that there was a model photo shoot at a local park coming up on the following weekend – on the 26th. I'd never photographed people before this, and I was most interested to try. This seemed like an ideal opportunity for this to happen.

Armed with my well-broken-in camera, my brand-new flash with remote cable, a pack full of lens filters, and $3 cash for the privilege of photographing a dozen models for four hours, I arrived at Pioneer Park in Anaheim that Sunday morning. The scene was surreal. Throughout the park there were a dozen isolated groups of dozens of photographers, all gathered around each model, with flashes lighting up the surrounding areas like a fierce electrical storm!

Had I mentioned before that I was painfully shy? While my personal relationships in college had significantly helped my confidence in the presence of women, these weren't just *any* women. These women were quite attractive *models*! Still, I put my insecurities aside and forged ahead with a faux confidence that seemed to work. I was very soon right in there among the other photographers, getting the model's eyes directed to my camera, and even suggesting poses!

These Southern California events, called "Photo Days", were a "win-win" for all participants. The model agencies would get a small amount of money from each photographer; the models would get experience posing and working with photographers; photographers would get experience using their cameras, working with light, and working with models. The models would also get 8x10 prints for their portfolios from the photographers when they entered their best photos into the contest associated with each Photo Day. The photographers with the winning prints, would see their names and photos published in Western Photographer Magazine, and they'd receive a trophy at the next logical event. Everybody won!

While there were perhaps a dozen Photo Day events around the Southern California region EVERY weekend throughout the year, it might be a month or two before the same agency showed up at a Photo Day with the winning trophies from a prior Photo Day's contest.

Despite my never having photographed a portrait before, I thought that some of the photos I created that first time weren't too bad, so I submitted a few to the contest. Imagine my considerable surprise when, at the next Pioneer Park Photo Day on January 18, 1981, they announced my name for *first place* in the color print category!

The agency owner asked me conversationally, "So how long have you been doing portraits?"

I told him, "Before this photo, I'd never done a single portrait."

He said, with caution in his voice, "Don't mention that to the other photogs.

Some of them have been trying to place in a contest for years!"

I kept my mouth shut.

And that was the beginning of my photographic adventures.

Over the course of the next five and a half years, I attended somewhere between three and six Photo Days every month, shooting an average of three rolls (108 frames total) of film per event. There were also quite a few Photo Days held at private outdoor locations where photographers could practice the creation of artistic nudes. The agencies associated with these "nude shoots" charged $25 per photographer to work with these models for the typical four-hour period. One of the more notable nude shoots was at an authentic western town attraction that the agency apparently rented for the day. There were a lot of great period props, including wooden fences, hitching posts, a saloon, wooden porches, an old-fashioned jail, and even some horses that we could use for posing the models. The nude models juxtaposed against the rough outdoor western backdrop in the light rain that day, made for a most compelling contrast, and really great images! For those who are curious, these models walked around the place the entire afternoon completely naked, except for the occasional partial outfit for a prop.

PHOTOGRAPHING MISS AMERICA

A year after I got my 35mm camera and began winning numerous awards for model portraits, I decided that I should probably take a photography class through a local community college – just to see what I'd missed through my self-education. I was a bit surprised that, not only had I covered everything in the instructor's curriculum, but she actually asked *me* to teach the section on night photography, as she hadn't done much herself, while I'd become rather accomplished with that particular technique.

We were given various assignments during this class. The subject matter wasn't the important part. It was the demonstration of a specific technique. For instance, we'd have to demonstrate the effects of using different apertures, or different shutter speeds, and how they affected the appearance of the images. With one such assignment to fulfill this one Saturday in September 1981, I decided to head down to the Disneyland Hotel, as it was very picturesque there, and not far from where I lived. I took many photos of a gazebo and various flowers on the grounds around the front and side of the hotel complex, and then I eventually ventured to the back where there was a lot of activity. At first, I wasn't sure what it was, as there were lots of television cameras, an announcer, and several events taking place in front of throngs of people all about.

Eventually I learned that it was an event called "H_2Olympics" – whose purpose still eludes me to this day. Anyway, it was rather warm under the direct sun where all of the activity was taking place, so I sought shelter in a nearby building on the grounds. As I had no schedule to keep, it felt good to enjoy the air conditioning for a while as I observed the activity through a tall window. After a bit a woman came up to me and asked if I was a photographer. Now, I've got my 35mm camera draped around my neck, and my full camera pack hanging from my shoulder, so it seemed somewhat incredible that anyone might seriously ask that question! With a touch of sarcasm in my voice, due to the obviousness of the situation, I replied, "Apparently."

She introduced herself, saying, "I'm Earlene Jones, director of the Miss Anaheim/Miss America Pageant Committee." She handed me a business card and continued, "Our official photographer hasn't shown up, so I was wondering if you'd be able to take pictures of my girls in the bikini show for us. It'll be starting in a few minutes."

I first had to consider my extremely busy schedule for that day, so it was probably something like a nanosecond before I replied as coolly as I could muster while trying to contain my excitement for this great opportunity, "Sure. I can do that."

"Good." She replied. "Let me get you an official press pass so you'll be able to get right up front."

She returned a moment later with a laminated card with a pin on the back to attach it to my shirt. It had "**PRESS**" emblazoned upon it in large, bold type. She introduced me to the current Miss Anaheim 1981, Dana Cody, so I'd know who to concentrate on, and then I gave Ms Jones my contact information. That done; I put on the badge and headed out to make my way through the sea of people. It wasn't long before the bikini show commenced with perhaps a dozen or so young women vying to become the next Miss Anaheim.

One of these beautiful, bikini-clad women was Debra Sue Maffett. She went on to become Miss Anaheim in March 1982, then Miss California in the summer, and, finally, Miss America 1983, crowned in late 1982.

Prior to Ms Maffett's ascent, Dana Cody remained Miss Anaheim for the remainder of 1981. In fact, she and Ms Jones showed up at one of the Photo Days in a local park later that year – one to which I'd brought a couple of friends from the photo club at work. The club members wanted to get more practice in portraiture, and they hadn't been to a Photo Day yet. I was basically their guide. This particular Photo Day had several local celebrities. Prior to the commencement of the regular activities this time the mayor spoke briefly. Then, Dana took the podium with a few words for the aspiring models. As she was walking down from the makeshift stage area, she caught sight of me. The club guys were standing there with me, mouths agape, as she came directly to me, greeting me by name! She asked me if I could take a few photos of her with her Miss Anaheim banner on. After we were done, the guys asked me how I knew her. I gave them the brief version of how I was recruited by the director of the Miss Anaheim/Miss America Committee. They were speechless!

I've since gone on to work with hundreds more models. I've become a Certified Professional Photographer, representing just 3% of all professional photographers, and I run my own professional portrait studio photographing families, newborns, high school seniors, boudoir clients and artistic nude models in my leisure time.

REMOTE CONTROL

Between September 22 and 28, 2007 I'd attended LightPro Expo on Captiva Island just southwest of Ft. Meyers, Florida. It was my very first opportunity to receive in-depth instruction and practice with studio lighting, but that was only a small fraction of the offerings at this event. There were several instructional seminars being given by several photography experts both in the classroom, and out on the beaches, and, most important, they had lots and lots of models that any photographer could "check out" from the queue and practice their art!

This model queue was very structured in order to be fair to all of the models. Basically, when a photographer requested a model, the agencies representing the models there would give that photographer the next model on the list – not one that he or she might wish to work with. At first, this took me somewhat aback. I mean, I prefer to choose the models that I'll work with. But, after giving it some thought, I realized that this checkout queue method was far more realistic for a photographer who intends to create portraits of random clientele. That is, we don't get a choice of photographing only the most beautiful people – and we're still expected to make all of our clients look their very best. So, I didn't complain when I got a male model, despite my preference of working with women. I felt that it would be a good challenge, and it was. I'm glad that I was made to work outside of my comfort zone.

When the speaker at the event orientation described the model checkout process, he said, "You'll check out models from the Model Room. You can only check out one model at a time and have to take the next model that's available in the list. If you don't like the model you've checked out, take her out to the Banyan tree, shoot a frame, and check your model back in so you can get the next one. Each time you check a model back in, you need to upload your memory card to a DVD for that model's portfolio."

Anyway, at some point while I was just finishing up photographing another model in one of the ten fully outfitted studio setups in the "Studio Lab", a "pack" of young girls came running up to me! I'd learn later that they were Zeanna (10 y/o), Yaileen (12), & Yasmin (13). Interestingly, Zeanna was the clear leader of this pack, and she spoke for the rest. They were looking for a photographer to shoot them (photographically, of course) on the beach. Although it was a bit unorthodox, since we'd be circumventing the formal model queue, since *I* hadn't picked *them*, rather, *they* had picked *me*, I felt it'd be okay in that way. The first thing I told them was to go get their mothers, both parents, or guardians, as there'd be NO WAY I'd be taking a group of young girls away from the hotel and down to the beach alone! That's just *trouble* with a capital "T", as you can never know what a minor might decide to unjustly accuse you of! Plus, I'd need a hand with the large 4' x 6' reflector that I'd also be checking out for fill light under the intense sun. Each day there it was around 100 degrees with very high humidity. In fact, each time I'd go outside with my equipment after the cool air conditioning inside, my camera lenses would fog up instantly!

The girls went back to the model room and changed into their bikinis. Once ready, they, and their mothers followed me, carrying my camera gear and the large reflector. We walked down to a nearby strand of beach about 10-minutes away and set up there for the shoot.

These girls were very inexperienced at modeling, so I had to work patiently with them. When we began the shoot with all three in front of the camera, they'd all *snap* their heads 90-degrees in the direction that I'd indicate, rather than making the very subtle shift I was expecting. Not only were they making nearly binary movements, with no fine adjustments at all, but they were all three doing the same movements in unison when I'd intended for only *one* of them to change her position slightly!

Instead of getting overly frustrated with these obviously eager, budding models, I decided to stop shooting for a moment and offer some instruction. From my position about ten feet in front of the trio, I asked them if they could see my eyes. Again, in unison, they called out, "No." I asked them to respond again, one by one, when I looked directly into each of their eyes. This time, only the one who I was looking at responded – thereby effectively disproving their prior statement. Next, without saying a word, or approaching them, I looked directly into Yasmin's eyes and tilted my head very slightly. She responded by very slightly tilting her head in the proper direction. Still silent, but just moving my eyes to make contact with Zeanna, I turned my hand as if unscrewing a light bulb. She responded by ever so slightly turning her head to the right, just as I needed it. Finally, looking into Yaileen's eyes, I tilted my head in a similar way as with Yasmin, and she complied. None of the others had moved from their fine-adjusted positions, so I took the shot, and it turned out great! It was just like having a "model remote control"!

PAINTING WITH FIRE

In 2009, I had the opportunity to work with an up-and-coming fashion photographer on a number of unique photo shoots throughout the year. Lindsay Adler is an energetic young photographer who started shooting portraits professionally when she was just 14. Shortly after she graduated college and started a small studio in Owego where my studio is located, she requested my help. Like me, she was largely self-taught, so I was eager to help her out. She had read an article I'd written about colorful night photography in Photo Techniques Magazine, and she was intrigued. She wanted to do some interesting "painting-with-light" (PWL) photo shoots incorporating fashion models, but she hadn't done much with light painting. I'd not only worked extensively with nighttime photography, but I'd also put my engineering skills to work and created proprietary light-painting apparatus that allowed us to achieve a most unique look.

The first PWL-inspired photo shoot where I assisted Lindsay was "Painting-with-Fire"! In the darkness of very early morning on September 23, 2009, we used tiki torches and very long exposures to achieve interesting patterns in the background with fashion models, Lari (Brazilian) and Jessica (Swedish), in the foreground. While they were in hair and makeup, Lindsay, Lisa (Canadian model) and I went outside just after midnight and started practicing our technique with the torches.

By the time Lari and Jessica were ready, we'd refined our methods, and started the official shoot out on the lawn at her parents' house starting at 2am, some in the local woods, and finally, we headed down to Hickories Park – at 5:30 in the morning! We began a series of long exposures using the torches to outline many trees, and then illuminating the two fashion models. We had to work fast, as the sun would be coming up soon. We wrapped up and started back to our cars just about 6:20am, just as we saw the headlights of another vehicle pull up. Getting closer, we saw that it was a local police car.

The officer got out of his car and met us partway down the hill as we were trudging up.

He said, "We received a complaint of 'suspicious activity, possibly witchcraft' from a couple of old ladies jogging through the park."

Lindsay brought up some of the images we'd just shot, on her camera, and replied, "We're shooting a fashion editorial here using tiki torches."

Once the officer had accepted this and the tension was relieved, Lari – the Brazilian model – took out her tiny point-n-shoot camera and asked someone to take a picture of her with the officer. He was gracious enough to comply before he headed back to his car. The finished images from this shoot would eventually find their way to a UK fashion magazine called McMag.

PAINTING WITH LIGHT

The next PWL fashion editorial Lindsay and I shot was done in New York City on October 26, 2009. This was the shoot where we used my custom-built "light brushes". These were basically small plastic boxes containing a colored LED (Light Emitting Diode), a couple of batteries, a pushbutton switch, and a small linear slit on the end. This caused the beam to come out as a wide, rectangular swath; much like an actual paintbrush would produce. It gave us considerable control over the beam during an exposure.

Again, we had two models, but this time we'd be working with them individually on separate days. On Day-1, when the first one was done with hair, makeup, and wardrobe, we set up one of my Canon 5D Mark II digital SLR cameras on my heavy-duty tripod to shoot the session. Lindsay had the older Canon 5D, and it didn't create quite as clean an image at the higher sensitivities as the Mark II. By now, Lindsay and I had practiced our technique sufficiently on test subjects to know how to produce optimal strokes with the light brushes. As it'd be totally dark once we opened the camera shutter, the first thing we had to do was to locate the model, and then her face – initially by sound, by asking her to speak, and then, once we were close, by feel. We then had to move the light brushes slow enough that they'd properly register on the camera's sensor, while being fast enough to reduce any natural movement of a live subject. As the eyes were the most important part, our rule was to illuminate them on a single, fairly quick swath in order to render them pin sharp. After showing one of the other crewmembers how to use my light brushes, we had him apply light swaths to the background. This combined technique resulted in a number of really great finished photos.

There was a slight glitch with the second day. We had the model, hair, and makeup people there, but the wardrobe stylist never showed up! What do you do when there's no wardrobe? The obvious solution is to shoot the model nude! With her agreement, that's what we did. Again, we used the same light painting techniques, but this time I decided to introduce some additional interest. As the shutter would be held open for between 25- and 45-seconds, we had time to move the model's head to radically different positions during the exposure. This created multiple faces, in-camera.

Our painting-with-light images from that two-day shoot have shown up in a number of publications, most notably on the cover of one of Lindsay's many photographic technique books, "Creative52".

THE RETIREMENT PARTY

Friday night, November 6, 2009, Lindsay called me up and asked, "What are you doing tomorrow?"

"I have a shoot in the morning, but I'm free after that." I replied. "What's up?"

"How'd you like to shoot video at a retirement dinner while I shoot stills?"

"Sounds like fun!" I responded. "Where and when?"

"It's at the Binghamton Country Club in Endicott." She said. "We need to be there at 6:30pm, and it'll probably go until about eleven o'clock."

While I don't shoot video often, my cameras have the ability to produce 1080p high-resolution video, so I agreed to do it. It really was your typical "dull dinner party", but they did have a rather good Frank Sinatra impersonator singing many of his classics, *and* they fed us!

Shortly after we arrived and found the huge room where the party would soon commence, a member of the country club staff came up to Lindsay and me asking what we each wanted for *our* dinner. Despite the fact that this was a "dinner party", nobody wants pictures of them eating! Therefore, we'd take a break after dinner began for the guests, allowing us to eat our own meal, and we'd resume once they were about done. After about two hours of photos and video of people chatting over hors d'oeuvres, one of the staff indicated to the guests that dinner was served.

This same staff person led Lindsay and me to another room for our dinner. I was expecting that we – as "the help" – would be taken to a small staff lunchroom. I was in for quite the surprise!

She led us to another room of similar enormity to the one we'd left. It was mostly dark, but I could see dozens of unset tables all around a single table illuminated solely by two tall candles. It was fully set up with white tablecloth and a complete formal table setting including crystal goblets, nice Chinaware, and about half a dozen utensils, the function of most being a mystery to me! The meal was incredible, made better only by great conversation.

One topic Lindsay brought up, *again*, was weddings. Up until that time I'd been petrified of shooting a wedding, as I knew what an enormous responsibility it was. She was constantly telling me how I really should start photographing weddings, and I continued to tell her that I didn't feel ready for it. She said that she had several weddings booked in the summer, and she was going to *make me* shoot one for practice, while she and her own crew did the official photography. How could I turn down such an offer?

After our meal, we returned to the main room and resumed our job, finishing shortly before 11pm. We got good photos and video of the event, and I now had plans to shoot a wedding with Lindsay in the summer! It was a fun and productive evening.

THE PRACTICE WEDDING

Summer came, and I had no excuse but to take Lindsay up on her offer to shoot one of her weddings with her. It was July 10, 2010, when I shot my first wedding. Even though Lindsay and her crew did the *official* photography, I still felt like I was responsible for getting great shots – and I *did* get them! Of course, by then she'd also prepared me quite well for what to expect, so there were no surprises. She's always been very good at teaching.

MY FAVORITE MODELS and BEST FRIENDS

I expanded my photographic capabilities significantly in 2010. First, in January, when Lindsay not only urged me to start offering boudoir portrait sessions at my studio, but she insisted on being my very first subject! She also gave me confidence in shooting weddings. Then, in June and October of that same year, a couple of beautiful young women – Michelle O'Neil and Vanessa

239

Davis, respectively – came to my studio to model artistic nudes. They would soon become great nude, boudoir, and pinup models, and also amazing long-term friends! The following year produced yet another long-term friend after Catherine Stone – the artist who produced all of the sketched illustrations for this book – modeled nude for me.

MICHELLE

Michelle O'Neil came to me in June, for a fun portrait session with a girlfriend of hers. But she was unlike any ordinary client. She brought a camera with her! I mean, did she think I wouldn't have one? When she wasn't in front of my lens, she was behind her own taking pictures. A few weeks later she started modeling for me on a regular basis, helping me to refine pinup and boudoir concepts. You can see an example of Michelle's modeling in the photo titled Michelle Modeling in the Mirror at the top of this chapter. She soon started helping me out at the studio, and it wasn't long before she'd indicated that she was also very interested in doing photography herself! Naturally, I was ecstatic to help her learn that which had been my own passion for three decades by then. She now runs her own portrait business, continues to model for me, we're always each other's "second shooter" anytime we do a wedding, and she's my *very best friend!*

ZOMBIE DEER

Michelle and I were deep in the woods up a steep hill behind my studio late at night on October 22, 2010, shooting an artistic nude "painting with light" scene. Once again, I was using my "light brushes" that I'd built for Lindsay's fashion shoots, to apply the colorful swaths of light as if doing a painting while Michelle posed, clinging to a section of a fallen tree. Because it takes time to properly make such a light-painting, each exposure was around 3-minutes long. Model movement during such an exposure would be impossible to eliminate except by my practiced technique of applying each color as briefly as possible. This shoot was further complicated by the fact that we could see our breath. Because of this, both Michelle and I would take a breath and hold it each time I applied a new swath of light so that the clouds of our condensed breath wouldn't pick up the light.

At around 11pm, after nearly an hour at this location, we wrapped up and prepared to head back down the steep hill. That's when it happened! We both heard a sharp "snap", as if from a stick breaking...only it wasn't coming from us. It was from deeper in the woods.

Michelle said, "What if it's a bear?"

In an attempt to quell her fear, I replied with a bit of levity, "I've never had any bears in my woods, but it could be a deer – and you know how carnivorous they are."

Without missing a beat, Michelle responded, "What if it's a *zombie* deer?! It'll want to eat our brains!"

On that note, we began a very rapid descent down the slope. Despite having flashlights, we still found ourselves tripping over much of the uneven terrain in the darkness. Each time one of us would tumble, we'd just come up laughing harder, which made it that much more likely that we'd take another spill. Ultimately, we made the ten-minute trip back to the studio in about three-minutes with only a few minor scrapes and bruises from virtually tumbling the whole way down the hill.

Was it worth it? Of course! Not only did we get amazing artistic photographs from it, but also this fun, and very real, story to share!

THE MOCK WEDDING

Early in 2012 Michelle and I decided to start advertising our respective wedding photography services. The only problem with this is that you can't advertise wedding photography until you've shot a wedding, and it's very difficult to book a wedding to shoot if you have no examples of your wedding photography. It's a literal Catch-22 scenario. Because I wasn't the official photographer at the wedding that Lindsay had me shoot with her for my practice in 2010, I didn't have rights to use those images for advertising. Michelle, therefore, proposed that we do a "mock wedding" with the specific purpose of generating photographs that we could use for advertising our wedding photography.

She directed me to a specific bridal shop where we might reach a trade agreement (apparel for photographs), while I came up with a venue for this "wedding". Michelle also rounded up models to play the various roles that we'd be photographing. I was more than just a bit surprised that the people at the bridal shop were so generous. For simply providing them with high-quality professional photography of their dresses modeled in a staged version of their actual intended use, they lent us an exceptionally beautiful (and *very* expensive!) wedding gown, three mostly matching bridesmaid's dresses, and a tux with vest, cummerbund, and shoes!

I decided to contact the priest at the Catholic Church where I shot beside Lindsay. This priest, too, was exceptionally gracious, and offered us their sanctuary for a few hours on Saturday, February 11, 2012. At that point, we had the wedding gown, bridesmaid's dresses, a tux for the groom, and a church in which to shoot it all! If you're keeping score, yes, we were short groomsmen apparel, but since we could only find one guy to participate – ostensibly as the groom – we hardly needed more formalwear. Apparently, men don't like to play dress-up as much as women.

Michelle loves modeling, so it wasn't long before she got caught up in the fantasy of dressing up as a bride and decided that she'd be the one to model the wedding gown! So much for her being *behind* the camera, but since this whole thing was mostly her idea, I figured I'd indulge her.

When the big day arrived, everybody converged at the church...except the guy who was to play the groom! I wonder if he realized that this was not a real wedding. Anyway, we had three women for bridesmaids, Michelle as the bride, and me to photograph it all. Now, we'd already solved the issue of not having an officiant. With the exception of certain very wide shots, an officiant (priest, in this case) wouldn't generally be in many of the shots, anyway, so we just kept the shots fairly tight and specific, focusing only on the bridal party. But, not having a groom for at least a few of the shots could be an issue!

While the women were getting their hair done and dresses on, we even discussed the possibility of making it a "lesbian wedding". We'd just have two bridesmaids, and the third would become the "groom". But, out of respect for the generosity of the church personnel and the sanctity of the church, we decided this wouldn't be a very good idea. Fortunately, I'd brought a remote shutter release device and tripod with me. As a professional photographer,

I always try to be prepared for just about any contingency. If this wasn't a contingency situation, I don't know what was! Of course, this meant that *I* would now have to be not only the photographer, but the *groom* as well… that is, assuming the tux would even fit me! I was most surprised to find that it all *did* fit!

In the end, we got a nice set of really great photographs that appeared as if they were from a real wedding, to use for advertising wedding photography! About a week after we did this shoot, and I'd long-since returned all of the formalwear of course, I delivered a CD containing all of the beautiful, finished images to the bridal shop, per our agreement. They were very happy with the results, also.

STATE SIGNS

In March 2014, I drove to Wisconsin and back – 13-hours each way. Now, I should mention that I'm not one who enjoys driving extremely long distances alone. In fact, I find it so unpleasant that I avoid it as much as I possibly can. I have no problem with one, two or even three hours in one sitting, but much beyond that, and I begin to be overtaken by an excessively strong, compelling desire to sleep! In my mind, driving and sleep are mutually exclusive activities, and it's a really bad idea to combine them!

Therefore, when a new nude/fetish model had contacted me from Wisconsin to set up a photo shoot, my first response was, "No way! Not unless you come to me!" She wasn't interested in that – maybe she falls asleep on long drives, too – so I'd considered that shoot a no-go and didn't think anything more about it…until I happened to remember that Michelle's very best girlfriend, Katie, lives in Wisconsin, too. I also knew that they hadn't visited each other in quite a while, so I figured that it might be a benefit both to her – to visit Katie and her family – and to me – to have Michelle and her son Brady ride with me to keep me alert – if we did the trip together. At the slightest mention of going to Wisconsin, Michelle was jumping for joy. I took that as a vague "yes", she was interested in accompanying me on this trip.

A couple of weeks prior to the date we'd selected for the shoot and this 3-day trip, I contacted the model again to confirm my travel plans and arrange to meet up there. I got no reply. I tried several more times throughout the following week – even the phone number she'd provided yielded no results – and still nothing. This wasn't looking good. I was, of course, a bit disappointed, but I really had no great problem canceling the trip if the model was going to be a no-show. I think I've mentioned how much I dislike driving extremely long distances. The problem was that I'd already promised Michelle a trip to see her friend, and I'm a man of my word. Whether or not I'd connect with this Wisconsin model, I wasn't about to take away Michelle's excitement about appearing at Katie's house for a surprise visit! The trip was a "go", either way.

I'd still be bringing my photography gear with me but considered it an infinitesimal chance of using it as intended. Contrary to prior long trips where I'd become very anxious as the date approached, since I knew how difficult it'd be, as the date for this trip approached, I was actually looking more and more forward to it. This is because I'd be doing a road trip with my very best friend, Michelle, and she just makes everything much more fun!

She's also friends with a family who has a very young child, Odin, afflicted with a series of debilitating, degenerative, and generally terminal conditions: West Syndrome, Krabbe's Disease, and Dopa Responsive Dystonia

Since Odin can't be away from the various apparatus needed to help keep him alive, he can't travel to see new places. As such, on this trip, Michelle made it her goal to help Odin travel vicariously through our adventure across several states that he might never see in person. Therefore, we stopped at the side of the road to take a picture of Michelle holding a sign proclaiming, "Odin Was Here!" next to the sign indicating entry to each new state. We did this at Pennsylvania, Ohio, Indiana, Illinois, and Wisconsin. Most of these signs appeared in fairly isolated, rural areas where pulling off on the shoulder wasn't any issue at all. There was plenty of space, the traffic was light to non-existent, and the scenes were generally bucolic.

But getting the Illinois sign was a challenge! They'd placed it just in front of an underpass with a high concrete wall directly to the right of the *very* narrow shoulder, and traffic was whizzing by very close and fast. Waiting for just the right moment when there was a break in traffic, Michelle and I jumped out of the car and ran up towards the sign. She posed with Odin's sign, and I snapped a couple of pictures. As the flow of traffic after that brief break continued, the noise level was so high that I couldn't hear anything she was trying to tell me until I was just a couple of feet from her. After getting the pictures, I had to wait for another break in the traffic to get back into the car, but we made it without incident.

Odin now has five more vicarious states.

The great thing about that trip – other than helping to create a virtual travelogue for Odin, and Michelle getting to visit Katie and family – was that I never even felt the slightest trace of fatigue throughout the entire trip either way! Brady (nearly 3 y/o at that time) was an amazing passenger, too! He never complained, and sat there taking in the scenery, sleeping, or looking at his books the entire trip. Michelle was basically the "entertainment director" for this trip. She kept my attention engaged by general chatting, or by playing games she'd make up, or making silly comments about the traffic or scenery. Since she was in charge of the entertainment, she also kept the music on the radio fresh through a long play-list from her phone. This also included a variety of comedy skits, as well. Even though the Wisconsin model never materialized (as I'd long-since accepted would be the case), I thoroughly enjoyed this trip because of my best friend Michelle.

MYRTLE BEACH

My youngest son, Bryce, had been living in Myrtle Beach, SC for a couple of years, and wanted to move back home to my place in NY in December 2014. He asked me to help him with this move. He'd indicated that he really didn't have enough stuff to bother with renting a moving truck and car trailer, as he'd estimated that everything should fit in a combination of his car and mine. My car at that time was a Pontiac Vibe, which I got specifically for its nice combination of high gas mileage, and reasonable cargo space with the back seats folded down.

Once again, I was looking at a 13-hour trip each way, so the first thing I did after, he asked me to help, was to contact Michelle! This time, except for it being Myrtle Beach, I could offer her no specific incentive to ride with me. Still, she accepted immediately! This time, however, we'd need to have the back seats folded down on the trip back in order to maximize the available cargo space, which meant we wouldn't be able to bring Brady along with us this time. She was able to arrange to leave him with her family for those few days, so we were set to go. Both to minimize the time she'd have to be away from Brady, and also to fit within my work's normal schedule (I currently get Friday off every other week), we'd be traveling south on Friday, packing Bryce's stuff into the cars on Saturday, and then traveling back north on Sunday.

As before, Michelle kept me entertained with a great variety of music and comedy skits, and kept me alert the entire way there and back!

Once my ex-wife, Kimberly, and our eldest son, Drew — both current residents of Surfside Beach, just 15-20 minutes south of Myrtle Beach proper — learned that I'd be coming down there ('cause I told them as soon as I'd begun to make plans!), they insisted on getting together... for breakfast, lunch, a concert, and dinner afterward — all on Saturday!

Let me tell you something about Kimberly, first. She is the *best ex-wife* one could imagine! We had our difficulties while we were married, but we're great friends now, and the kids and I have done vacations (a Caribbean cruise, and a visit to Disneyworld, for instance) with her, her great new husband, Robert, and their cute and precocious adopted Chinese daughter, Mia. It's always a great pleasure to visit with them all.

So, the plan had been to meet the family for lunch on Saturday. Then Drew told me that he couldn't make it at lunchtime, as he would be practicing for a Christmas concert that they were putting on that evening. He'd meet Michelle and me for breakfast. Then, we simply *had* to go to Drew's concert where he'd be singing, and, naturally, to dinner after that! This didn't leave a lot of time to pack up the cars, but we did actually manage to complete that task in approximately 1.5-hours between lunch and the concert!

Between breakfast and lunch, we actually had a couple of hours with nothing specific scheduled, as Bryce wanted to take that time to do some final packing of his stuff into boxes. Michelle and I, therefore, decided to take advantage of that time and do something we'd seen a billboard for on our way to breakfast. She had never been in a helicopter. Being a helicopter pilot myself, I found this nearly inconceivable, or at very least tragic, and we simply had to remedy that. The advertisement we'd seen earlier was for helicopter rides along the beach, so I decided to treat her to such an adventure! Michelle had also found several discount coupons for helicopter rides in a booklet in our hotel room, which she'd cut out to use for this purpose (the coupons, not the room!). No, I wouldn't be piloting this helicopter. I was simply along for the ride, as it were, and to share (and capture in pictures) Michelle's first helicopter experience!

She absolutely *loved* it, even the scary part that she wasn't prepared for when our pilot came in for a landing much faster than she'd expected, thereby pulling several Gs just before coming to the landing pad. I'm fairly sure he did this radical maneuver (not what I'd call "tourist-friendly") because he knew I was a pilot and wanted to provide a bit of the thrill that I'd experienced when I was flying as a student.

Another thing that Michelle wanted to do while we were there was some souvenir shopping and go to the beach. The last time she'd been to Myrtle Beach was when she was a little kid. We did both. Of course, in early December, the temperature had "dropped" to only about 70 degrees, and the beaches were all vacant except for a few locals walking along the surf wearing heavy parkas and staring oddly at Michelle and me in our bathing suits!

VANESSA

Vanessa Davis came to me in October that year. She was most impressed by some of my earlier work with boudoir and nude models, particularly those I'd done outdoors, and she told me as much in an eloquent and quite lengthy e-mail letter of introduction. She was a nude/fetish model. Her modeling talents helped take me to an entirely new level of artistic nude photography. The techniques and poses we were exploring could also apply to some client boudoir and artistic nude photo sessions. After nearly a full year of frequent photo shoots, we compiled the best of the resultant images into a beautiful glossy coffee table book titled "Extreme Art Nudes: Artistic Erotic Photo Essays Far Outside of The Boudoir". For that book project, I'd adopted the pseudonym, "Victor Navarre" – a name that she created for me. Vanessa became my other best friend.

BANNERMAN CASTLE and THE STICK SHIFT

The juxtaposition of a beautiful, flawless model against the crumbling remains of a tumbledown castle can produce most compelling images. This was apparently the picture that Vanessa had in her mind when she began corresponding with the caretaker of Bannerman Castle in the middle of the Hudson River near NY City in January 2011. She wanted to get permission from him for us to do a photo shoot by the castle ruins once it warmed up in April or May. Once she'd done the introductions, I followed up with the proprietor in the areas of fees and lodging. Finally, everything was set. We'd be staying a night at the castle caretaker's Bed & Breakfast, "The Swan" in Beacon. After checking in on the evening of May 6, we headed to the rendezvous point on the Hudson where we'd meet the people who'd boat us over to the island where the castle resided. We shot for about an hour and a half, until the sun set, and then we returned to the B&B where we had a very nice, nearly private candlelight dinner at around 9pm. After dinner we headed back to our room and packed up in preparation to return home the next day immediately after another few hours shooting at the castle that morning.

During those two days (May 6 & 7), we got all of the planned shots. Despite the fact that Vanessa was nursing a raging cold at the time, we created some spectacular imagery.

She'd intimated several times in the prior month about wanting to learn to drive a stick shift vehicle, but she didn't have one to practice on, and nobody who did have one, wanted to teach her. My vehicle has a stick shift, and I was happy to teach her, but I hadn't expected it to happen while we were hundreds of miles from home! That's right; she brought it up again just as we were leaving the B&B!

I drove us over to a large parking lot and gave her as much verbal instruction as possible before she'd just have to feel it out for herself. Switching seats, she now sat on my left. I don't know of anybody – myself included when I was 16 – who doesn't have some problem initially learning to coordinate the clutch with the gas. That's right, it was no surprise that she stalled my car a number of times when at first attempting to find this delicate balance. I was quite pleasantly surprised, however, at how quickly she finally did figure it out! With that early success, she then asked if she could drive the entire way – about 3-hours – back to my studio near Binghamton. I could find no reason to object, so that's just what she did!

Of course, since a majority of the trip was highway driving, she never had to shift once getting up to speed. This created its own problems, though. After a while of driving without having to shift, when we'd come to an exit, she'd forget that she'd have to shift! I'd remind her, of course, and all was well – until the one time we came to a rest stop and she forgot to put in the clutch when coming to a stop. Well, we needed the engine stopped there, anyway! After that trip, anytime she'd be over for a shoot, and we'd have to drive somewhere – even to the corner store – she'd ask to drive. In time, she actually became a rather good stick shift driver!

STEAK

Both Michelle and Vanessa are fantastic cooks. Michelle makes me great meals routinely, and they're always wonderful. Vanessa has only prepared two meals for me – a breakfast, and a dinner – but they were both amazing! This is about the steak dinner.

Vanessa is a substantial carnivore. She loves her steaks. She also loves her wine. We got into a discussion one time about these two items – in fact, during the drive to Toronto, which you'll get to soon. I mentioned that I didn't like the taste of any wines that I've had, and I don't eat steak much because I simply haven't found one prepared in a manner that I've found worthwhile. She took this as a challenge, saying, "I'm going to prepare a steak meal, along with some wines, that I know you'll love!"

When she said a "steak meal", she truly meant a complete meal, including a variety of steaks, a couple of sumptuous side dishes, a few different bottles of wine, and dessert. The night before this special meal, Vanessa began preparing the dessert; chocolate mousse and whipped cream, all made completely from scratch, by hand. Both the mousse and the fresh whipped cream needed to chill overnight. Because I didn't have an electric mixer, we both took turns whipping the cream with a wire whisk. We were up until about 2am, May 8, 2011, before this very vigorous whisking action finally resulted in an almost magical transformation of this runny heavy cream into thick whipped cream! We put the bowl of freshly whipped cream into the freezer, and the bowl of still-soupy mousse into the fridge to chill before serving after the meal.

Michelle showed up around noon for me to do her maternity photo shoot. She was nearly eight-months pregnant, and Vanessa painted a floral pattern onto her for a unique look. Once done with her part, Vanessa headed to the kitchen while I worked with Michelle. A few hours later, after Michelle had showered off the paint, and gotten dressed, Vanessa called to us saying, "Dinner is served!"

She'd made fillet mignon and rib-eye steaks for the three of us, plus a 9x13 casserole dish filled with quartered, buttery, roasted potatoes, and a large bowl of French-cut green beans in an amazing white sauce with melted parmesan cheese! Just after I saw down, I nearly committed what I'd very soon learn was a major faux pas in the presence of an expert chef like Vanessa. Before I'd tasted anything, I started to get up to fetch salt and pepper! She glared at me with a look that could have peeled the paint off of the walls, and said, "You don't need it! Trust me. Taste everything; you don't need it!" Suitably put in my place, I sat back down, and vowed never to insult the chef again with such an act of apparent treason.

Three bottles of wine were set upon the table, as well. While I still didn't care for two of them, the third was "palatable". It certainly wasn't something that I'd ever crave, but I could at least drink a glass of it without finding it overly offensive. But the meal…this meal was absolutely exquisite! She'd certainly outdone herself, and I actually DID love the rib-eye steak the way she'd prepared it – in butter and bacon grease!

After suitably satisfying ourselves on this incredible meal, Vanessa then served us all the chilled chocolate mousse – now with substantial structure to it – with the semi-frozen hand-whipped cream! Together, this was yet another incredible taste sensation.

These are just some of the things that best friends do together!

BOLDT CASTLE and THE DISTRESSED DRESS
Late on May 21, 2011, Vanessa, Michelle and I drove up to a hotel in

Watertown, NY in preparation to visit Boldt Castle on the St. Lawrence River the next day. Prior to this trip, Vanessa had gone to a thrift store and purchased an old prom dress for next to nothing. She wanted to pose in this dress at the castle…rather she wanted to pose in what was left of it after she'd "prepared it" to look the way she wanted.

The next morning, we traveled the remaining 40-minutes up to Alexandria Bay where the castle resides. We'd catch a ferry over to the island and do our photo shoot there.

When we arrived at the ferry that would take us over to the castle, Vanessa pointed to a parking space that edged up against a small dirt hill. Seeing my confused look, she told me that she wanted the dress to have a "distressed look" to it. Therefore, after she'd dunked it briefly into the bay, she carefully set it out upon the dirt hill just in front of one of my car's front tires. She asked me to run over it and spin my wheels on it several times. I did. We got some odd stares, but she was quick to put their concerns at ease by telling them that she was having me distress her dress for a photo shoot. Once she'd determined that I'd satisfactorily distressed it in that way, she asked me for my pocketknife. After we boarded the boat, she then proceeded to cut long slices into the dress, letting the tulle inside spill out in spots. Satisfied with its appearance by the time we arrived at the castle, she put it on, posing upon one of the castle's balconies as a fair damsel in a distressed dress apparently awaiting her prince. In reality – in this image – since I believe that women are very strong and capable in their own way, she's not waiting around for any prince; she'll defend her castle by herself!

Again, we got amazing photos not only on the castle balcony, but all about the grounds such as when she was wading – in the same dress – in a shallow pool, posing in a tree, relaxing in one of the many gardens, or reclining on the edge of another pool.

Michelle came with us partially because she'd suggested the idea of doing a photo shoot there, and because she'd never been before. She posed for a few shots, but it was just fun having her there with us. She also shot some kickass images and was *very* pregnant at the time!

TORONTO and THE TRAFFIC STOP

In April 2011, Vanessa had booked five photo shoots with four photographers in Toronto. One of them wanted to do both an evening shoot and a sunrise shoot. She'd arranged to stay with one of them over the weekend. As a nude/fetish model, this could be a very dangerous prospect if she wasn't so good at researching and checking out the credibility and reputation of each and every photographer before meeting with them...including me! She'd done her due diligence with this shoot but had only heard back from one of the three models she'd contacted who'd worked with one of these five photographers. That one model had reported nothing bad. Just a few days before she was about to head for Toronto, she received much less than stellar reports about this photographer from the other two models. As luck would have it, the bad reports were related to the photographer she'd planned to stay with! She called me up asking my advice. She didn't want to cancel and lose all of the money that she'd otherwise earn from these shoots, but none of the other photographers were in a position to offer her accommodations, and she couldn't afford a hotel before being paid.

One of the things I enjoyed most was traveling with Vanessa – much like Michelle. It was during these trips that we had the greatest opportunity to chat and learn more about each other, invariably bonding. Given the opportunity, Vanessa would chat incessantly, and it was very refreshing to me! I suppose it suggested to me a greater degree of trust, to share her very personal stories.

Given her quandary, I told her not to cancel the photo shoots, and that I'd just take her, while acting as a protective escort as well as providing a hotel room. She liked this idea, so I booked a hotel for that Friday!

Even though I'd picked her up around 3pm, due to Friday afternoon traffic we didn't get to Toronto, and the location of the first photo shoot, until around 9pm. Following brief introductions, I sat out of the way in a corner reading a book while keeping a loose eye on Vanessa to be sure she was still okay. This shoot lasted until nearly 2am Saturday. We had to be back to that same location at 6am for the sunrise portion of the shoot, so, by the time we checked into the hotel, got to sleep, and got up again with enough time so that she could prepare her hair and makeup to be ready for this early shoot, we'd get just over two hours of sleep!

We headed to the next photographer's location immediately after finishing the early shoot. I've detailed this particular photo shoot in Chapter 21, titled "ESP?: Experiment #2". We had about an hour between this shoot and the next, which we used to get some lunch. At the final shoot, it turned out that this photographer had seen, and greatly admired, some of my photography with Vanessa, and appeared to be virtually star-struck at having me grace his presence. I'd insisted that I was to be completely ignored, as HE was the photographer in charge of the shoot (I hadn't even brought a camera!), but he kept deferring to me for lighting and exposure guidance, and posing suggestions. Anyway, I think, between his having the opportunity to work with the amazing and incredible Vanessa Davis, as well as having me there to help guide him through the shoot, we'd really made his day!

After that shoot, we immediately headed back for the States. Only we weren't headed back to the Southern Tier where we'd begun. We were planning to go to a party at a club in Rochester, NY that Vanessa and I had been to a few times previously. But, first, we had to find our way out of Canada. The GPS in my phone didn't work outside of the US, and Vanessa's dedicated GPS unit that she brought, was giving information that conflicted with the maps I'd printed out from Google. After some while of probably going around in circles, I did finally stop and ask directions, as well as purchase a map that covered the area. Between these two things, we were able to make it to the Rainbow Bridge, across to the USA.

Soon afterward, we began looking for someplace to catch a quick dinner, as it was around 9pm by then, and we hadn't eaten since before noon. I took the first exit from the Thruway that appeared to have a chance of having some restaurants. Without realizing it, I'd chosen the Depew exit – that which leads directly to the town where I'd grown up as a kid! Now remember, not only were we hungry, but also significantly sleep-deprived, and even more tired from driving a few hours. This is when it happened!

I was traveling down Transit Road (aka: Route 78) in the center of three lanes carrying uncharacteristically heavy traffic headed towards Main Street when I saw a Tim Horton's coffee shop/restaurant off to the right, only a few car-lengths in front of us. Checking my mirrors to be sure I had space, I then signaled my lane change, and, now in the right lane, immediately signaled again while stomping on the brakes to slow enough to make the immediate right turn into the restaurant's driveway. It was a fast move, but executed – in my mind – completely legally. This is why I was so surprised to immediately find flashing blue and red lights behind me!

I pulled over in the parking lot, and he pulled up at a 45-degree angle just in front of me. I might mention that this was the *very first time that I'd ever been pulled over!* He stormed over to my open window and bellowed, "*WHAT* the *HELL* was that?!?!?!"

Knowing that my quick maneuver *could* have been dangerous, all I could think to do was apologize. I replied, "I am SO sorry!"

He said, "All you had to do was use the next entrance down the road a bit."

I said, "I realize that now. I just hadn't seen it then."

He wrapped it up saying, "Please drive more safely!"

I thanked him, and he went back to his car.

I have no idea what Vanessa was doing, other than looking stunning in the passenger seat – after having been made up for the photo shoots, and then further touched up in anticipation for the party in Rochester.

Once the officer had left, I drove us over to a proper parking space and we went inside to get some food. Because my legs refused to work properly after this potentially difficult encounter with the police (probably due to the adrenaline still coursing through my body!), Vanessa had wrapped her arms around me to help me across the parking lot. She kept repeating to me, "It's OKAY! It's over now. You're fine!" Unfortunately, I couldn't get my legs to believe it until a while after we'd been seated.

PANCAKES

Vanessa and I were talking about pancakes one day. She described making them completely from scratch – using flour and such, not the pancake mix like I'd use – and a sweet strawberry glaze. I told her that the pancakes sounded delicious, but I always use maple syrup on mine. She said that I would love these pancakes with only her glaze. I wasn't so sure. With that, the challenge was on! She said she'd make these pancakes with her strawberry glaze, and I'd love it!

We went to the store and picked up the ingredients that afternoon. She wouldn't let me put maple syrup in the cart, but I was still able to sneak it into my purchase. Let's just say that I wasn't completely convinced that the glaze would adequately replace my favorite syrup, so I just wanted to be prepared – just in case I was right.

It was June 1, 2011, and Vanessa and I were doing a painting-with-light photo shoot, therefore we had to wait for darkness to make it most effective. We started the shoot around 10pm, and finally got the look we were after just before 11:30pm. After that, I helped her prepare the strawberry glaze, since she wanted it to chill overnight. By helping, I mean I was taking pictures of the process while she was slicing strawberries and mixing up the glaze – all while she was totally nude. Bright and early the next morning – around 10am – she started the pancakes. At that time, Vanessa was *not* a morning person! For her, ten in the morning was extremely early! Anyway, as she was making a stack of pancakes for us, she discovered my maple syrup in the fridge! She wouldn't let me put it on the table, ensuring that I'd have to use her glaze, instead.

Now wearing only a vintage apron, she served me my pancakes, and ladled on a generous portion of glaze. All I can say is "I was wrong!" I do NOT need maple syrup when I have something as amazing as Vanessa's strawberry glaze! It was incredible!

MY BEST FRIENDS

Both Michelle and Vanessa are the two most amazing, caring, giving, beautiful, and intelligent people I've ever known, and I'm proud to call them my very best friends! I'm also pleased to call Catherine another of my best friends.

What do you mean, I can't have *three* "best" friends? When you have a favorite kind of ice cream, do you expect that only a single tub of that brand will taste that great, and all others will pale in comparison, or will all of that type and brand be considered the best to you? I think it's the same with friends. Mine are really sweet and a bit nutty, and they never fail to make me happy anytime I'm either around them or talking with them! Ipso facto: three best friends are allowed. They make my life far more fun and interesting than it'd be otherwise.

Chapter 21 – ESP?

EXPERIMENT #1

Bill and I had both bought our very first personally owned cars in mid-1980. As an experiment in ESP (Extra-Sensory Perception), we'd intentionally *not* mentioned to the other what make, model, color or anything else about the car we were each planning to get. There was also no mention of ferrets.

I bought a midnight blue metalflake, 1980 Pontiac Sunbird hatchback with a manual transmission, air conditioning, and a sunroof.

Bill bought a midnight blue metalflake, 1980 Pontiac Sunbird hatchback with a manual transmission and air conditioning.

The only difference was the sunroof!

In February 1985, our cars would meet for the first time, in front of a hotel in Bakersfield, California. We were both in Bakersfield to perform figure skating routines at the large, regional Goldskate competition. The nearly identical cars that nearly identical people drove amused members of our respective skating clubs from both the north and south!

EXPERIMENT #2

Many, many years later, in fact it was April 2011, as an attempt to disprove this as ESP, I had the opportunity to perform yet another experiment – only this time, it *wasn't* with my twin! Since twins are always said to be prone to ESP with each other, I decided to try it with someone who wasn't even related to me.

I was up in Toronto with my very good friend and model Vanessa Davis. We'd done quite a few photo shoots together prior to this, and I'd clearly noticed some very odd situations where one of us seemed to be reading the other's mind! Since I wasn't the photographer at this particular shoot in Toronto – I was just escorting Vanessa to keep her safe with unfamiliar photographers – I was sitting in a loft area reading a book. I could see the area where the photographer was working with her, and that there were about a dozen different items hanging from a pegboard behind her. I'd anticipated that the photographer would eventually ask her to select one of the items to pose with it. While she was looking at the photographer, I briefly diverted my eyes from my book to make a quick mental selection of one of the items from the pegboard and waited.

The photographer did, in fact, ask her to pick an item, so she turned around and studied the pegboard for a moment. Finally, she made her selection. It was the very item I'd already selected in my mind. Just after that, I made a second selection without even looking, as I already knew what the items were by then, and, again, waited. When done with the first item, the photographer asked her, once again, to select a different item. After turning around again to hang up the first item, she briefly studied the pegboard. That's when she started to go for a different item than the one I'd locked into my mind!

At this point, with her back still to me, I was watching the scene unfold, so I felt a slight concern that the experiment was about to fail. Then she suddenly withdrew her hand from the wrong item and moved it over to the item I'd actually picked! WOW! This was intense, but I still don't believe in ESP! I'm quite certain that what people call ESP is simply a similar development of thought patterns through similar experiences either independently, or together. Therefore, given new stimulus, the likelihood of making the same choice is greatly increased.

Chapter 22 – A MONTH IN HAWAII

Working on the SSP Kaimalino

PREPARATION FOR THE TRIP

It was February 1982. I'd been granted a Top-Secret DoD clearance a month or so prior and was working on a project related to sonar systems. My lead engineer came up to me and asked, "How'd you like to go to Hawaii?" After only about a 1.37 nanoseconds hesitation, I replied that I'd love to. He continued, "We'll be doing sea trials of this system, and could be there a few weeks." This certainly didn't reduce my enthusiasm. In fact, it only increased my desire to go.

The secretaries on this program definitely earned their keep, at least when it came to arranging travel for us engineers. It was Friday, February 12 when more than a dozen people filed into the program conference room. I'd never even seen about half of them before that day. It turns out they were the basic support people: forklift drivers, welders, mechanics, crane operators, and logistics people. On the table, next to each seat around the long table, there was a thick folder with a name on it in heavy black marking pen. I took the seat next to my packet.

Inside, I found my personal itinerary, a copy of a map of the Hawaiian island of Oahu, open-ended airline tickets to Honolulu International Airport, a confirmation of my open-ended hotel reservation on Waikiki Beach, a thick stack of traveler's cheques in $20, $50 and $100 denominations to pay for the hotel, food, etc., and about $150 in cash, for initial expenses on the way to the hotel! It was an incredibly short meeting. Once everyone had found their seat, the program manager announced, simply, "Take your packet, sign the reference line on all of your traveler's cheques before you leave today, and have a safe trip to Honolulu on Monday!" The program secretaries had arranged all of our reservations, obtained all of our cash and traveler's cheques, and organized it all into these concise, neat packets for each of us! It was most amazing.

Unbeknownst to me at the time, having a reservation at a hotel on Waikiki Beach was actually a bit of a joke, as we'd only see the hotel maybe a total of ten times during the entire month we'd end up working in the area. We arrived in Honolulu and checked into the hotel Monday, February 15, 1982. As we'd all be carpooling, only three or four of the entire contingent were given rental cars. That evening, dining at a nice Japanese steakhouse in Waikiki, it felt like I was on vacation. The next morning, we all congregated at a pancake house for breakfast in Old Honolulu. There, our local contact, a native Hawaiian, gave us some pointers for the next few weeks that we'd be in the islands. The point that sticks most in my mind was this; he said, "When you're out and about, *do not look like a tourist*. If, instead, you look like a local, then the street vendors won't take advantage of you...as much" He went on to explain that oversized, flowered shirts, in particular, are a total "tourist" look! He also gave us a quick lesson on how to pronounce Hawaiian words, particularly the street signs. You pronounce every vowel and add a glottal stop between similar-sounding letters. For instance, "Kauai" is not pronounced like "cow-eye". Instead, you speak it like, "cow-ah-ee".

After breakfast, we drove through the Pali (the main mountain range dividing the island's north and south sides) to Kaneohe Marine Corps Air Base. The most unique feature that I remember about this base was the "jet crossing" gate. It was a standard railroad crossing gate across the road to the base, only, instead of train tracks on the other side, it was the main runway! If the gate was down and flashing, then we'd have to wait for a jet to take off or land. Once the jet had passed, and the gate went up, then we could drive across the runway to the main buildings on the base.

THE SSP KAIMALINO

When we got to the dock, I saw the most unusual-looking ship I'd ever seen. It wasn't long with a pointed bow like most ships. It was, in fact, very much like a floating rectangle, with a very wide, blunt nose. Conceived in the 1960s, and built in 1975, I was looking at the SSP Kaimalino, the very first practical SWATH (Small Water-plane Area Twin Hull) SSP (Stable Semi-submerged Platform) ever built. It was about 88 feet long, and about 50 feet wide, with a 193-ton displacement. Its primary propulsion was provided by two 2,230 horsepower refurbished helicopter gas turbine engines geared through a chain drive to controllable pitch propellers, with secondary propulsion provided by a pair of diesel/hydraulic engines to be used for close quarters maneuvering. None of the main hull area came into contact with the water except in high sea state conditions. It was supported above the water by two long, narrow pontoons that plunged deep into the water from four large stanchions – one at each corner of the ship.

Even the bridge was unlike that of a normal ship. It strongly resembled the bridge of the starship Enterprise from the popular "Star Trek" TV series. It had thick leather swivel chairs and panels of electronic displays and flashing pushbuttons where analog gauges might have been otherwise. One of the most notable attributes about this bridge, in addition to the technology and coolness factor, was what was below it! I'm not certain about the right side, but the front-left pontoon had a ladder that extended from the bridge down some 15-feet to the base.

It was like another world down there. The front of the pontoon was made of a thick clear acrylic material about 6.5 feet in diameter, allowing an unprecedented view below the surface. In order to make this experience even more enjoyable, there were two, front-facing, thick leather reclining chairs, side-by-side, fixed to the floor. I watched dolphins swimming ahead of the pontoon when we'd be moving along.

That entire day was spent preparing the ship. The crane operator hoisted the large "electronics van" (the size of a small trailer) up onto the deck where it was welded down. We loaded huge spools of hydrophone-equipped cable and mounted an enormous pulley to the stern of the ship. That evening would be the last we'd see Honolulu, and our hotel rooms for a few days, as bright and early the next morning, after driving to the base again, we were headed out to sea.

SLEEP ANYTIME, ANYWHERE

As the ship was small, we had sufficient provisions for just 3-days at a time, only enough fresh water to allow the grimiest workers to have an occasional shower, and enough berths (built-in beds below deck) to accommodate *just* the ship's crew. The rest of us were issued sleeping bags and air mattresses. We were told – and strongly encouraged – to "sleep anywhere and anytime that you can, because we can't predict when you'll be needed." While the sole woman along for these tests was given the captain's quarters, it was actually pretty common to find someone sacked out in their sleeping bag at our feet underneath a worktable!

As I was one of the five or six engineers (hardware and software) onboard, my main job was to operate the electronic processing equipment when we were actively engaged in a test run, as well as to analyze the data we'd collect, all inside the air-conditioned electronics van. That also meant that, not only did I *not* qualify for the occasional shower, but most of the time I would be out on deck in my bathing suit with the other engineers, helping to pay out and retrieve the mile-long hydrophone cables. See the photo titled Working on the SSP Kaimalino at the top of this chapter.

One night out at sea I was sleeping on my air mattress inside the electronics van, but it had deflated – my mattress, not the van. So, I stepped outside of the air-conditioned van into the humid tropical air, causing my glasses to fog up instantly! Removing them for the time being, I groped my way to the engine room where I knew they had an air hose that I could use to re-inflate the mattress. As I approached the open hatchway, I felt a strong pull like a suction into the engine room. Holding onto a railing, I was able to stabilize myself and fill the mattress, but I soon realized the source of this incredible suction. Both of the turbine engines were running, and they took in air from the engine room!

"Everybody move away from the aft deck!" came the announcement from the bridge. A moment later, we could hear the unmistakable whine of the high-speed starter for one of the two turbines, and then the roar of that engine kicking in. Once the first was stable, they'd repeat the process for the other one. Once both were running, we were allowed back to finish what we were doing on the stern. When I asked why we had to evacuate the back of the ship when they started the engines, I was told that they're more prone to exploding during start-up than any other time. I respected this, of course, but still felt that it was rather unlikely that any shrapnel from an exploding engine could make its way through the inch or two thick deck plating...that is, until a chain broke on one of the engines!

I was sitting on the aft deck casually removing hydrophones from a cable we'd just pulled in after a test run. We were cruising along on the turbine propulsion. That's when I found myself suddenly propelled a couple of inches off the deck at the same instant as a gunshot-like sound! Immediately, a large plume of thick black smoke came billowing out of the affected engine. This chain, apparently running at ten or twenty thousand RPM from the turbine, was propelled up towards the deck, forming a notable dent in the extremely thick plating just inches from where I was sitting! The smoke plume was actually normal on shutdown for these engines, since they were running on diesel fuel. The engine had shut down automatically when sensing the fault.

THE AIRBORNE KETCHUP BOTTLE

Another time we were experiencing high seas when several of us were down in the galley waiting for the ship's cook to prepare lunch. There was a large, glass ketchup bottle setting on a table one moment, and the next, it was flying up into the air where it soon crashed down and shattered on the floor. You'll recall that I'd mentioned that the hull of this ship was normally several feet above the water's surface. Well, when we'd be pitched about with high sea conditions, the ship's hull would come down and *smack* hard against the water. That kinetic energy was then transferred through the floor and into the table's pedestal. Since all of that was bolted down, the only thing that was free to be launched was the ketchup bottle. It really was quite the sight!

SEEING STARS DURING THE DAY

Have you ever seen the stars during the day? I have. I was working out on the deck, and I looked straight up into the sky. It was maybe 2pm, so the sun wasn't directly overhead. There wasn't a cloud in the sky, and we were perhaps 100 miles from any land, therefore the sky was completely free from any pollutants. At first, I was amazed at how dark blue the sky looked – nearly black! Then, after a moment, I started to actually see stars! My best guess is that the atmosphere right there was so free of any particulates that even the typical blue from refraction through moisture wasn't obscuring the view directly into deep space! It was pretty amazing.

We'd be out at sea for three days at a time, and then come back into port re-provision at the end of the third day. We'd head back to our hotels for the night, take a luxurious-feeling shower, and have dinner in Waikiki, then repeat. This continued for 31-days straight! No, we didn't take off weekends, or *any* days, for that matter. We didn't sleep 8-hours straight at any point while aboard ship. If we were lucky, we'd get 3-4 hours before we were needed again. We did hard work outside, even in the rain. But we did it in our bathing suits under the sun, it was incredibly fun, and it all just felt like a really long tropical vacation! Oh, and since we were getting paid for 80-hours straight time per week, for that *one month* I earned the equivalent of $9,000 in today's currency!

THE GARDEN ISLE

On the Friday (March 19) when everyone else was getting on the first flight they could catch back home, I decided, since I was already in "the islands", that I'd take a puddle-jumper over to Kauai. I'd read about "The Garden Island" and was determined to get a glimpse of it while I was already so close. I booked my flight from Honolulu back to LAX for 11pm, and then headed off to Kauai! I rented a car there and headed southwest on route 50 up to Kalalau Lookout at the top of the Kaunuohua Ridge that forms Waimea Canyon. Taking in the view for a second or two, I then jumped back into the car and proceeded to negotiate the numerous switchbacks back down the mountain and back to the airport in Lihue in record time, just before my flight was about to depart. Back then the "terminal building" at

Lihue airport on Kauai was little more than an open shack with a thatched grass roof, and the car rental lot was only a few feet away, so even though I was cutting it close, I wasn't too concerned. It would be nearly a decade later before this airport lengthened and paved its packed dirt runways, installed a much larger terminal building with automated baggage claim, and became an international airport capable of accommodating aircraft larger than the DC3.

Despite the whirlwind nature of my Kauai visit, the seed had been planted. I *needed* to go back someday to photograph the amazing grandeur of the lush rain forests, pristine beaches, and spectacular array of flowers on this beautiful island!

Chapter 23 – COMPETITIVE FIGURE SKATING

Skating Free Dance with Jessica

SKATING BACKWARDS

I had both been roller-skating for quite a few years, just as a means to maintain a certain degree of aerobic activity. I skated as a kid at roller rinks near Buffalo. I roller-skated all through college. And I roller-skated when I moved to California. In all of those years, though, I'd never learned to skate backwards. This was about to change. It was around December 1982, and I was 24 when I started taking roller skating lessons at a local rink with the specific intent of learning to skate backwards!

It really didn't take very long before I was skating in any direction you could imagine like a pro...something that certainly didn't escape the notice of my instructors. Unbeknownst to me my instructors (called skating pros) also ran a skating club at the rink where members participated in advanced figure and dance skating competitions. My pros were always on the lookout for new talent. They knew that I was also into gymnastics, so they saw a strong young man who skated well and who, if coupled with a partner, might compete in dance skating competitions and shows, earning their skating club trophies.

What they *didn't* know until shortly after I'd joined the club, was that, after almost three and a half years of very heavy gymnastics, including a number of times landing on my back across the side vault after failed front handsprings, I was nursing chronic neural pain down one of my legs due to a pair of lumbar discs that were preparing to rupture. This would severely limit my lifting abilities.

THE SKATING CLUB

It was just about February 1983 when I joined my rink's skating club. There, I was introduced to the existing members consisting of, most notably, Debbie Flippen, Mike Hauk, Christine & Michelle Sceglio (identical twins), Jessica Amber, Tom Jacobson, and Selena. Deb was just a year or so younger than me, but she was already paired with Mike. The twins were 15 at the time, and while quite friendly, they weren't interested in partnering – although I'm quite sure that their mother had a strong desire, once her daughters turned 18, for them to marry my brother and me after she'd heard that I had a twin. I think it was just one of those "twin things"! That left Jessica, age 11. She was small, light, and already an accomplished singles skater – the perfect skating partner, in the eyes of my pros (Belson and Czarina Sanchez), for one who has back problems!

There were basically three levels of skate competition. Singles skaters perform solo routines consisting of a series of jumps, spins, and complex footwork, in coordination with music. Free-dance skaters perform similar skating routines, also coordinated to music, but the male of the pair also lifts his female partner all about, but not over his waist level. Pairs skaters are doing all of this, *plus* the guy will toss and twirl the girl all about, *over his head*. Because over-the-head lifts were not going to agree with my back problems at the time, Jess and I were relegated to the free-dance routines.

While much of the choreography for the free-dance routine that Jess and I did was created spontaneously in conjunction with the music, Bel and Czar showed us a number of lifts that would give the routine its necessary appeal. Once the full routine was defined, Jess and I practiced it a couple of times during each practice session, refining it as we went along. Our goal was to be ready to perform it at the upcoming, large annual, regional skating competition called "Goldskate" held each February in Bakersfield, California in February 1984.

RUPTURED DISCS & MY TWO DAYS AS A PARAPLEGIC

It was Thanksgiving weekend, 1983, and my Aunt Dorothy and Uncle Don Howlett were visiting family in Southern California. As I'd wanted to show them the routine that Jessica and I been polishing for the February 1984 competition, they came by the rink for a bit. We performed it flawlessly for them. They took off, and Jess and I went back to practicing. Just as I was bending forward, holding Jess in my arms while moving along the skate floor, it happened! I'd learn later that two of my lumbar discs (L4/L5 & L5/S1) had just ruptured... badly! I couldn't bend at all without severe pain shooting all up and down the back of my left leg, so Jessica had to unlace and remove my skates for me! Still in severe pain, I managed to drive her home, and get myself home safely, where I just deposited myself on my bed, and tried not to move too much, until I could get to a doctor the following week.

They sent me to the hospital for a CAT scan the next Monday. Late in the evening after this scan, I got a phone call from the hospital. It was the orthopedic surgeon I'd seen who'd scheduled the CAT scan, calling me personally! Not his office. Not an assistant or a secretary. The surgeon, himself, called me and told me not to eat or drink anything after midnight, and for me to get to the hospital at 7:00 the next morning! He told me that I had the worst rupture of these two discs that he'd ever seen, and that he'd scheduled me for surgery at that time!

That Tuesday afternoon, after the surgery, I remember lying in the bed in my semi-private hospital room. Bill had flown down from Sunnyvale and was sitting there when I became mostly lucid. The most notable thing that I remember was that I couldn't feel or move my legs!

Ironically, my first thought as the reality of this situation began to sink in was that I'd never again do my favorite back handsprings and whip backs! Eventually, I realized that this also extended to walking! Now I was starting to get a little bit panicky...that is, until I remembered that ALL of my life short stories have happy endings. This immediately turned my thoughts from the pessimistic visions of life as a paraplegic, to optimistic thoughts of how to overcome this!

With supreme effort, I tried to cause any movement at all in my legs, feet or toes. Nothing! I wasn't going to quit so easily, though. All through the night I kept on trying. Very early the next morning, was able to wiggle some of the toes on my right foot! This was the encouragement I needed to push even harder for even more progress! By that afternoon I was able to lift my right leg slightly and had seen movement in my left big toe. With each new movement below my waist, I was further encouraged to push even harder to get more function back! It had become a personal competition with my own nervous system, and I was determined to win!

It's now Thursday morning – two days after the surgery – and I was finally able to move my right leg a little more than the prior afternoon, but the most notable improvement was the slight movement I'd been able to achieve in my left leg. Soon after I'd mentioned this to the nurse, she helped me get out of the bed, and supported me while I maneuvered myself up to the wheeled walker that she'd brought in. My legs were not able to support me at all, but since I still maintained my substantial upper-body strength, I just held myself upright like I was on the gymnastics parallel bars, while I did what I could to move my legs in a crude walking manner. It took two full weeks before I could walk unassisted, but, except for a lingering, significant paralysis in my left calf, I'd won! It took me another two months after I got out of the hospital before I was back to doing back handsprings and whip backs again...only with some modification to accommodate the left-calf issue.

MATCHMAKERS

Because of lifting restrictions, I wasn't allowed to resume free-dance skating until about April 1984. When I resumed practicing the routine with Jessica, I noticed that the club had some new members; most notably, Kim Quinn. Bel and Czar weren't only instructors at the rink, but they also fancied themselves as matchmakers! Apparently, Kim had lamented to one of them about her senior prom coming up in May, and she had nobody to go with. So, as I'd been told much later on, our pros schemed to put a plan into action. Out on the floor, Czarina offered to help Kim with some footwork, while at the same time Belson wanted to show me some new move to put into the routine. It was actually a ruse...an opportunity for Belson to tell me that Kim wanted me to take her to her prom, while Czarina was telling Kim that I was interested in taking her. In fact, neither of us had said these things. They were just setting us up! Still, it worked. I'd never gone to a prom, so I figured it might be my only opportunity to experience one. Kim was just 17, but since I had no ulterior motives, this wasn't an issue for me. I took her to her prom, and we actually had a pretty good time.

In or around September 1984 I'd decided that I wanted to find a new place to live, as my apartment complex in Anaheim was starting to get a bit run down, and there were increasing break-ins and thefts in the car ports. Once again, as soon as Bel and Czar had gotten wind of my search for a new place to live, they set their matchmaking wheels into motion! They knew that Deb had just broken up with her fiancé and needed a place to live. It seemed logical for them to direct her to me. For the next month or so Deb and I looked at houses and apartments together, with the intent of being roommates. We were looking very seriously at a new housing complex down in Irvine, but I simply didn't have enough for a house down payment at that time. Finally, we ended up in a very picturesque 2-bedroom "garden apartment" in Placentia, just a couple of miles from the old place.

In the meantime, Jessica and I continued to practice our free dance routine. Finally, delayed a year by my ruptured discs, we performed the routine in front of a large audience in an arena in Bakersfield. See the photo titled, "Skating Free Dance with Jessica" at the top of this chapter. While my back wasn't bothering me anymore, I was having issues with nervousness about performing in front of so many spectators! Call it stage fright, if you will, but I was definitely not feeling very good about skating out to the center of the huge floor with a spotlight trained on just the two of us! Ultimately, I just did what I'd always done with my gymnastics moves; I let my body do what it'd been prepared to do, and I stopped thinking about it. Once the music began, and we began our routine, everything else was just completely automatic. We did a flawless performance, and it was actually a lot of fun!

THE STUBBORN TRAFFIC LIGHT

After we'd all done of our performances, everybody congregated to celebrate at one of the hotels where one of the skating clubs was staying. It was very late by the time I drove back to my hotel. I'd been asked to take one of the young women from another skating club back to her hotel that was closer to mine, so she rode with me. Now, Bakersfield wasn't really much more than a truck stop in the middle of California, so there was never very much traffic on the roads, and far less at about 1am when we approached one particular traffic light. I had to make a left turn, and there wasn't a soul on the roads anywhere in sight, and yet this light remained red in our direction.

After a couple of minutes had passed my passenger said, "There's nobody around. Why not just go through it?"

I replied, "Because, the moment I do, a police car will somehow magically appear out of nowhere!"

Another minute passed, and I was actually starting to consider her urging.

About four or five minutes after we'd pulled up to this totally vacant intersection in the middle of nowhere in the middle of the night, I finally decided that the light had to be stuck, and that I'd be justified if I were to go through it after making absolutely sure that it was clear. The moment I took my foot off of the brake, I saw the other side go to yellow, and then red. We got the green light...finally! Just after I'd turned onto the intersecting road, I saw a police car sitting there partially hidden behind a low billboard! I could only imagine that he had some kind of control unit for the traffic signal, and was intentionally making it appear to be stuck, and then he'd ticket those unfortunate enough to take the bait! I'm glad that I'd made the right decision by waiting instead of giving in to my passenger's impatience.

THE BEST ROOMMATE

Since Deb was a college student, we didn't split the rent right down the middle. Instead, I only asked her to pay a small portion of the total rent and make up the difference in basic house cleaning. She readily agreed to this but ended up going far above my expectations when she'd also prepare most of our meals, as well! She was the very best roommate I'd ever had! With very few exceptions, we lived like we were husband and wife. While we'd each date other people independently, anytime Deb and I found ourselves without a date, and we wanted to do something with someone, we'd just do it together. From this we actually made a pact; if we were both still single by the time we both turned 30, we'd just marry each other.

Alas, this was not to be. In January 1986, a few months before Kim Quinn turned 19, we began dating. That summer, I proposed, and we were married in April 1987.

Chapter 24 – WAVES IN THE PARKING LOT

If you've ever been walking along a large, nearly empty parking lot or a paved road during an earthquake, then you've probably experienced this. If not, you probably won't believe what I'm about to say.

I believe it was 1984. I was walking across the large, sparsely populated parking lots between buildings where I worked in Anaheim, California on a sunny day when I thought I was seeing an illusion. The pavement was "rolling towards me" like waves in the ocean! I saw the few cars that were there hop up and down as this wave passed beneath them. Once it reached me, it nearly knocked me off of my feet!

What I'd just experienced was a fairly mild, earthquake exhibiting Rayleigh (up/down) wave motion. What was most unusual about this experience was that the pavement around me that had acted like a fluid just moments prior had no signs of damage! There were no new cracks, breaks, or crumbling! Once it had passed, it was as if it'd never happened!

Chapter 25 – TEN DAYS IN KAUAI

Hanakapiai; The Perfect Beach!

After my very brief taste of the stunning beauty of Kauai back in 1982, I'd planned to return, only this time I'd bring my brother to share the experience, and we'd bring our cameras to record it. Due to various factors, not the least of which being that we didn't have enough vacation time available to make such a trip later in 1982, we decided to try for November 1983 after we'd both get fresh vacation time, and we'd also have more time to save up for this expensive trip.

Unfortunately, my back wasn't cooperating around that timeframe, as I ended up rupturing two lumbar discs and having major surgery. This meant we'd have to put it off into 1984, after I'd fully recovered.

I'd recovered from my surgery, but then Bill's back decided to act up, requiring another surgical procedure – called the chymopapain injection – to help reduce the disc swelling in the same lumbar region of my rupture. This occurred sometime around March or April of 1984, further delaying our plans for the Kauai trip.

Finally, with both of our backs cooperating for at least the time being, we scheduled the Kauai trip for June 1984. We made reservations *only* for our flights, the rental car, and the resort condominium where we stayed in Princeville. Beyond that, the entire ten days we'd be on Kauai were totally unscheduled – a completely blank slate. In doing so, we had the flexibility to sit on Tunnels Beach for three hours just to capture the sunset over Bali Hai Peak, or spontaneously do the Kalalau Trail hike to Hanakapiai Beach and back, or thoroughly explore the peaks of Waimea Canyon – all without any concern of having to rush to the next attraction.

THE KALALAU TRAIL & THE PERFECT BEACH

We DID prepare to hike. We DID bring canteens for water. In fact, they were in the condo when we headed out to where Route 56 ends at Ke'e Beach. But the sign at the trailhead for the Kalalau Trail indicated that there were two segments, and the 2-mile portion seemed like it'd be simple enough...even without our canteens. For the record, I'd like to say that this was *not* one of my better decisions. While it turned out to produce incredible experiences that we'd repeat numerous times in the future, the lack of hydration did... well, what it does. We'll get to that in a moment.

Backpacker Magazine rates the Kalalau Trail as one of the ten most dangerous hikes in America. The Sierra Club rates it a 9 out of 10 for its difficulty. This is ostensibly for the entire 11-mile length all of the way to Kalalau Beach, but since the trail has numerous elevation changes, up to as much as 800-feet and back to sea level, throughout its entire length along the Na Pali coastline, it wouldn't be unreasonable to rate the first 2-mile section as at least a solid 6 for the average person.

Bill and I were both carrying full camera packs. No, these weren't as huge as a full hiking backpack, but they also weren't like a tiny single-camera bag, either. Inside each of our camera packs we had a Minolta XD-11 35mm camera, two or three lenses, a flash, lots of film, many lens filters, and a tripod strapped on sideways. Oh, and, of course, a towel – an important item for any hiker! All together, we were each carrying about 25 pounds of equipment on our backs.

Had this not been our very first time hiking this trail, we'd have made much better time. But to be consistent with our "no schedule" philosophy, we took our time, savoring the spectacular sweeping vistas, and capturing

275

them photographically. Unlike decades later, when foot traffic on this trail is almost like a busy freeway at rush hour, that first time in 1984 we didn't see a single person along the entire path, until we reached Hanakapiai beach – *the perfect beach!* Others may contest this designation, but *for me*, it was the most perfect beach I'd ever encountered.

Still on the trail, about 200-feet above the water, and nearly two hours later, we got our first glimpse of the beach. It was a wide section of white sand nestled comfortably between a pair of vertical cliffs rising hundreds of feet above the sea. There's also a long rocky line defining a stream from Hanakapiai Falls further inland. This stream meanders along the north edge of the beach and deposits its fresh water into an 18-inch-deep depression in the backside of a natural rise in the sand before it runs into the ocean at the south end. This shallow accumulation is pleasantly heated from the sun, making it bathtub warm, and the ideal way to rinse off salt from the ocean. We could also just make out a total of three ant-like figures currently occupying the beach! See the photo titled Hanakapiai; The Perfect Beach at the top of this chapter.

Before getting down to the beach, you will now find rather ominous signs warning of dangerous rip currents, even giving a count of the number of those who've drowned as a result. When we first went there the only warning signs posted simply stated, "Strong swimmers only!" We were 26, accomplished gymnasts, and competitive figure skaters at the time. We were in prime physical condition. As such, we felt imminently qualified to proceed to the water…with reasonable caution, of course.

After making our way down the steep incline and crossing the rocky stream, we found ourselves on the beach. Shrugging off our camera backpacks and depositing them on the sand, we proceeded to the water. This is where we met the other three inhabitants of this perfect beach, close-up. They were two very naked women, and a guy. Had I mentioned that this was the perfect beach? Anyway, they welcomed us, and reiterated the presence of the strong undertow.

Because the slope from the beach is so shallow, we had to wade out perhaps a hundred feet before the water reached…uh…let's just call it *chest*-height for us all. As there was a very strong, constant wind blowing towards the beach, it wasn't long before a wave came along that was just right for bodysurfing. I have never before ridden so many waves so far! In fact, more than a couple of times, my ride took me so far up the beach that I was actually deposited, rather unceremoniously, onto nearly dry sand! Had I mentioned that this was the perfect beach?

We continued this physically demanding, yet immensely satisfying activity for about an hour before returning to our backpacks. Digging them out from the sand that had blown over them, we took some pictures, and then bathed for a bit in the freshwater to rinse off the salt. At this point, we'd gone three hours without water while engaged in strenuous activities in hot and humid conditions, and we were still facing another couple of hours to get back to civilization!

We didn't dawdle on the way back, so we made good time, but at about the 1.5-miles point the dehydration was starting to affect me. I nearly blacked out once and had to sit down and rest a bit while splashing water over my head from one of the streams that run across the trail. Feeling better, we continued...until my vision started to fade yet again! Like the last time, we'd just approached another stream, but this time, in addition to dousing my head, I also thoroughly cooled my legs with the refreshing water. After a moment, my vision cleared and I was now feeling fully refreshed, so we both sprinted off at a dead run for the remainder of the rigorous winding trail! While our rental car was parked at the Ke'e Beach trailhead, it didn't help a lot, as it was like a thousand degrees inside until the air-conditioning became effective, and we still needed water! We had to drive to the Dry Caves parking area, about a mile away, before we found an ice cream truck! Seldom before had ice cream and cold water been so welcome!

TUNNELS BEACH

Later in the day we decided to check out a secret beach that we'd learned about the night before from someone at the condo. He'd told us that it's known only to the locals and isn't marked in any way. It's called Tunnels Beach. It is the best place for snorkeling. Our directions were basically, "Head west, and go over several one-lane bridges. When you cross a double set of one-lane *wooden* bridges with a white horse next to it, then it'll be on your right in about three miles – just look for cars parked along the road."

Despite our doubts, we did, in fact, find a *real* white horse grazing in a field next to the double wooden bridge, and soon saw a few cars pulled off of the road. Of course, today, a LOT more people have heard about this amazing beach, so, due to complaints from residents in the area, parking is no longer allowed along the road. You'll have to park at Haena Beach and walk the quarter mile back to Tunnels.

Passing through a section of woods, we exited onto a beautiful beach with a great view of Bali Hai Peak! Just beneath the water's surface there were a series of partially formed tunnels, apparently formed by lava flow. Most had a small open area along the top that was just big enough to look through, but not enough to fit through. We took turns where one of us would act as a spotter at the surface and watch the other as he swam through a tunnel. This worked well until I came upon a tunnel with a fork. It had two passages. I'd already gone straight through the one passage, but I wanted to try the fork to the right the next time. Again, while Bill waited and watched my progress from above, I entered the main tunnel and made the right-turn into the new one. After a moment, my shoulders started to scrape the sides, and finally, I could proceed forward no further. At this point, I simply paddled backwards until I was back in the anteroom where I'd be able to locate the main tunnel out...once the silt I'd just stirred up had settled.

I just sat there, quite comfortable for the next 30-seconds or so, until I could get my bearings, and then I swam out. Bill, on the other hand, wasn't quite as relaxed. He'd seen me enter the side tunnel, but, after a bit, and the cloud of silt, couldn't tell what was going on after that. I think he was worried or some silly thing like that, as I met him swimming down to the main entrance just as I was coming out.

THE HELICOPTER TOUR

That evening the activities director at the condo suggested that we might like to take a helicopter tour the next day. This sounded like fun – I mean we always like flying in any of its many manifestations, and we'd only ever been in a real helicopter, for about a 3-minute ride, just once before while in college. The next day, we drove to the place where this particular helicopter tour company was based. We covered a fair portion of the island in the 45-minutes of this flight. This pilot did something, however, that didn't seem exactly typical of most tour companies. He asked us if we'd like to experience an autorotation (power-off) landing! Knowing very little about helicopters at that time, while the concept was exciting, I also thought that it seemed to be rather dangerous. He went into the autorotation, anyway, and we soon found ourselves hovering just inches above the ground that was rushing up to us so quickly just moments prior. I think it was that bit of thrill, plus the complete maneuverability that the helicopter could achieve that finally helped us to decide what type of aircraft we *ultimately* wanted to fly!

Our remaining time on the island was spent photographing a wide variety of exotic flowers at Olu Pua Gardens, and everywhere else we went about the island. We got the classic shot of Wailua Falls that appeared on the opening of the weekly television series, "Fantasy Island", and we headed back to Kalalau Lookout at the top of Waimea Canyon – also known as "The Grand Canyon of the Pacific". There, we photographed the spectacular, panoramic vistas.

These ten exceptionally relaxing, schedule-free/pressure-free days had given us both a new love: The island of Kauai. We'd, therefore, find our way back to the island many times over the decades.

Chapter 26 – FLYING REAL HELICOPTERS, SOLO!

Bob Flying a Helicopter Solo

Remember that dream we'd had when we were five years old? We'd desperately wanted to fly! It took that dream, plus 22-years of determination and good choices that allowed us both to become sufficiently successful, plus a tantalizing taste of the amazing capabilities of a helicopter in Kauai months earlier, in order for us to make that dream a reality.

Why helicopters? Consider John F. Kennedy's famous speech in 1962 about going to the moon. He said, "But why, some say, the moon? Why choose this as our goal? ... We choose to go to the moon in this decade and do the other things, not because they are easy, but because they are hard; because that goal will serve to organize and measure the best of our energies and skills..."

Compared to regular, fixed-wing airplanes, helicopters are notably much more difficult to fly. But, similar to the quest for the moon, the rewards of achieving this goal are far greater, as well. With the exception of the Harrier and the V22 Osprey military aircraft, and perhaps a few others, airplanes just cannot hover, fly sideways, fly backwards, and go straight up like helicopters can. Quite simply put, helicopters are extremely versatile and excessively FUN to fly! To master this mechanical marvel that simply doesn't *want* to fly, is nothing short of organizing and measuring the best of our energies and skills!

Just six-months after our Kauai adventure, Bill and I had both begun helicopter flight training. He flew out of San Jose, and I started my training in Santa Ana, finishing in Long Beach, all in California.

NEITHER EASY NOR CHEAP

It was December 16, 1984, when I first sat in the pilot's seat of a real helicopter at Pacific Coast Helicopters (PCH) at John Wayne/Orange County Airport in Santa Ana. It was a 2-seat Robinson R22-HP light helicopter with a 25-foot 2-inch semi-rigid, two-bladed main rotor, a 42-inch tail rotor, and a 160-horsepower Lycoming piston engine. This is the aircraft that would soon enable me to fully satisfy my dream of flying with full control, but it wouldn't be easy, or cheap!

The Federal Aviation Administration (FAA) requires a minimum of 40-hours of flight time, comprised of 20- to 30-hours dual flight instruction and 10-hours solo flight time. Additionally, they require 40-hours of ground school instruction. The purpose of the ground school is to teach student pilots the basic physics of flight, airfoils, lift and drag, how to compute weights and balances for the aircraft, how to interpret weather data, how to navigate effectively, how to read and interpret the aircraft's instruments, and, of course, rules, regulations, and procedures. It's also necessary to pass a written "pilot knowledge exam" covering these and other concepts sometime prior to registering for the oral exam and check ride – the practical flight final exam – but they suggest taking it soon after the student's first solo cross-country flight. In addition, a student pilot is required to pass a flight physical exam prior to their first solo flight.

These are the *minimum* requirements, and most fixed-wing students earn their private pilot license with just 40-hours, *nobody* gets a *helicopter* pilot license in just 40-hours! The Certified Flight Instructor (CFI) who last signed off your logbook is substantially responsible for your actions as a pilot, so they'll hold off until they're absolutely sure that you are a safe pilot before they'll recommend you for the final check ride. This means *lots* more flight hours than the minimum.

Because I flew just once or twice each weekend, I had precisely fifty lessons in an eleven-month period. In that time, I flew 67.2 hours, averaging 1.3 flight hours per lesson, in four different Robinson helicopters, with three different instructors at two different flight schools. I passed both my knowledge test and oral/check ride final in just one try each, thereby earning my Private Pilot Rotorcraft/Helicopter License on November 19, 1985!

The costs do add up! There's ground school, the medical flight exam, the pilot knowledge exam, the oral & check ride exam, books, manuals and other study material. There's also the flight computer, a personal helicopter headset, and, of course, I had to pay for the flight instructor fees and helicopter rental costs. Altogether, this amazingly satisfying and fun endeavor cost me just short of $10,000. This is just over $22,000 in today's dollar value.

The reason I've included all of this information here, including the costs, is to emphasize why it was so very important for us to make good choices, and pursue our interests that translated into very lucrative and successful careers. It is because we both became very successful with our engineering careers, that we were able to pay for our flight training as we went along, rather than going into debt with large loans. When you are successful, you too, can enjoy life's little extras.

ONE IN TEN THOUSAND

Bernt Torgerhagen was my first flight instructor. Bill's was Tor Gunnar Salbu. As both were Norwegian, we concluded, from this huge, scientific sampling, that they must have a LOT of helicopter pilots in Norway! It was my second lesson (January 1985) before I met any of the other students at PCH. I was considerably surprised, and quite pleased, to make the acquaintance of Karen Kim. I was quite pleased because she was very cute, but I was surprised because female helicopter pilots are almost unheard of. They're an extremely rare breed. To put this into perspective, consider some statistics from an FAA report about pilot licensure in 1985. Helicopter pilots made up just 1% (1 in 100) of ALL general aviation pilots. Women made up just 1% of all helicopter pilots. Therefore, *female helicopter* pilots made up just 0.01%

(1 in 10,000!) of all general aviation pilots! Considering how unique she was, I felt almost like I was standing in the company of royalty! I'm sure I acted just about as nervously as I would with royalty, as well!

HELICOPTERS ARE SAFER

It wasn't very long before I learned how much safer helicopters are in comparison to fixed wing airplanes, when flown within the proper operating parameters. Let's dispel a very common myth right now. Most people believe that a helicopter will drop like the proverbial brick if the engine should quit. Nothing could be further from the truth! In fact, in an engine failure scenario, I would MUCH rather be in a helicopter than a fixed wing airplane! Why? Well, let's look at such a situation.

Both the airplane *and* the helicopter will continue to glide and can maneuver considerably (depending upon initial altitude), with no power when flown by a competent pilot. The huge difference comes in when you get near the ground. In a small airplane like a Cessna 172, you need to find an airport runway, a grass landing strip, a large open field, or a long, straight section of road or highway (300 – 700 feet) to land on. In a small helicopter like the Robinson R22, it's necessary only to locate a space just slightly bigger than the helicopter itself (about 40 feet)!

In fact, during my training, I performed about 224 power-off (autorotation) landings in the helicopter. Is the helicopter just that unreliable, that the engine keeps on quitting? No! It's because my instructors kept rolling off the throttle at random intervals! This is actually quite normal in ANY pilot training. They do this with every student to keep us alert, and to sharpen our emergency procedures. While most of these autorotations were terminated in a hover to spare the landing gear excessive wear and tear, I did experience about half a dozen full touchdown power-off landings. We bounce! Because of these frequent, unexpected throttle-chops, as a pilot you develop a very interesting attitude.

When you get into your car, I'm sure you don't *expect* it to quit. As such, you're very surprised when it does, and you might not always know what to do if it should happen while you're driving along the highway. When you fly an aircraft, *any* aircraft, you DO expect it to quit! You *have* to. If you didn't, then you might not be prepared when it does. As such, you fly it in a manner that ensures maximum safety at all times. For instance, while a helicopter *can* take off and land straight up and down, this wouldn't be the safest condition if the engine were to quit. Therefore, anytime we can, we take off and land with a running profile similar to an airplane. In doing so, if the engine were to quit at either takeoff or landing, then we've got sufficient velocity to perform an autorotation landing safely – which, itself, as already indicated, takes a very small space to set it down.

REALIZING MY DREAM; FIRST SOLO FLIGHT!

Bernt had accepted a helicopter tour job in Hawaii in mid-February, so my new instructor, for the next several months, would be Karl Schultz.

It was Saturday, March 30, 1985, at 3:41pm when I flew a helicopter alone for the very first time in my entire life! The weather: 73 degrees with 10-knot winds from the west, and clear blue sky with 40-mile visibility. I first flew an hour with Karl, just like any other lesson. Then he asked me to set the helicopter down in the sod, and he got out. Beneath the roar of the powerful engine and spinning rotors beating at the air, Karl showed me a few hand signals that he'd use to communicate to me which hovering maneuvers he wanted me to do before taking it up much higher. He stood about 50-feet away. He had me pick it up to a five-foot hover, then set it down three times. Next, he had me take it back up to a hover and perform a left pedal turn, and then a right, setting back down again. He came over to me and asked if I felt like taking it around the traffic pattern a few times. I said, "Sure!"

Karl reached inside, slipped on his headset for a moment, and called up the tower. He said, "Orange County Tower, Helicopter Six-Zero Juliet. I'm sending a student up for his first solo. Take care of him." The tower responded back, "Will do." Once Karl was back at a safe distance, it was up to me now to call back the tower and request permission to depart into right closed traffic. As soon as it was clear, they radioed back with, "Helicopter Six-Zero Juliet, you're clear to proceed. Good luck!" And I was off – on my very first solo flight… well, one with more than five-feet of altitude, anyway.

I executed a textbook departure, turned to the right for my crosswind leg, and another right into the downwind portion. I was told to do a mid-field approach. This meant that, instead of heading to a point beyond the start of the runway where a regular approach would begin, I'd execute my base leg just over the control tower, and then align for final approach to a grassy area parallel to the runway.

At first, I was simply too thrilled to give much thought to the fact that I was actually flying – alone! But then, just as I was descending through about 300-feet over the tower, preparing to turn into my final approach, the full force of the reality finally hit me! I suddenly realized that I was truly alone… in a $150,000 aircraft (equivalent to $335k today) …with nobody next to me to take the controls if something went wrong! I was in *complete control* of this aircraft, and of my life! A wave of adrenaline swept through my body at that moment but dissipated rapidly as I knew that I had sufficient training to maintain control. I soon came to a five-foot hover in the same spot where I'd departed and looked over at Karl for his hand signal. He gave me a thumbs-up, so I requested permission from the tower for another departure. After completing three trips around the pattern – thus qualifying as an *official* first solo flight – I set it down in the sod, and Karl came over to me.

"How do you feel?" he asked.

"Great!"

"How'd you like to take it around three more times?"

I replied, "Sure!"

Even after I climbed into my car after this amazing day that I'd dreamt of and prepared for the past 22-years, I felt like I was still floating! See the photo at the top of this chapter taken shortly after this first solo flight.

THE LETTER FROM THE FAA

Both Karen and I had our pilot knowledge exams scheduled for April 20, 1985. Therefore, the prior week she and I got together with Karl for a few intense study sessions. After feeling terribly unprepared, I was surprised at how easy the exam actually was for me. Ferrets won't typically do as well. And then came the waiting. Ten days later I received a letter from the FAA in the mail. Terror swept over me as I gazed at the outside of the envelope. I so badly wanted to see that I'd passed, but I also so badly did *not* want to see that I'd failed! It was the universal dilemma. I set that envelope on my kitchen table for an hour before I finally got up the courage to *tear* it open as quickly as I could, and search for the words I wanted to see! After the interminable second or two that it took me to find the results, I finally saw it: "PASSED" Considering how easy the exam was to me, I shouldn't have had the slightest concern, but there's always just that slightest little bit of doubt. Karen called me later saying that she, too, had passed. We were both extremely happy about these results.

QUICK-STOPS

There are few things more fun than quick stops in a helicopter! Once I was cleared to solo, I'd spend hours out in the practice field by the tower doing hovering maneuvers – fine coordination skills that helped to refine my control of the helicopter. After a while, I started making up games. I'd sit there hovering stationary just five feet over the grass while watching the 747 jets take off and land on the main runway. I'd do an exercise called "square the pad", where I'd have to maintain a nose-in attitude in a five-foot hover, while moving laterally around a square concrete pad, paying particular attention to the corners. A similar exercise was done around a tire on the ground. I'd also hover-taxi all about, as well. This led naturally to the quick stop. When in a five-foot hover, I'd get up to about 60-knots (69mph) just above the grass in the practice field, and then pull back on the cyclic control stick quickly while, in a coordinated motion, I'd drop the collective lever so I didn't "balloon" (suddenly soar high), but I'd maintain altitude while stopping immediately, still in the hover. That was a "normal" quick stop. Again, since the helicopter is an amazingly versatile machine and my imagination was fully in control during those "maneuver refinement hours", I decided to modify it just a bit. In order to stop much more quickly, I'd have to pull *way* back on the cyclic control. Of course, with a tail boom and its associated rotor sticking out some 20-feet behind me, doing so would drive the tail into the ground – not a preferred action! Therefore, I naturally swung the helicopter around at the instant of stopping, thereby causing a brief tail-high attitude, and I'd be facing in the direction that I came from. Now this is called FUN!

THE FLYING MOTORCYCLE

Have you ever ridden a bicycle, a mini-bike, or a motorcycle through bike trails in the woods? Bill and I did this a lot out back in the woods behind our parents' house. But it was never like this! There were similar bike trails through various woods in the Southern California hills, and they didn't have a lot of trees nearby. Sometimes, again while practicing maneuvers, I'd fly the helicopter over to these wooded areas and follow the bike trails – only I'd be around ten-feet above them! The Robinson R22 helicopter is extremely agile, and maneuvers very much like a motorcycle, except you have the option to go up and down in addition to left and right! Following bike trails with the helicopter provided me with much enjoyment!

Z-AXIS; DENIED!

If you've ever driven in any of the high-congestion areas like Boston Massachusetts, Washington DC, Northern Virginia, San Francisco California, or the highways around Los Angeles California, and a few other areas, I'm sure you've been caught in frustrating stop-n-go traffic. I was no stranger to this phenomenon living in Anaheim. One day, just after I'd left the airport following a flight lesson, I was in just such a traffic condition. Not thinking about it, I found myself reaching down to my left side with the intent of pulling up on the collective pitch lever that isn't there so I could just hop over all of the traffic! Once the traffic cleared, I could move in the X (left & right) and Y (forward & backward) coordinates, but my Z-axis (up & down) that's so very natural in the helicopter just isn't there in a car! I suddenly felt *very* surface-bound!

THE CHECK RIDE & POWER-OFF LANDING

Remember, I'd told you about autorotation – power-off – landings? They can take many forms. You might have found a nice landing spot shortly in front of you, so you do a straight-in auto. Sometimes you'll have just passed the best place to put it down, so you execute a 180- or 360-auto (like a corkscrew), depending on your altitude and the wind direction. If you're hovering just a few feet above the ground, you go into a hovering auto.

During my check ride, with the FAA examiner sitting next to me, he asked if he could take the controls shortly after I'd reached cruising altitude. At that moment, I felt sure that I'd done something that caused him to become so concerned that he didn't want me on the controls anymore, thereby causing me to fail the exam! I was significantly relieved after several minutes when he asked me to take the controls back. Now I was just confused...until he announced, "power failure!" Unlike my instructors, who just rolled off the throttle to an idle, the examiner had the courtesy to let me roll it off, on his command. Now we're flying through a very congested area between Fullerton and Long Beach California, so prime landing spots are few and far between. I automatically went instantly into an autorotation maneuver – choosing a 360. As I'm starting to turn the helicopter, he asks, "Where you gonna set it down, Bob?" I replied, "We just passed a church that has a large yard." Maneuvering to be sure I'd use up just enough altitude to line up with the yard, and making sure I'd be landing into the wind, I was down to about 100-feet when he said, "Okay, that's good. Abort the maneuver." He didn't want to go all of the way to the ground in a populated area. We'd do full touchdown autos back at the airport.

Another of the school's helicopters, Six-Niner Delta had been completely renovated between December and April, beefing up the power, and sporting a beautiful new paint scheme. The base color was a metallic silver-gray, and it had a bright baby blue and coral swirl along the sides. It'd been flown quite a bit since then, though, and once, as Karl and I were coming in from a cross-country flight, the engine started sputtering. We set it down fine, but we couldn't duplicate the issue at that time. We had the maintenance crew check it over, but they couldn't find anything, so Karl just told us (all of the student pilots) to be aware of it, and simply perform an autorotation landing if it should happen again. No problem.

So, this one time, when I was flying Six-Niner Delta, practicing maneuvers at the airport solo the mystery sputter returned! Before it happened, I'd hover-taxied from just outside of the hangar to the edge of the tarmac. Sitting there in a five-foot hover I radioed, "Orange County Tower, Helicopter Six-Niner Delta requesting permission to transition runways, for right closed traffic maneuvers."

A moment later, the tower replied, "Helicopter Six-Niner Delta, cross without delay the taxiway; hold short of runway one-nine right."

"Six-Niner Delta" I replied to indicate that I understood.

Just before I applied forward cyclic to begin crossing the taxiway, the engine began to sputter again! I couldn't maintain altitude, so I immediately executed a hovering autorotation landing while simultaneously radioing the tower; "Orange County, Helicopter Six-Niner Delta canceling transition request." Just as I was about to touch the ground, the low RPM warning horn began blaring at me. While it was not a soft landing, it was one of the gentlest full touchdown *autorotation landings* I'd ever done – and it was a real one, at that! After adjusting the choke and throttle a bit, the sputtering stopped, so I got back up into a five-foot hover again. This time, I was able to get across the runways and do my practice after new permission was granted by the tower.

AIRWOLF & SOME PHYSICS

One of my lessons with Karl at Orange County happened to fall on "Helicopter Awareness Day". Air Logistics at Long Beach Airport was hosting a helicopter show to commemorate the day. I asked Karl if he'd mind if we took a quick trip over there as part of my lesson. As he was also interested in checking it out, he agreed. When I contacted the tower to request permission to land there, I was told, "Land at your own risk." Well, then! That sounded rather encouraging. I set up my approach and set the helicopter down in an open space among a line of other parked helicopters. It was almost like parking a car into a parking space – except that we became an "exhibit" to the swarms of people milling around, in the process. There were about 30 helicopters on the ground, and several buzzing about in the air. One of the more notable helicopters on exhibit was the Bell 222 helicopter with its unique black and white (killer whale) paint job that was used in the filming of the TV series "Airwolf".

For those who aren't familiar with the "Airwolf" show, it featured this uniquely painted helicopter as a "secret weapon" to fight crime and bad guys trying to destroy the planet, and such. One of the special features that they exploited in the show was a "turbo-boost" capability that was supposed to hurl the helicopter to supersonic speeds.

Since that show's been off of the air for decades now, I feel that I can reasonably point out a certain fallacy in their turbo-boost system. Helicopters fly by way of a rotary wing – the main rotor. Because it spins, the only time that lift is symmetrical about the wing is in a stationary hover. When flying at any speed beyond this, the blade that advances into the direction you're heading will have more lift than the retreating blade. At a certain speed – for the Bell 222 helicopter used in Airwolf, this is just 135kts (about 155mph) – the retreating blade will stall, and the advancing blade will have an enormous amount of lift, thereby forcing the helicopter into a rapid roll. Whether by continuing to accelerate normally, or by way of any sort of a jet-like boost system, the results will be the same...and they're not pretty. Of course, it was just for entertainment, so they can violate physics at will while exercising their creative license.

MOM'S AMAZING SECRET LIFE

You might recall, when we were seven, I'd mentioned that our mother would frequently wear an ancient weather-beaten leather flight jacket when she'd do her gardening, and when we were thirteen, she sat down and tapped out flawless, high-speed Morse code for us. Maybe Bill and I just weren't that observant, or we simply didn't connect the dots, but it wasn't until 1985 after we'd both earned our helicopter pilot licenses that we'd learn that our mother was *also a pilot!* She flew many search and rescue missions in New York State with the Civil Air Patrol (CAP) during the 1940s in fixed wing airplanes. Back then, the primary means of communication in an aircraft was with Morse code. Now – finally – it all fits together! Our mother was certainly a woman well ahead of her time.

Chapter 27 – RAISING A FAMILY

You'll probably notice that this chapter occurs after most of the crazy and exciting adventures. This, too, was part of my grand plan. I'd always known that priorities would shift from *me* to *us* as soon as I was married and had a family – as it rightly should. Therefore, I wanted to be sure that I had accomplished most of my planned life goals that would use a considerable amount of my time, effort, and money before it would be properly diverted to the family.

Kim and I were married in April 1987. We'd moved to Sunnyvale, California in November 1986, so our first son, Drew, was born in that area in 1988. We moved again in late 1989 to Omaha, Nebraska. I'd designed certain high-speed electronic equipment in Sunnyvale, which was installed at Offutt Air Force Base – home of the US Strategic Command, formerly Strategic Air Command (SAC) – and nearly a dozen other bases around the world, and agencies in and near Washington, DC. In Omaha in 1990, our second son, Bryce, was born.

At this point, Kim and I had created a pair of "living legacies" in our children. With that done, I now needed to start working on some positive *durable* legacies. It was time to pursue publishing opportunities. I began working on an action-adventure novel substantially based upon my flying days. While I've had many other pieces published since then, that novel isn't one of them – yet! One day...

We'd move yet again in 1995. This time it was because I felt that I was starting to lose my electronics design abilities since I was only maintaining the equipment I'd designed years earlier. I wanted to get back into the active design arena, which meant, for that project, that I'd need to head to Northern Virginia.

I'd like to say that everything was all roses and butterflies at that time, but it wouldn't be true. For a variety of obscure reasons Kim and I began to drift apart – to the point where we separated in 1997 and divorced in 1999. Our primary intent was to keep things amicable between us so it wouldn't create undue stress on our kids. Once the divorce was final, she married a very nice guy, ironically also named Robert, whose birth date is the same as mine, except one year off. To this day, Kimberly remains one of my best friends. In fact, our entire – split – family has occasionally vacationed together! We're all *much* happier now. Did you notice how even this short story chapter in my life, despite the troublesome period leading to divorce, had a happy ending?

Chapter 28 – THE TOP SECRET MISSION

When I was living in Northern Virginia in the late 1990s, I had complete, unescorted access to a number of three- and four-letter agencies, including CIA, DIA, NRO, NPIC, the Pentagon, and a place called simply, "Area 58". This was, of course, in addition to a fair number of air force bases both in the US and abroad where we'd installed our equipment. This access was necessary for the project I was working on at that time.

For the record, and to dissuade anyone who might have unfavorable intentions after reading this section, I no longer retain ANY useful information from back then, and that which I had known has long since been declassified and is now available in the public domain.

A MONTH AT THE CIA

Okay, there IS one thing that I still vividly recall from the month that I spent working at CIA Headquarters while supporting the equipment I'd designed and installed there. They had a Sbarro's Pizza place among several other fast-food establishments within their in-house food court which prepared the *most amazing* Gourmet Mushroom pizza I'd ever had! The crust was nearly an inch thick – like light, fluffy cake – and I believe they used Portobello mushrooms, giving it a heavenly tang!

You're probably thinking that since it was at a standard pizza chain, that this very same pizza would be available elsewhere. Not true! I'd tried ordering it at other Sbarro's in the area, and they simply don't have the Gourmet Mushroom pizza on the menu. I even tried their regular mushroom pizza, but it pales in comparison! Therefore, I'm compelled to say that the best-kept secret at the CIA was, in fact, this Gourmet Mushroom pizza!

CHRISTMAS AT THE PENTAGON

Christmas day, 1996: I got a phone call at home that morning from my manager's manager indicating that some of our equipment at the Pentagon was down, and, so far, the technicians there hadn't been able to fix it.

He wanted me to know that I might be needed later on if they were still unsuccessful in repairing it in a few more hours. Kimberly, the kids, and I did the Christmas tree thing, unwrapping gifts in the morning, and we'd just finished our Christmas meal shortly after 2pm when the manager called again. He said that the techs still hadn't been able to fix the problem, and he needed to "call in the big guns now". Apparently, that meant me. I headed up to the Pentagon and spent the next eight-hours – on Christmas Day! – fixing and trying to obtain a proper signal level on a couple of fiber optic lines that had broken. Finally, successfully getting the system back online, I left the Pentagon at 11pm!

TOP SECRET DELIVERY

One day in 1999 I had to courier a top secret, 10.5-inch diameter computer tape from Washington, DC to McDill AFB down near Tampa, Florida. The problem with such a scenario is that once the digital tape is double wrapped into a pair of concentric, separately sealed envelopes, it couldn't be opened until it was delivered to an individual with the proper level of access, within an approved Sensitive Compartmentalized Information Facility (SCIF). This meant that it couldn't be opened for airport security in DC, and I couldn't allow it to be X-rayed, either! Clearly, this could cause a dilemma, even prior to the heightened airport security requirements imposed after 9/11 in 2001.

The solution was to have an Air Force captain from the Pentagon, who was our project liaison to the Air Force, meet me at Reagan National Airport. He presented the required credentials and information to the head of airport security before I'd arrived, and they both escorted me around the security checkpoint. Of course, once I was on the plane, I had to ensure that I never let the package out of my sight, which was a bit more difficult than you might imagine. For instance, I had to bring it with me when I used the rest room, and I couldn't just toss it down by my feet. I literally had to hold it for the entire flight, and I couldn't allow myself to doze off. At Tampa International Airport, I rented a car, and drove down to McDill Air Force Base. Only once I was securely inside the proper SCIF there, could the package be considered delivered and opened.

Chapter 29 – KAUAI WITH FAMILY

Drew, Bryce, and Bob Ready for SCUBA

KAUAI WITH MY KIDS

August 2003 was the last time that I went to Kauai as of the writing of this book. I took my sons Drew (15) and Bryce (13) with me that time, to introduce them to the island that gave me such fun and exciting memories over the prior decades. We'd be meeting my brother, his wife and their granddaughter there.

Consistent with every prior visit (except for my very brief introduction in 1982), I took them on the 2-mile Kalalau Trail hike to Hanakapiai Beach and back. Unlike 1984 when Bill and I first hiked the trail, this time there was a steady stream of foot-traffic in both directions. Also, unlike that first time, we brought plenty of water. We even found and tried some natural-growing guava along the trail, but no kumquats. I put that last bit in for Michelle, by the way, as an inside joke. This hike was a significant challenge for my kids, but I'm proud that they made it.

We also did a helicopter tour, in two choppers. While neither my brother nor

I are qualified to fly the turbine helicopters they had there, he did know one of the pilots rather well. While I was satisfied with my Private Pilot helicopter license, my brother went on to get his Commercial Pilot certification and became a Certified Flight Instructor (CFI). With that, he taught student helicopter pilots to fly at Nice Air, a flight school at Reid-Hillview Airport in San Jose. It was there that he met and became friends with another CFI, Nobu Yamauchi. Nobu was one of our tour pilots on Kauai. Nobu invited us all to come over for dinner at the end of the week to meet his family while we were there. After a most amazing meal more helicopter pilots began to show up. There were five pilots (Nobu, Marty, Luka, Gary, & John) from Inter-Island Helicopters, one (Bill – not my brother) from Jack Harter Helicopters, and, of course, my brother and me. Get eight helicopter pilots in a room together, and there'll be some fantastic stories exchanged! We had a fantastic time!

80-LBS OF METAL

We had also scheduled a catamaran tour up the Na Pali coast with Blue Dolphin Tours. As my brother and his wife had been SCUBA diving before, they chose to snorkel when the ship arrived at a beautiful location just offshore, west of the island, while Drew, Bryce and I had signed up to SCUBA dive. A dive instructor familiarized the three of us with the SCUBA gear and went over the procedures while we were en route. Just before we arrived, he'd helped us into our heavy tanks, regulators, lead weight belts, fins, and masks, adding about 80 lbs of metal to each of us. See the photo titled Drew, Bryce, and Bob Ready for SCUBA at the top of this chapter. Since Drew and I wear glasses normally, we were quite pleased when the instructor produced a -2-diopter mask for Drew, and a -3-diopter mask for me to wear. With these, we could actually see without our glasses!

Once the ship anchored, they put down a wide metal grate at the stern of the ship, allowing the snorkelers to sit on it at water level, and slip in at their leisure. Not so for us! Our instructor opened a section of the railing around the deck and jumped in – expecting us to follow. Now let me put this into perspective for you. We're each carrying around 80-pounds of extra weight in the form of our Self-Contained Underwater Breathing Apparatus (SCUBA) and such, and we're expected to basically walk the plank from a height of ten to fifteen feet above the water! Not knowing for sure if I'd be able to breathe under the water, or whether I'd just sink straight to the bottom or perhaps bob to the surface, I was, shall we say, hesitant – okay, maybe terrified is the better word – about just jumping right off of the deck. Of course, my kids were gracious (or scared?) enough to let me go first! Finally, I jumped. Let me just say that the trepidation I'd felt upon that precipice was matched only by the elation of discovering that I could breathe beneath the water, and that I came easily back to the surface!

Even swimming just beneath the surface, while breathing without a snorkel felt rather magical to me, but that was only the beginning. The three of us gathered at a rope from the ship where the instructor was waiting. He first had each of us clear our masks of water while submerged. Next, we had to remove our regulator mouthpieces under the water and then re-insert them without getting water in our mouths. The final task before we could head for the bottom was to go to a depth of about 10-feet and then equalize the pressure in our ears. We all accomplished the first two tests, but Bryce was unable to get one of his ears to clear when trying to equalize. Unfortunately, this disqualified him from participating in the dive any further, for his own safety. While I understood the safety concern, after all, the pain he'd suffer at depth even if he didn't burst his eardrum would be excruciating, I still felt really, really awful that he couldn't share this experience with us!

THE SCUBA EXPERIENCE

With deep regret for Bryce, I joined Drew and the instructor, and we descended until we were skimming just over the rocky features below. To me, SCUBA diving felt almost like flying! I was able to soar gracefully over, under, and around the landscape, along with the extremely colorful fish, or just hover in place at will. The water was slightly cool but by no means cold, and crystal clear, allowing us to see incredible distances! After 30-minutes immersed in the fantastic aquatic environment, we made our ascent. I'd glanced occasionally at my depth gauge, but once we broke the surface, and Drew spat his regulator mouthpiece out, he reported with considerable glee that we'd reached 52-feet! This was most notable, as the deepest I'd swum prior to that experience was about 15-feet.

Chapter 30 – THE ULTIMATE SPARKS

What does high-energy particle physics research, high-speed digital signal integrity in circuit boards, and parenting technique all have in common? They can all be accomplished with a Marx High-Voltage Pulse Generator.

AN EXPERIMENT TO INTEREST MY KIDS

In 2005, when my youngest son, Bryce, was in his mid-teens, I wanted to show him some of the more fun, interesting and exotic aspects of one of my favorite topics, electronics. As a parent, who was also a child once, I knew that the very last thing that he'd want to do was anything that interested me, unless it was just too fun for him to resist. I knew that teens liked things that were loud, bright, and dangerous. I'd recently discovered the concept of the Marx generator, and felt that this would certainly satisfy all of that, while also complying with my interests in electronics.

The Marx high-voltage pulse generator concept was first proposed by Irwin Marx in 1924 with the express purpose of producing subatomic particles for physics research. This was before the Cyclotron, Synchrotron, or even the linear accelerator existed. It was the only device that could produce these particles for physicists to do their research.

While I'd actually built two versions, I'm going to refer only to the second one here, as it produced twice the output as the first, and it was also much nicer looking.

Using parts available around the house, plus a handful of common electronic components from a local store, I was able to construct a device that would produce an ear-shattering, quarter-million Volt, nine-inch-long electrical discharge three times a second when energized! While I was capturing spectacular photos of the spark entering a shallow bowl of water, creating very interesting tendrils along the surface, I was also catching my son's attention.

ASYMMETRY LEADS TO RETURN CURRENT DEMO

While this was a fascinating display of the "skin effect" – a characteristic of high-frequency signals in conductors – I was bothered by the asymmetrical patterns I was getting. It wasn't long before I realized that the tendrils more strongly favored a path along the surface which mirrored the shape of the long ground wire I'd placed beneath the water. Suddenly recalling a portion of a refresher class on high-speed digital circuits that I'd taken earlier that year taught by Dr. Howard Johnson, I realized that I was seeing what amounted to a return current path, like those he'd described to us in his class.

The concept I was recalling was that which stated that the return current of a high-speed digital signal will travel through a solid ground plane inside of a printed circuit board directly below the signal trace. That is, it will *not* spread out to use the entire plane's area like a stable Direct Current (DC) will do. This is an esoteric concept that's been taught to engineering students who learn transmission line theory for ages. But, nobody's ever actually *seen* the return current in a plane before, not even ferrets!

I soon set up an experiment with the express intent of very clearly, visually demonstrating this most elusive concept. Instead of a solid metal plane, however, I created an equivalent plane on one side of a sheet of Plexiglas comprised of hundreds of tiny conductive squares. The spaces between the squares would allow the very high voltage from the Marx generator to jump from square to square, tracing a bright path along the way. The other side of the sheet contained a single copper trace in a complex shape. The result was so amazingly conclusive, that I had to send Dr. Johnson the pictures. He published these in his high-speed digital signal integrity newsletter in 2005. I later refined the experiment to represent a circuit board with more than two layers. I've only recently had this profusely illustrated article published. Those who are interested can check it out in "New Electronics", a UK engineering magazine.

Chapter 31 – DISPLAY MONITOR METRICS and WHO'S THE EXPERT?

In the late 1990s I'd been tasked with the replacement of new high-resolution display monitors for our project. As such, I learned all that I could about monitors, CRTs, and display metrics so that I could do an in-depth, meaningful, and fair comparison among several monitor vendors. I was surprised then at how much human physiology there was to consider when designating monitors that will be used by image analysts eight hours a day, every day.

One of my first surprises was the definition of "light". You'd think that it'd be obvious, but it's not. Sure, light comes from the Sun, as well as from many other sources like light bulbs, LEDs, and display monitors, but not *everything* they produce is light. In fact, only about 13% of what shines down upon us from the Sun can be called "light", and it wouldn't exist at all without us. No, I'm not saying that we're somehow in control of the Sun, although it would be really cool if we were! Actually, we've defined light with us as part of the equation. Light, by its technical definition, cannot exist unless a human *observes* it. Have a look.

Light \lit\; That portion of radiation within the electromagnetic spectrum that evokes a psychophysical response in the human visual system.

What is a "psychophysical response"? It's the combination of the retina sensing the radiation, and the brain interpreting the retinal sensations as bright, dark, and colorful. Our retinas are tuned to detect a very narrow slice of the spectrum from about 400 nanometers for deep blue, to 700nm for deep red, with green right around 530nm, and all of the other colors we know in between.

The level of light emitted from the display monitor's screen has to be adjusted to a very specific intensity in order to reduce operator fatigue. To understand the significance of this, it's necessary to know how the eye responds to light. The human eye operates in three distinct modes: photopic, mesopic, and scotopic. During daylight, it operates in the photopic mode, engaging the iris and eye lids to regulate the bright light. When it gets dark, the iris dilates, and the retina "dark-adapts", significantly increasing the sensitivity. This dark-adaption process can take as much as 20- or 30-minutes to achieve maximum sensitivity and involves a complex chemical process in the retina.

Both the constriction of the iris in bright light, and the dark-adaption of the retina in the dark, use energy. It may not be a lot, but it is enough to cause fatigue in the form of eyestrain in someone who might be experiencing such transitions frequently during their work shift. Therefore, in order to reduce fatigue, display monitors used for long periods of image analysis should be adjusted to operate within the middle range – the mesopic mode. This is an intensity that is bright enough that the retina doesn't dark-adapt and yet dim enough that the iris won't have to constrict. It produces the least amount of fatigue.

I found much of this to be quite fascinating, which is probably why I remained involved with monitor calibration and metrics for the next several years.

A year or two after I'd made my final selection of the manufacturer who would be building the monitors to replace our aging systems, I had a technical question about display metrics. I called up the National Information Display Lab (NIDL) in Princeton, as they'd defined many such parameters and measurements while they were developing the 1080p high-resolution television systems that we have now. About an hour or so later I received a call from an imaging scientist in Los Angeles, but it wasn't the answer; he was asking *me* the question that I'd posed! I soon learned that the director of the NIDL had called up the monitor maker on Long Island, who called up one of the imaging scientists in Rochester, who called up this imaging scientist on the west coast...who called ME! This is when I learned precisely where I fell in the display metrics food chain!

By the way, just for fun, and to give your tongue a bit of a workout, I happened to put the following two words together one day and found the pair to be remarkably difficult to say. Try saying this phrase a few times fast – or even just once! I think it's one of the most difficult word-pairs I've ever encountered.

"Scotopic stochastics"

Although – fortunately – such a phrase would probably never occur in the wild, but if it ever did, its meaning might be, the probabilistic prediction of seeing something in the dark.

Chapter 32 – Self-Improvement Engineering Excel Spreadsheets

(UPDATED) In Section 1, I provided a way to improve yourself physically by using my Weight-Loss Tracking spreadsheet in conjunction with a structured weighing, diet, and workout plan. I know it works, because I developed this spreadsheet tracker during my very own very successful, recent weight-loss journey.

In this chapter I will provide a way to improve yourself intellectually without the need to spend thousands of dollars or many years on additional school or other training. I know this also works because I developed the following tutorial spreadsheets during my very own very successful recent re-education journey.

> ***These self-improvement tutorial spreadsheets were developed specifically to refresh (or build new) knowledge in electronics engineering and advanced math – things I need for my work. Some of them can also benefit people working in other engineering disciplines and the sciences in general. The basic concepts exploited in these spreadsheets can benefit virtually anyone by understanding how to recognize trends***

I graduated college with my engineering degree about 42-years ago. I worked exclusively in digital circuit design for the first 30 years of my career. Digital circuits are computer-related binary logic circuits, processors, memory. This required very little math and almost none of the analog circuit theory I'd learned in school. As clock speeds continued to climb throughout the mid 2000s, effective digital circuit design started to require a good understanding of analog circuit theory. Analog circuits are those that handle signals with continuous levels, sinusoidal waves, and curves associated with linear algebra, exponential decay, and calculus.

To remain current, I started refreshing my knowledge of analog circuit theory on a circuit-by-circuit basis by referencing my old books from school and looking things up on the Internet. Essentially, just covering my specific needs at that time. Eventually, I determined that I needed something a bit more structured, but I didn't have the time or desire to enroll back into any course of engineering study that might help me with this. So, I naturally decided to tutor myself with the assistance of self-developed Excel spreadsheets.

This allowed me to run an unlimited number of different scenarios, formulas, whatever and observe the results in a large number of different analog theory and mathematical categories. In doing so, I was able to make mental connections, and see trends, and patterns between the theory and the results displayed as a simulated reality. This visual reinforcement helped me enormously to easily understand some of the most esoteric concepts of analog circuit theory, and some of the more challenging math problems.

What I discovered during this process is a method of learning that I had never experienced before. I found that I could understand just about any formula or equation without someone explaining it simply by seeing *three different problems* using the equation worked out completely with numerical values.

Since this self-reeducation after developing my engineering analytical tool spreadsheets, I'm now considered an expert in analog circuit theory and design!

Why does this work?

Most equations are given with variables in order to give them a general-purpose utility. You just drop in some numbers, and voila! An answer appears. Well, that's how it's supposed to work, but if I have no familiarity with the equation in the first place, then it's quite difficult to know what values to put where, and how these different values will affect the result.

For me, if I'm trying to understand an unfamiliar equation, I look for places where the equation is used – reference books, Internet sites, etc. – specifically where it's fully worked out with numbers in place of the variables. This helps me *start* to understand how to use the equation, but I still need more information before I can understand it fully.

After I saw it worked out once, I'll then work it out myself using different numbers and look at the result. Obviously, the result will be different, but I still don't know for sure which variables I changed made the result go to the new value.

To determine this, work it out a third time! This time the result will provide a value that indicates a trend. Observing trends in the results of an unfamiliar equation is remarkably beneficial in understanding how to use it effectively. A trend is the direction the result goes, either higher or lower, when the magnitude of each of the variables is changed in specific directions.

In order to effectively observe and make sense of these trends, it's important to be able to work out the equation numerous times in a relatively short period, and this is where the Excel spreadsheets come in. By implementing equations in a spreadsheet, it allows me to enter new values and observe the results instantaneously.

For those who are interested a variety of mathematical and electronics engineering concepts and would like to rapidly build new knowledge or refresh waning knowledge in those subjects, you will find a description of the spreadsheets I've developed (and you can use, yourself), here. They greatly benefited me, and so I'm now sharing them with you. To find out how you can get a copy of these analytical tool tutorial spreadsheets for yourself, please go to the end of this book (see: **Request Self-Improvement Excel Spreadsheets**).

While I have made them as user-friendly and generic as possible, it should be well understood that I built these tools to benefit my quest to improve my analog circuit theory skills, and so they will not appear quite as polished as some application you'd pay hundreds or even thousands of dollars for. Despite the unpolished appearance, I can assure you that they are very functional at what they do.

1. 1ˢᵗ-Order Integral Calculus – Line Integrals
    a. Defines definite and indefinite line integrals
    b. Indicates two methods for solving line integrals
    c. Provides standard calculus rules and identities with helpful mnemonics
    d. Solves numerical results of definite line integrals, resulting in area under the curve

2. 2nd-Order Integral Calculus – Surface Integrals

   a. Defines the method of 2-dimensional integration

   b. Indicates two methods for solving surface integrals

   c. Solves numerical results of definite surface integrals, resulting in volume under the surface

3. 1st-Order Differential Calculus – Derivatives

   a. Defines the standard derivative as slope of a portion of a curve

   b. Provides standard calculus rules and identities with helpful mnemonics

   c. Solves numerical results of derivatives at any point on a curve

4. Nodal Circuit Analysis and Simultaneous Equations

   a. Provides a step-by-step method to create a matrix from a series of circuit nodes

   b. Illustrates how to solve the matrix

   c. Solves numerical results for voltage and current at each node in circuits that cannot be solved with Ohm's Law, alone

   d. Provides a step-by-step method to solve 3 equations with 3 unknowns

   e. Solves for numerical result of x, y, & z, and numerical result of each equation

5. Circuit Superposition with Two Voltage Sources

   a. Illustrates how to solve superposition circuit analysis with two voltage sources

   b. Solves for numerical result of current and voltage at a specific node

6. Bipolar Transistor Characteristics and Biasing

   a. Generates transistor family of curves

   b. Superimposes load line, quiescent point, saturation point, and cutoff point

   c. Provides suggestions for Class-A bipolar transistor biasing

   d. Provides ability to measure (showing waveforms) various points in a Class-A-biased bipolar transistor circuit

7. Resistor, Inductor, Capacitor (RLC) Filters

a. Provides step-by-step derivation and definition of a transfer function

b. Provides Bode & Nyquist plots illustrating phase & gain of eight different RLC filter types

c. Gives access to all of the complex math used to determine phase & gain

d. Provides all of the equations involved in a number of example RLC filter transfer functions

8. Resistor Capacitor (RC) and Cascaded RC Circuit Analysis

   a. Provides numerical result of a single charging capacitor at any point in time with

      i. A fixed voltage source

      ii. A current-limited, fixed voltage source

      iii. A stepped voltage source

      iv. Either a linear or exponentially rising voltage source

   b. Provides numerical result of two charging capacitors in a cascade configuration at any point in time with

      i. A fixed voltage source

      ii. Either a linear or exponentially rising voltage source

9. 2D Field Solver

   a. Provides a visual representation of electric field vectors and magnetic field vectors surrounding metal traces in proximity to one another and/or one or two ground planes in a printed circuit board, and also for charged particles

   b. Provides numerical field strength at any vector location

   c. Provides numerical result of crosstalk in an adjacent printed circuit trace while rotating traces for least broadside coupling area

10. Wire, Cable, & Trace Characteristics

    a. Provides transmission line impedance in the following printed circuit board configurations

       i. Single-ended microstrip

       ii. Single-ended embedded microstrip (thin & thick)

     iii. Single-ended symmetric stripline

     iv. Single-ended asymmetric stripline

     v. Differential microstrip

     vi. Differential embedded microstrip

     vii. Differential symmetric stripline

     viii. Differential asymmetric stripline

  b. Determines the following transmission line characteristics in a circuit board

     i. Wavelength of periodic signal inside the medium

     ii. Signal rising edge electrical length

     iii. Signal rising edge critical length

     iv. Whether or not controlled impedance trace is required

     v. Maximum distance between a signal via and an inter-plane stitch

     vi. Maximum intra-pair length disparity for high-speed differential pairs

     vii. Signal rate of propagation inside the medium with specified dielectric constant

     viii. Dielectric constant given the propagation rate

  c. Determines the following circuit board trace characteristics

     i. DC resistance given trace length, width, and copper weight

     ii. AC resistance of trace due to skin effect at specified frequencies

     iii. Current-carrying capacity through a surface trace

     iv. Current-carrying capacity through a buried trace

  d. Determines the following single wire characteristics

     i. DC resistance given wire length, gauge, and stranding configuration

     ii. AC resistance of wire due to skin effect at specified frequencies

     iii. Current-carrying capacity through a single stranded wire at a specific gauge

iv. Current-carrying capacity through a stranded wire at a specific gauge tightly bundled with other wires

e. Provides resistivity of several metals common to electronics

f. Determines the following characteristics of wires

   i. Single wire in free space

     1. DC resistance

     2. Inductance

     3. Signal delay

g. Determines the following characteristics of transmission lines comprised of...

   i. Parallel wires separated by a specified distance

   ii. A wire over a ground plane, separated by a specific distance

   iii. A coaxial cable with specific dimensions

     1. DC resistance

     2. Inductance

     3. Conductance

     4. Capacitance

     5. Loss tangent

     6. Attenuation factor

     7. Signal delay

11. Power Distribution Network (PDN) analysis

a. Determines resistances and voltage drops across circuit board plane shapes given voltage sources, load currents, plane shape, copper thickness, via parameters, and temperature

b. Generates visual 3-dimensional surface plot of voltage gradients across power plane

12. Op Amp instability

a. Illustrates how the addition of delay in an operational amplifier's feedback loop causes instability through divergent response

b. Provides a demonstration of organic gain through negative feedback

c. Provides Bode and Nyquist plots of op amps in a variety of functional configurations

d. Provides transfer functions of op amps in a variety of functional configurations

EPILOGUE

*D*espite what you've just read, I have not lived a perfect life. I've made mistakes. But unlike those whose lives seem to be defined more by their failures than their successes, I've learned from my missteps to make much better decisions. Like I've said throughout, life is like a series of short stories. All good stories have some conflict, distress, peril, or hardship that makes them interesting. But, consistent with my optimistic approach to life, I choose not to dwell on the bad parts, since doing so might threaten to redefine my otherwise positive future. I simply make every effort to try and make the very best choices that I possibly can from the information available to me at the time.

Life is ALL about choices! Choose to make yours great!

EDUCATION ALERT GLOSSARY

1. Perhaps I should elaborate about the milk chute for those who didn't grow up in the Stone Age. Back then, it was common to have your milk delivered by a milkman. We would place empty glass bottles into the chute from inside the house, and the milkman would remove those via the tiny door to the outside, and replace them with full bottles of milk, or other items from the store if so requested in a note left at a prior visit.

2. Until just the past decade, a television receiver contained radio-frequency oscillators for tuning, intermediate-frequency oscillators to separate the audio signals from the video, low-frequency horizontal- and vertical-oscillators which are fed into power amplifiers to deflect the electron beam of a very large, evacuated, glass Cathode Ray Tube (CRT) for display with phosphor coating the inside of the screen, audio- and video-amplifiers to increase the level for the sound and picture signals, low-voltage (6.3Vac, 45Vdc, 90Vdc), B+ supplies (350Vdc-450Vdc), and high-voltage (20kV-25kV) power to drive all of the other circuits. The "later" TVs with digital displays and controls also employed a variety of digital circuitry. Today, with flat-screen LC and LED Displays, much of this still exists. With the change of the display technology, the power supplies have changed the most, and microprocessors are used heavily to control the remaining circuitry.

3. A word about the danger of this enormous, specialized tube; until flat panel TVs and computer displays became popular sometime after 2005, all of these devices contained a CRT to display the picture. Cathode Ray Tubes are so called because they use an electron gun to generate a stream of electrons, also

called "cathode rays". From there, this beam is accelerated to fair fraction of the speed of light by high-voltage accelerator plates, and deflected by electromagnets to scan a raster pattern (back and forth, up and down) onto a phosphor-coated screen inside of a large, very fragile, evacuated glass tube in order to create a picture. This sounds like an incredibly dangerous item to be casually placed into nearly every home and business in the developed world, but, due to the inherent dangers, numerous safety measures were eventually developed. The three primary safety features were: 1) The use of nearly 1-inch thick safety glass on the front, 2) Containment within a wooden, metal, or, since the about mid 1970s, a plastic cabinet, 3) A tension band around the perimeter of the screen.

4. The government and military commonly used the DD FORM 1149 for material requisitions, which includes quantity, part number, description, unit cost, extended cost, total, and a variety of authorization signature fields.

5. This is the standard EIA resistor color code:
    Black = 0 Brown = 1 Red = 2
    Orange = 3 Yellow = 4 Green = 5
    Blue = 6 Violet = 7 Gray = 8
    White = 9 Gold = 5% Silver = 10%

6. The technically attuned reader might notice that I'd listed light bulbs for indicators, instead of LEDs. This is because LEDs were so fantastically expensive back then that most stores didn't carry them. The first Light Emitting Diodes (LEDs) that appeared in 1968 electronics catalogues were priced from $49.50 to $135 – EACH! – depending upon the style and power dissipation. That's in 1968 dollars. Today, that would be like paying $285 to $780 for a single red LED! Yes, just red. No other *visible* color was yet available, and infrared LEDs never really caught on for indicator lights…well, not for humans, anyway. In case you didn't get that, we can't see infrared. LEDs became conspicuously absent from the electronics catalogues for the next few years, finally showing

up again in 1972 once their prices had dropped dramatically. Green and yellow LEDs came onto the market in 1975, but the practical production of a blue LED represented a significant technical challenge. This meant that we wouldn't see blue LEDs until around 1991, which, coincidentally, is the very same time that Mars candies started selling blue M&Ms! Is there a common chemical or technical process between the two? I wonder.

7. As the name suggests, binary is a two-state number system. One **binary digit** – a bit – is either "on", or it's "off". Each bit carries a specific "weight", depending upon its position within a set of bits. The right-most bit in a set has a weight of 1. The next bit carries a value of 2. The one to its left is 4, then 8, 16, 32, 64… Each bit to the left has a value twice that of the bit to its right. A collection of eight bits is called a "byte", while four bits is a "nibble". In this way, any decimal number between 0 and 15 can be represented in just four bits, or one nibble.

8. Three hundred Volts will start an arc less than 1/64th of an inch long, according to the basic rule of thumb where it takes 10,000 Volts to jump just a single centimeter in dry air! Not much of an arc, really.

9. Let's make some definitions. I've used the terms "sparks" and "arcs" almost interchangeably so far. This is because we weren't exactly particular whether we created fleeting or lasting discharges, so long as they were bright and physically long, but there really IS a rather substantial difference. Sparks are momentary, high-energy discharges, while arcs are continuous. Also, arcs usually generate a great deal of heat, while sparks do not. To clarify, a spark can easily have enough energy to vaporize the metal it's conducting to, but due to its instantaneous nature, it creates very little measurable *ambient* heat around it. The attribute that sparks trade for heat is sound. Many sparks can have a nearly ear-splitting CRACK when they go off!

10. You'll undoubtedly have noticed that I've never said "infrared light" or "ultraviolet light" in any chapter. This is because it

would be incorrect since each of those two phrases is, in fact, an oxymoron; they contradict themselves. It might seem silly to look up the definition for "Light". I mean, it just seems so very obvious. Right? If you did look it up, however, you might be surprised to find that "Light is that portion of radiation within the electromagnetic spectrum which evokes a psychophysical response in the Human Visual System (HVS)." "Infrared" literally means "below red", while "Ultraviolet" literally means "above violet". Neither of these regions of electromagnetic radiation is within the visible region for humans. Therefore, they cannot evoke either a physical response in our retinas, or a psychological response in our brains. As such, they are not "Light". The proper references are Infrared Radiation and Ultraviolet Radiation.

11. A flying-spot scanner is the poor-man's television (video) camera. One could be built fairly easily using just a standard TV receiver modified to display only a white raster (an all-white rectangle), and a photodetector tube or a photocell with the applicable circuitry to amplify the signal from either device. The TV would be placed in a facedown attitude with a lens to focus the scanned raster onto a table. The photosensitive pickup device is positioned to receive any light that is reflected from the table surface. Usually a photograph will be placed on the table where the raster is focused, thus producing a signal in the reflected light and photo sensor that is proportional to the tones from the photograph. This varying signal is amplified and then fed into another TV modified as a monitor, where it will display the photograph. An alternative method is to place a transparency directly upon the surface of the picture tube of the raster-scanning TV, and the photo sensor is placed on the opposite side of the transparency – no lenses needed, but a darkened environment is a necessity. A common use for the flying spot scanner was with "Slow-Scan TV", since a still picture was typical with such a scanner device, and slow-scan required an unchanging picture. While many different modes exist today, back in 1974 there was basically one mode. Unlike a normal 1970s vintage TV that would paint a

complete frame on the screen in 1/30ᵗʰ of a second, a slow-scan image was created in *8 seconds* – hence the name "slow scan". The benefit of such low-speed images was that their video signals required a tiny fraction of the bandwidth of standard broadcast video, thus allowing hams to send pictures over their standard audio-bandwidth radio transceivers!

Resources

Help for drug and alcohol addiction: http://www.recovery.org

Help for video game addiction: http://www.recovery.org/topics/video-game-addiction-recovery

Help for gambling addiction: http://www.recovery.org/topics/gambling-addiction-recovery

Help for pornography addiction: http://www.recovery.org/topics/porn-addiction-recovery

Help for mental health issues: http://www.nami.org

References (based upon information in 2014)

1. Bachelor of Science Degree Income Versus Bachelor of Arts Degree Income: http://www.npr.org/blogs/money/2013/09/10/219372252/the-most-and-least-lucrative-college-majors-in-1-graph

2. Minimum wage worker statistics: http://www.pewresearch.org/fact-tank/2014/09/08/who-makes-minimum-wage

3. Cost of a pack of cigarettes in NY State: http://www.ibtimes.com/price-cigarettes-how-much-does-pack-cost-each-us-state-map-1553445

4. Statistics of heavy smokers and drinkers: http://www.ons.gov.uk/ons/dcp171778_338863.pdf

5. Cost of crack cocaine: http://www.reddit.com/r/Drugs/comments/1f2n2d/street_price_for_crack_in_the_us

6. Cost of crystal meth: http://www.crystalmethaddiction.org/Crystal_

Meth_Prices.htm

7. Cost of video game addiction: http://kotaku.com/5384643/i-kept-playing--the-costs-of-my-gaming-addiction

Request Self-Improvement Excel Spreadsheets:

To request a copy of any of my Self-Improvement Excel Spreadsheets (either any of my numerous **engineering tutorials**, or my **customizable weight-loss tracker with database**), or to send me comments, please e-mail me your request at the e-mail address provided below.

If you are purchasing one of my spreadsheets, I will reply with instructions for how to PayPal me $1.00 for each spreadsheet requested – just to offset the cost of the time I need to dedicate to replying to the bulk of messages I receive each day.

Once I've received this token payment, I'll e-mail you the most up-to-date version of the Excel spreadsheet(s) that you've requested. They perform equally well on either Mac or PC systems. Please ensure that you have Microsoft Excel installed on your computer and you are able to use it, before placing a request.

Please be civil in your messages. There is absolutely no reason to be rude. I'm just passing along my experiences for your benefit. If this somehow offends you, then you *don't* have to follow it; you *don't* have to keep reading the book; you *don't* have to send me a nasty message telling me what a load of crap you think it is. Again…it's entirely *your choice*.

Request your copy of engineering tutorial spreadsheets, or the weight-loss tracking spreadsheet with database, or send me comments about my book here:

YourSuccessChoiceBook@gmail.com